Macs

PORTABLE GENIUS

Macs
PORTABLE GENIUS

by Paul McFedries

WILEY

Wiley Publishing, Inc.

Macs Portable Genius

Published by
Wiley Publishing, Inc.
10475 Crosspoint Blvd.
Indianapolis, IN 46256
www.wiley.com

Copyright © 2008 by Wiley Publishing, Inc., Indianapolis, Indiana

Published simultaneously in Canada

ISBN: 978-0-470-29052-1

Manufactured in the United States of America

10 9 8 7 6 5 4 3 2

For general information on our other products and services or to obtain technical support, please contact our Customer Care Department within the U.S. at (800) 762-2974, outside the U.S. at (317) 572-3993 or fax (317) 572-4002.

Wiley also publishes its books in a variety of electronic formats. Some content that appears in print may not be available in electronic books.

Library of Congress Control Number: 2008929123

WILEY

About the Author

Paul McFedries is a Mac expert and full-time technical writer. Paul has been authoring computer books since 1991 and has more than 60 books to his credit. Paul's books have sold more than three million copies worldwide. These books include the Wiley titles *Teach Yourself VISUALLY Macs*, *Teach Yourself VISUALLY Computers*, 5th Edition, and *The Unofficial Guide to Microsoft Office 2007*. Paul is also the proprietor of Word Spy (www.wordspy.com) a Web site that tracks new words and phrases as they enter the language.

Credits

Senior Acquisitions Editor
Jody Lefevere

Senior Project Editor
Cricket Krengel

Technical Editor
Brian Joseph

Copy Editor
Lauren Kennedy

Editorial Manager
Robyn B. Siesky

Vice President & Group Executive Publisher
Richard Swadley

Vice President & Publisher
Barry Pruett

Business Manager
Amy Knies

Senior Marketing Manager
Sandy Smith

Project Coordinator
Kristie Rees

Graphics and Production Specialists
Carrie A. Cesavice
Alissa Ellet
Jennifer Henry
Jennifer Mayberry

Quality Control Technicians
Laura Albert
Melanie Hoffman

Proofreading
Tricia Liebig

Indexing
Broccoli Information Management

Special Help
Jama Carter
Sarah Cisco

For Karen and Gypsy.

Acknowledgments

The only thing more fun than using Macs is writing a book about them! That's particularly true for an interesting project such as this book, which was made all the more pleasant by the great people I got to work with. They include Acquisition Editor Jody Lefevere, who was kind enough to ask me to write the book; Project Editors Cricket Krengel and Sarah Cisco, whose just-so suggestions and penetrating questions made this a better book; Copy Editor Lauren Kennedy, whose eagle-eye for all things ungrammatical made me look like a better writer than I am; and Technical Editor Brian Joseph, whose knowledge of the Mac world is nothing short of amazing. Many thanks to all of you for outstanding work on this project.

Contents

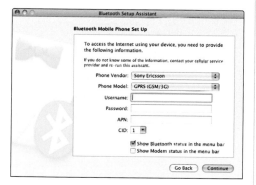

How Can I Get More Out of the Web?   80

How Do I Use My Mac to Organize My Real Life?   106

chapter 7

Can My Mac Help Me Communicate More Effectively? 166

How Do I Use My Mac to Organize My Online Life? 138

How Do I Keep My Mac Running Smoothly? 198

chapter 9

Can I Upgrade My Mac? 228

chapter 10

How Do I Solve Mac Software
Problems? 258

chapter 11

How Do I Solve Mac Hardware Problems?

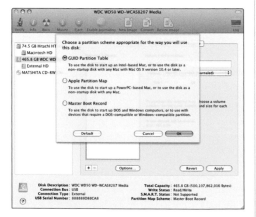

appendix a

appendix b

Introduction

Some less-than-charitable folks insist on calling Mac users a "cult." Why? Well, who knows, really? Perhaps it's because people who use a Mac actually *enjoy* using a computer, as opposed to folks using other systems who seem to wage a daily war to stop themselves from putting a fist through their screens. Perhaps it's because Macs just work: you take them out of the box, plug them in, and within minutes you're doing your thing. Perhaps it's because Macs just look so darn good that we can't help but admire (and point out to others) their stylishness and innovative design. Whatever the reason, in the end it doesn't matter: we love our Macs and no amount of name-calling is going to change that.

Some folks also insist that love is blind, so we Mac users need to be careful that our love for all things Mac doesn't blind us to the Mac's limitations, annoyances, and even its failures. Yes, it's true: the Mac isn't perfect. Sure, the Mac is dead simple to use out-of-the-box, but some of its most useful and powerful features are hidden away in obscure parts of the operating system. Sure, the Mac doesn't get in your way when you're trying to be productive or creative, but sometimes it does something (or forces you to do something) that just makes you want to scratch your head in wonderment. Sure, the Mac's robust design makes it a reliable machine day after day, but even the best built machine can have problems.

When they come across their Mac's dark side, many people make an appointment with their local Apple Store's Genius Bar, and more often than not the on-duty genius gives them good advice on how to overcome their Mac's limitations, work around its annoyances, and fix its failures. The Genius Bar is a great thing, but it isn't exactly a convenient thing. You can't just drop by to get help; you may need to lug your Mac down to the store; and in some cases you may need to leave your Mac for a day or two while whatever problem gets checked out and hopefully resolved.

What Mac users really need is a version of the Genius Bar that is easier to access, more convenient, and doesn't require lugging or leaving the Mac. What Mac users really need is a "portable" genius that enables them to be more productive and solve problems wherever they and their Mac happen to be.

Welcome, therefore, to *Macs Portable Genius*. This book is like a mini Genius Bar all wrapped up in an easy to use, easy to access, and eminently portable format. In this book you learn how to get more out of your Mac by learning how to access all the really powerful and timesaving features that aren't obvious at a casual glance. In this book you learn how to avoid your Mac's more annoying character traits and, in those cases where such behavior can't be avoided, you learn how to work around it. In this book you learn how to prevent Mac problems from occurring, and just in case your preventative measures are for naught, you learn how to fix many common problems yourself.

This book is for Mac users who know the basics but want to take their Mac education to a higher level. It's a book for people who want to be more productive, more efficient, more creative, and more self-sufficient (at least as far as their Mac goes, anyway). It's a book for people who use a Mac every day, but would like to incorporate that Mac into more of their day-to-day activities. It's a book for people who pooh-pooh the notion that Mac users are a cult, but if someone decided to start an actual Mac cult, they'd join anyway. It's a book I had a blast writing, so I think it's a book you'll enjoy reading.

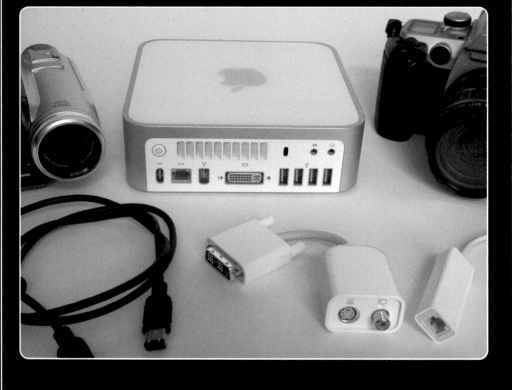

You love your Mac because it doesn't require you to be a genius to accomplish basic, everyday tasks. Got a new mouse? Just plug it into any free USB port and it's ready to use within seconds. Nice! Unfortunately, there are some devices that are more ornery and require a bit of extra effort on your part to get them connected and configured. In this chapter, I take you through a few such devices, including an external display, printer, fax, digital camera, scanner, camcorder, and even another Mac!

Using an External Display

If you have an extra external display — a monitor, television set, or projector — kicking around, you can connect it to your Mac in various scenarios:

- **As a new desktop monitor.** You can use the external display as a replacement for the monitor that came with your desktop Mac.

- **As a notebook alternative.** You can use the external display instead of the built-in monitor on your Mac notebook.

- **As a desktop extension.** You can use the external display to extend the desktop of your Mac. To do this with a Mac Pro or a Power Mac G5, you need to either add a second graphics card, or you need to replace the existing graphics card with one that supports two monitors. See Chapter 9 to learn how to replace or add a graphics card.

Fortunately, all of these connection types are plug-and-play (meaning that after you plug in and turn on the external display, your Mac recognizes the new device right away). That's the good news. The bad news is that although using an external monitor is plug-and-play, the *plug* part isn't as straightforward as you might like because there are many different ways to connect a Mac and a display. The next few sections provide you with the details you need to make things happen.

Understanding external display connections

To connect your Mac and an external display, you need to know the various ways these connections can occur. For starters, you need to get familiar with the four main connector types: DVI, Mini-DVI, VGA, and video.

DVI connections

The standard video connection type on modern-day Macs is called DVI (digital video interface), which is now common on most LCD monitors and on some televisions and projectors. That sounds simple enough, and it is — on the Mac side. Unfortunately, external displays such as LCD monitors and televisions can use different DVI connectors. There are actually three types:

Note

What's the difference between single-link and dual-link? DVI uses a transmitter to send information along the cable. A single-link cable uses one transmitter, while a dual-link cable uses two transmitters. This means that dual-link connections are faster and offer a better signal quality than single-click connections.

- **DVI-A.** This connector works with only analog signals (see figure 1.1).

- **DVI-D.** This connector works with only digital signals and it comes in single-link and dual-link versions (see figure 1.2).

- **DVI-I.** This connector works with both analog and digital signals and comes in single-link and dual-link versions (see figure 1.3). Mac Pros, MacBook Pros, Mac Minis, and Power Mac G5s all use the DVI-I dual-link connector, as do some versions of the PowerBook G4.

1.1 A DVI-A connector

1.2 DVI-D single-link (left) and dual-link (right) connectors

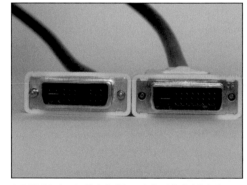

1.3 DVI-I single-link (left) and dual-link (right) connectors

As you can see, each type of DVI connector uses a slightly different pin arrangement, so when you're matching your external display, DVI cable, and Mac, you need to make sure that they all use the same type of DVI connector.

Genius A dual-link DVI connector plugs in to (and works with) a single-link DVI port. Unfortunately, the reverse isn't true: that is, you can't plug a single-link DVI connector into a dual-link DVI port. Note, too, that a DVI-D connector can plug into a DVI-I port, but a DVI-I connector won't fit into a DVI-D port.

Mini-DVI connections

The Intel-based iMac, the MacBook, and most 12-inch PowerBook G4s don't use regular DVI connectors. Instead, they use a different connector called a Mini-DVI, shown in figure 1.4.

To connect your Mac's Mini-DVI port to a DVI port on an external display, you need to purchase at least the Apple Mini-DVI to DVI Adapter. I say at least because the Mini-DVI to DVI Adapter uses a DVI-D connector. This is either good news or bad news depending on your external display port:

1.4 A Mini-DVI connector

- ● **DVI-D port.** This is good, because it probably means you have a DVI-D cable, which connects to both the adapter and the display. In this case, the adapter is all you need.

- ● **DVI-I port.** This isn't so good, because it probably means you have a DVI-I cable, and that cable won't fit the adapter's DVI-D connector. In this case, the adapter on its own won't cut it. To solve the problem, you either need to buy a DVD-D cable, or you need to hunt down a DVI-D to DVI-I adapter so you can use your DVI-I cable.

Note

In high-tech cable and port connections jargon, a connector with pins is described as *male* and a connector with holes is described as *female*. The Apple Mini-DVI to DVI Adapter has a female DVI connector, which means you can't plug it directly into an external display's DVI port, given it is also female. In other words, you need to run a DVI cable — which is male on both ends — between the adapter and your external display.

VGA connections

All CRT monitors and many LCD monitors and projectors come with a VGA connector, shown in figure 1.5.

1.5 VGA connectors are standard on CRTs and common on LCDs.

Note Older Mac models such as the iMac G5, iBook, eMac, and some 12-inch PowerBook G4s come with a Mini-VGA port. To connect a VGA external display to any of these Macs, you need to purchase the Apply VGA Display Adapter, which offers a Mini-VGA connector on one end and a VGA connector on the other.

To connect your Mac to an external display that only offers a VGA connector, you have two choices depending on your connector:

- **DVI connector.** You need to get the Apple DVI to VGA Display Adapter, shown in figure 1.6.

- **Mini-DVI connector.** You need to get the Apple Mini-DVI to VGA Adapter, shown in figure 1.7.

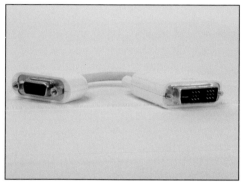

1.6 Use the Apple DVI to VGA Display Adapter to connect your DVI Mac to an external display's VGA port.

1.7 Use the Apple Mini-DVI to VGA Adapter to connect your Mini-DVI Mac to an external display's VGA port.

Video connections

If your external display is a television or projector (or even a VCR), it likely has either a Composite (yellow RCA) connector or an S-Video connector; both are shown in figure 1.8.

1.8 Composite (left) and S-Video (right) connectors are common on televisions, projectors, and VCRs.

Note

For older Mac models such as the iMac G5, iBook, eMac, and some 12-inch PowerBook G4s that use a Mini-VGA port, you can use the Apple Video Adapter to connect a Composite or S-Video external display.

To connect your Mac to an external display that only offers either Composite or S-Video connectors, you have two choices depending on your connector:

- **DVI connector.** You need to get the Apple DVI to Video Adapter, shown in figure 1.9.

- **Mini-DVI connector.** You need to get the Apple Mini-DVI to Video Adapter, shown in figure 1.10.

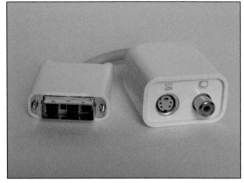

1.9 Use the Apple DVI to Video Adapter to connect your DVI Mac to an external display's Composite or S-Video port.

Setting the external display mode

The hard part about using an external display is getting the correct cables and adapters and ensuring they fit into the appropriate connectors on both your Mac and on the display. After you've got that set, however, the rest is a breeze because as soon as you connect the external display and turn it on, your Mac recognizes it and starts using it. That's more like it!

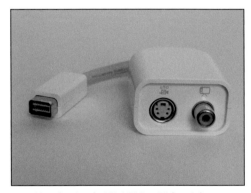

How you use the external display depends on what you want to do with it. Your Mac gives you two choices:

1.10 Use the Apple Mini-DVI to Video Adapter to connect your Mini-DVI Mac to an external display's Composite or S-Video port.

- **Video mirroring.** This external display mode means that the same image that appears on the Mac's main or built-in display also appears on the external display. This is useful if you want to use a larger monitor to work with your Mac notebook, or if you want to show the desktop on a projector so that other people can see it.

● **Extended desktop mode.** This mode means that your Mac's desktop is extended onto the external display. This is useful if you need more screen real estate to display your programs. For example, you can have your main application open on one display and an application that you're monitoring — such as Mail, iChat, or Safari — on the other display.

To switch between these external display modes, follow these steps:

1. **Click System Preferences in the Dock.** The System Preferences window appears.

2. **Click the Displays icon.** The display preferences appear, and you see one set of preferences for each screen. Figure 1.11 shows the preferences for the main display, and a similar window appears for the secondary display.

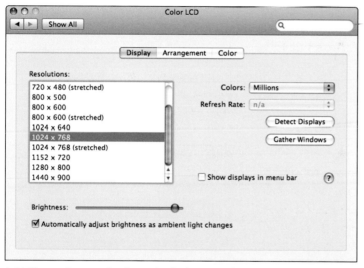

1.11 The preferences for the main display. A similar window appears with preferences for the secondary display.

3. **Click the Arrangement tab to select the external display mode.**

   ● To turn on video mirroring, select the Mirror Displays check box.

   ● To turn on extended desktop mode, deselect the Mirror Displays check box.

Genius

After you connect your external display, you should calibrate the display so that the colors of images appear correctly. To calibrate a display, open its display preferences, select the Color tab, and then click Calibrate. This launches the Apple Display Calibrator Assistant, which takes you step by step through the calibration process.

4. **If you turned on extended desktop mode, use the objects in the Arrangement tab to configure the screen layout (see figure 1.12).** To set the relative screen positions, click and drag the screen icon to the positions you prefer. To set the location of the menu bar, click and drag the white strip to the screen you prefer.

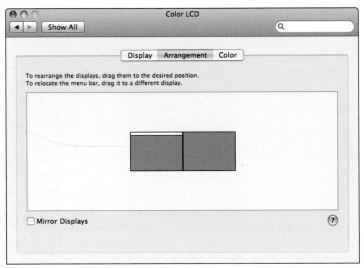

1.12 Use the objects in the Arrangement tab to configure the screen layout in extended desktop mode.

Connecting Two Macs Directly

If you've got a couple of Macs kicking around, it's natural to want to share things between them: documents, Safari bookmarks, iTunes libraries, downloads, and more. The standard way of sharing data between computers is to create a network. However, that requires having a central connection point for the computers, usually a switch, router, or wireless access point. If you don't have such networking hardware handy (for example, you're in a hotel room or on a plane), you might think that sharing is off the table, but that's not true. There are actually several ways that you can connect two Macs directly: with a network (or crossover) cable, with a FireWire cable, or by creating an ad-hoc wireless network. The next three sections provide the details.

Connecting two Macs with a network cable

The easiest way to connect two Macs directly is to string a network cable between them. A network cable is also called a *twisted-pair* cable (because it consists of four pairs of twisted copper wires that together form a circuit that can transmit data) and it comes with an RJ-45 jack on each end. As you can see in figure 1.13, a network cable's RJ-45 jack is similar to — but much larger than — the RJ-11 jack used by a telephone cable.

The RJ-45 jack on a network cable plugs into the corresponding ethernet port on your Mac, as shown in figure 1.14.

So far so good, and at this point you might be tempted just to plug any old network cable into the network ports of your Macs. Unfortunately, there's a good chance that this won't work. On some Macs the network ports get confused if you use a regular (also called *straight-through*) network cable because they only can connect using a special *crossover cable*. The Macs that require a crossover cable include:

- eMac
- iBook
- iBook (FireWire)
- iMac
- iMac (17-inch Flat Panel)
- iMac (Early 2001)
- iMac (Flat Panel)
- iMac (Slot Loading)
- iMac (Summer 2000)
- iMac (Summer 2001)
- Power Mac G4 (AGP Graphics)
- Power Mac G4 (PCI Graphics)
- Power Mac G4 Cube
- Power Macintosh G3 (Blue and White)
- PowerBook (FireWire)
- PowerBook G3 Series (Bronze Keyboard)

1.13 Network cables have RJ-45 connectors (top), which are similar to, but considerably larger than, the RJ-11 connectors used with telephone cables.

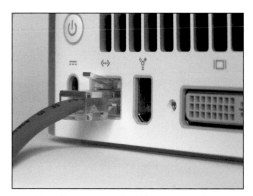

1.14 You plug a network cable's RJ-45 jack into the corresponding ethernet port on your Mac.

All of these Macs require a crossover cable only if they're connecting to another Mac from the list. For example, if you're connecting an iBook to an iMac, you must use a crossover cable. If you're connecting to any Mac not on the list, you can use a regular network cable. This is the case, for example, if you're connecting an iBook to a MacBook Pro.

From a distance (or, heck, sometimes even up close), crossover cables look identical to regular network cables. To help you identify them, many crossover cables come with a label such as CROSS taped to them. If you don't see such a label, add your own. However, if you didn't do that and now you're not sure which of your cables is a crossover, there's a way you can tell. Take the connectors on each end of the cable and place them side by side so you have a good view of the colored wires inside. (A clear plastic covering helps here.) Make sure you hold the connectors with the same orientation. (It's usually best to have the plastic tabs facing down.) If the layout of the wires is identical on both connectors, then you've got a regular network cable.

Genius

If you need to buy a straight-through cable or a crossover cable, check the cable category. Because most Macs support 100 Mbps transmission speeds, you need a category 5 or higher cable to transmit data at that speed.

If you see, instead, that two of the wires — specifically, the red and the green — have switched positions (see figure 1.15), then you've got a crossover cable.

Besides getting the right kind of network cable, you also have to make sure that your Macs are configured to share files. Follow these steps:

1. **Click System Preferences in the Dock.**

2. **Click the Sharing icon.** The Sharing preferences appear.

3. **Turn on file sharing.**

    - **OS X Leopard.** Select the File Sharing check box, as shown in figure 1.16.

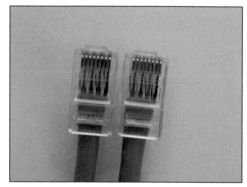

1.15 In a crossover network cable, the position of the red and green wires is swapped in the two connectors.

    - **Earlier version of OS X.** Select the Personal File Sharing check box.

4. **If you feel like it, you can also use the Computer Name text box to edit the name of your Mac, which is the name that will appear in the Network window of the other Mac.**

To see the other Mac, open Finder and then choose Go ⇨ Network (or press Shift+⌘+K). Double-click the Mac's icon, click Connect As (in Leopard) or Connect (in earlier versions), and then enter a name and password to connect to the other computer. Figure 1.17 shows a connection to another Mac named Karen's Widow.

1.16 To exchange files over the network cable, you must turn on file sharing on both Macs.

1.17 A successful computer-to-computer connection over a network cable.

Connecting two Macs with FireWire

If you don't have a network cable lying around, but you just happen to have a FireWire cable on hand, that's great because you can use it to connect two Macs via their FireWire ports and share files between them (see figure 1.18). I'm assuming here, of course, that both Macs have FireWire ports.

1.18 You can use a FireWire cable to connect two Macs via their FireWire ports.

The connection is basically the same as with a network cable, so I'll just give you the barebones steps here (see the previous section to flesh out the details):

1. **Connect the FireWire cable to both Macs.**

2. **Turn on file sharing on both Macs.**

3. **Use Finder's Network window (choose Go ➪ Network) to connect to the other Mac.**

Connecting two Macs wirelessly

If you don't have a network cable or a FireWire cable, or if you're sick to death of cables, you can still connect two Macs directly using a wireless network. I'm not talking about a standard wireless network that uses an access point (also called an *infrastructure wireless network*). I'm talking about a *computer-to-computer wireless network* (also called an *ad hoc wireless network*) that doesn't use an access point. As long as you have two (or more) Macs with wireless networking capabilities, it's very easy to set this up:

1. **Click the AirPort status icon in the menu bar and then click Create Network.** The Create a Computer-to-Computer Network dialog box appears.

2. **Type a name for the new network in the Name text box.**

3. **Leave Automatic selected in the Channel list.**

4. **If you want people to enter a password to join your network (a good idea), select the Require Password check box.** The dialog box expands, as shown in figure 1.19.

5. **In the Security list, select either 40-bit WEP (to use a 5-character password) or 128-bit WEP (which requires a 13-character password).**

6. **Type the password in the Password and Verify text boxes and click OK.** Your Mac sets up the computer-to-computer network.

To connect to your new network from another Mac, click the AirPort status icon in the menu bar and then click the name of your network (in this case, the network is called AdHocNet), as shown in figure 1.20. If you set up a password for the network, you're prompted to enter the password.

1.19 Use this dialog box to create your computer-to-computer network.

1.20 Your new computer-to-computer network appears in the list of available wireless networks.

Connecting and Sharing a Printer

Nine times out of ten — it's probably more like 99 times out of a hundred — connecting a printer to your Mac is a no-brainer: You plug it in to the USB port, turn it on, and presto! — your Mac and your printer have already become fast friends and you can start printing right away. How can you be sure? There are a couple of ways to tell:

● **In any application that supports printing, choose File ➪ Print.** In the dialog box that appears, you should see your printer's name in the Printer list, as shown in figure 1.21.

1.21 If your Mac and your printer are getting along famously, the printer appears in the Printer list.

● **Click System Preferences in the Dock, and then click Print & Fax.** In the Print & Fax preferences that appear, you should see your printer's name in the Printers list, as shown in figure 1.22.

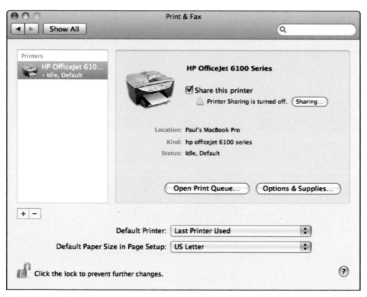

1.22 If your Mac recognized your printer, it appears in the Printers list in the Print & Fax preferences.

Genius

Surprisingly, Windows doesn't have a monopoly on annoying behavior. One of the senseless things that OS X does is set the default printer to whatever printer you used or added most recently. To fix this, choose System Preferences ➪ Print & Fax, then use the Default Printer list to choose the printer you want to use as the default.

Connecting a printer manually

What happens on those rare occasions when your Mac doesn't recognize your printer? In that case, you need to do a bit more legwork and install the printer manually. Here's how it's done:

1. **Connect and turn on the printer if you haven't done so already.**

2. **Click System Preferences in the Dock, click Print & Fax, and then click the + icon.** Your Mac displays the list of connected printers.

Note   You can also display the list of connected printers from any application that supports printing. Choose File ➪ Printer, open the Printer list, and then select Add Printer.

3. **In the Printer Browser's list of available printers, choose your printer.**

4. **In the Print Using list, choose Select a driver to use and then choose your printer in the list that appears.** If you don't see your printer in the list, you need to install the printer driver by hand as follows:

   ● Insert the disc that came with your printer.

   ● Choose Other in the Print Using list.

   ● Open the printer disc (or the folder where you downloaded the printer driver), choose the printer driver, and then click Open.

5. **Click Add.** Your printer is now connected.

Note   If you don't have a printer disc, or if the disc doesn't contain Mac drivers, visit the printer manufacturer's Web site and download the drivers you need.

Adding a shared network printer

If your Mac is part of a network, one of the big advantages you have is that you can connect a printer to one computer, and the other computers on the network can then use that computer for printing. That saves you big bucks because you don't have to supply each computer with its own printer.

To use a shared network printer, you must first add it to your Mac's list of printers. Follow these steps if the printer is shared on another Mac (see the next section for Windows printers):

1. **Click System Preferences in the Dock, click Print & Fax, and then click the + icon.** Your Mac displays the list of connected printers.

Genius If you can't get drivers for the printer (annoyingly, many printer manufacturers don't bother writing Mac drivers), you may still be able to use the printer by choosing Generic PostScript Printer in the Print Using list.

2. **In the Printer Browser's list of printers, select the shared printer you want to use.** There are two ways to recognize a shared printer:

   - **OS X Leopard.** The Kind column displays Bonjour Shared, as shown in figure 1.23.

   - **Earlier versions of OS X.** The Connection column displays Shared Printer.

3. **Click Add.** You can now use a shared network printer.

1.23 In OS X Leopard, look for Bonjour Shared in the Kind column.

Adding a shared Windows network printer

If the shared printer you want to use is part of a Windows network, follow these steps to add it to your Mac's list of printers:

1. **Click System Preferences in the Dock, click Print & Fax, and then click the + icon.** Your Mac displays the Printer Browser.

2. **Display the list of Windows workgroups on your network.**

   - **OS X Leopard.** Click the Windows tab.

   - **Earlier versions of OS X.** Click More Printers and then use the top list to select Windows Printing.

3. **Choose the workgroup that contains the computer you want to work with.**

4. **Click the computer with the shared printer you want to add.**

5. **Log on to the Windows computer.**

6. **Click the shared printer you want to use.**

7. **In the Print Using list, choose Select a driver to use and then choose the printer in the list that appears.** Figure 1.24 shows an example.

8. **Click Add.** You can now use a shared printer on a Windows network.

Sharing your printer with the network

If you have a printer connected to your Mac and you'd generously like other folks on your network to use it, you can share it by following these steps:

1. **Click System Preferences in the Dock.**

2. **Click the Sharing icon.** The Sharing preferences appear.

3. **Select the Printer Sharing check box.**

4. **Click Show All.**

5. **Click the Print & Fax icon.** The Print & Fax preferences appear.

6. **Share the printer.**

- **OS X Leopard.** Click the printer you want to share and then select the Share this printer check box.

- **Earlier versions of OS X.** Click the Sharing tab, select the Share these printers with other computers check box, and then select the check box beside each printer you want to share.

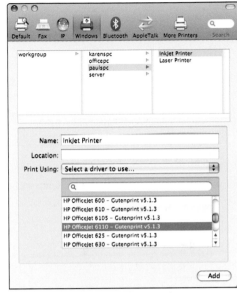

1.24 You can add a shared printer from a Windows computer.

Connecting and Sharing a Fax

Even in this age of e-mail, instant messaging, and chat, the need to fax things comes up surprisingly often for some of you. Dedicated fax machines bit the electronic dust many years ago, and no wonder given fax modems enable you to send and receive faxes from the comfort of your Mac. For this to work, you need to connect a fax modem to your Mac. In the following sections, I show you how to do this three different ways.

Connecting a fax modem

If your Mac doesn't come with a built-in fax modem, you need to connect an external fax modem — such as the almost too-cute Apple USB Modem shown in figure 1.25 — to your computer.

1.25 You can connect the Apple USB Modem to your Mac to add faxing capabilities.

After you've connected the modem, follow these steps to add it to your Mac's list of printers and faxes:

1. **Click System Preferences in the Dock, click Print & Fax, and then click the + icon.** Your Mac displays the Printer Browser.

2. **Display the list of faxing devices.**

   - **OS X Leopard.** Click the Fax tab. A list of attached faxing devices appears, as shown in figure 1.26.

   - **Earlier versions of OS X.** Click the Default Browser tab.

3. **Click the device you want to use for faxing.**

4. **Click Add.** Your fax is now connected to your Mac.

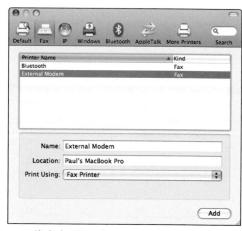

1.26 Click the Fax tab to see your attached faxing devices.

Adding a shared network fax

To use a shared network fax, you must first add it to your Mac's list of printers and faxes. Follow these steps:

1. **Click System Preferences in the Dock, click Print & Fax, and then click the + icon.** Your Mac displays the Printer Browser.

2. **Display the list of faxing devices.**

   - **OS X Leopard.** Click the Fax tab. A list of attached faxing devices appears, as shown in figure 1.26.

   - **Earlier versions of OS X.** Click the Default Browser tab.

3. **Select the shared fax you want to use.** There are two ways to recognize a shared fax:

   - **OS X Leopard.** The Kind column displays Bonjour Shared.

   - **Earlier versions of OS X.** The Connection column displays Shared Fax.

4. **Click Add.** You are now ready to use a shared network fax.

Sharing your fax with the network

If you have a fax modem connected to your Mac and you'd like other folks on your network to use that fax, you can share it by following these steps:

1. **Click System Preferences in the Dock.**

2. **Click the Sharing icon.** The Sharing preferences appear.

3. **Select the Printer Sharing check box.**

4. **Click Show All.**

5. **Click the Print & Fax icon.** The Print & Fax preferences appear.

6. **Share the fax.**

   - **OS X Leopard.** Click the fax you want to share and then select the Share this fax check box.

   - **Earlier versions of OS X.** Click the Sharing tab and then select the Let others send faxes through this computer check box.

Working with Imaging Devices

Your Mac is a graphics powerhouse, so you should take advantage of that power by connecting various imaging devices, including digital cameras, digital camcorders, and document scanners. Most of these devices connect without a hassle, but there are a few things you need to watch out for, and a few extra steps you need to follow to make sure each works as it should. In the next few sections, I take you through all this, as well as show you how to set up a camcorder or digital camera as a Webcam.

Connecting an imaging device

Connecting an imaging device to your Mac is mostly a straightforward bit of business that begins at the beginning by attaching the device:

- **Digital camera.** Attach a USB cable to the camera and to a free USB port on your Mac.

- **Digital camcorder.** Attach a FireWire cable to the video camera and to a FireWire port on your Mac.

- **Scanner.** Attach a USB cable to the scanner and to a free USB port on your Mac. Note, too, that you must also install the software that came with the scanner. This installs the scanner device driver as well as the scanning application — sometimes called the TWAIN software — that operates the scanner.

For most digital camera and camcorders, your Mac will immediately connect to the device and perhaps even offer to download images (via iPhoto) or video (via iMovie). However, with some cameras and most scanners, you need to perform some extra steps to complete the connection:

1. **In Finder, choose Applications ⇨ Image Capture.** The Image Capture program appears.

2. **Choose Devices ⇨ Browse Devices (or press ⌘+B).** Image Capture displays a list of available devices.

3. **If necessary, double-click the branch containing the device you want to connect.** For example, to connect a scanner, open the TWAIN devices branch.

4. **Choose the device you want to work with.**

5. **If you're working with a scanner, select the Use TWAIN software check box to use the device's application to scan images rather than Image Capture.**

6. **Connect the device.**

   - **OS X Leopard.** Select the check box in the device's Connected column.

   - **Earlier versions of OS X.** Click the Connect button (see figure 1.27).

1.27 Some imaging devices — particularly scanners — require a few extra steps to complete the connection.

Caution Most FireWire-compatible digital camcorders are compatible with Macs, but not all. For example, most Sony digital camcorders don't work with Macs. If you're looking to buy a camcorder, be sure to do some research on the Web to make sure the camera you want is Mac-friendly.

Connecting to a network imaging device

When you set up a network for your Macs, you might expect to share devices such as a printer and a DVD drive, but did you know that you can also share imaging devices? This is a great feature because it enables you to view and download a camera's pictures, import a camcorder's video, or operate a scanner, all without having any of these devices connected directly to your Mac. Follow these steps to connect to a share imaging device:

1. **In Finder, choose Applications ⇨ Image Capture.** The Image Capture program appears.
2. **Choose Devices ⇨ Browse Devices (or press ⌘+B).** Image Capture displays a list of available devices.
3. **Double-click the Remote Image Capture devices branch.**
4. **Double-click the branch that contains the imaging device you need.**
5. **Choose the device you want to work with.**
6. **Connect the device.**
   - **OS X Leopard.** Select the check box in the device's Connected column.
   - **Earlier versions of OS X.** Click the Connect button.

Sharing an imaging device

If you have a digital camera, digital camcorder, or scanner connected to your Mac, you can share that device with your network pals.

How you go about this is quite a bit different in OS X Leopard than in earlier versions of OS X, so I'll treat them separately. First, here's how to do it in Leopard:

1. **In Finder, choose Applications ⇨ Image Capture.** The Image Capture program appears.
2. **Choose Devices ⇨ Browse Devices (or press ⌘+B).** Image Capture displays a list of available devices.
3. **Click Sharing.**
4. **Select the Share my devices check box, as shown in figure 1.28.**

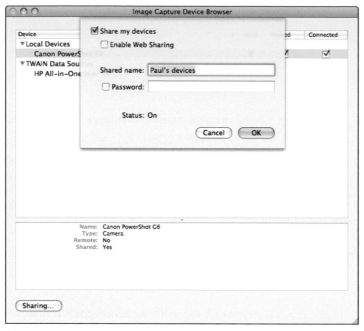

1.28 Select the Share my devices check box to share one or more of your Mac's imaging devices with your network.

5. **Edit the Shared name if you feel like it.**

6. **If you want folks to enter a password to use the devices, select the Password check box and then type your password.**

7. **Click OK.** The Image Capture Device Browser window now appears with a Shared column.

8. **For each device you want to share, select the check box in the device's Shared column.**

Now here are the steps for sharing an imaging device in earlier version of OS X:

1. **In Finder, choose Applications ➪ Image Capture.** The Image Capture program appears.

2. **Choose Image Capture ➪ Preferences.** The Image Capture Preferences dialog box appears.

3. **Click the Sharing tab.**

4. **Select the Share my devices check box.**

5. **Select the check box for each device you want to share.**

6. **Edit the Shared name, if so desired.**

7. **If you want to protect your devices with a password, select the Password check box and then type your password.**

8. **Click OK.**

Configuring a camera as a Webcam

A *Webcam* is a camera that's accessible over a network or the Internet that takes a snapshot every so often (for example, once a minute). This enables you to remotely monitor whatever scene the camera is pointed at, which can be handy for security or just to watch something interesting from afar. Webcams normally require special software, but you can configure your Mac's Image Capture program to handle all the hard work, as I show you in the next few sections.

Enabling Web Sharing for the camera

In the previous section, I covered sharing imaging devices over the network. To set up your Webcam, you need to go a step further and enable Web Sharing for your imaging devices. You do this by following essentially the same steps as in the previous section, with the following differences:

● **OS X Leopard.** In Image Capture, click Sharing, select the Share my devices check box (if you haven't done so already), and also select the Enable Web Sharing check box. Image Capture displays an address below the check box, as shown in figure 1.29. Make note of this address, because you'll need it later to connect to the Webcam over your network.

1.29 Select the Enable Web Sharing check box to turn on your Webcam.

- **Earlier versions of OS X.** In Image Capture, click the Sharing tab, select the Share my devices check box (if you haven't done so already), and also select the Enable Web Sharing check box. Again, Image Capture displays an address below the check box, which you need to make note of.

Viewing the Webcam over your network

With Web Sharing enabled, you're ready to check out your Webcam. First, be sure to point your camcorder or digital camera at whatever site you want to view. Now, on the remote network computer, launch Safari and enter the address that Image Capture displayed when you selected the Enable Web Sharing check box in the previous section. Safari opens a page named Digital Cameras on *Computer*, where *Computer* is the name of the Mac that's got Web Sharing turned on. Click the Remote Monitor tab, and the camera takes a snapshot that's then displayed in the tab, as shown in figure 1.30.

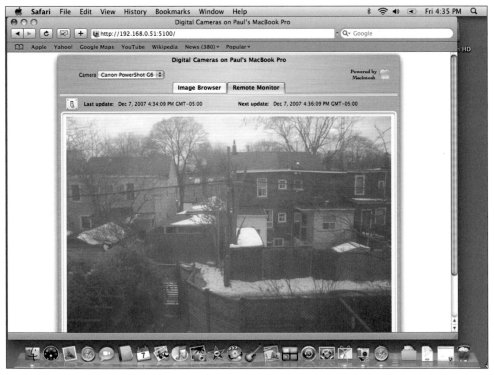

1.30 Use the Remote Monitor tab to view the scene with pictures that update periodically.

Note

By default, the Remote Monitor takes a new picture every minute. To change the frequency, click the light switch icon that appears to the left of the Last update text. Type the number of times per hour you want a new picture taken, and then click Set.

Viewing the Webcam over the Internet

If you want to view your newfangled Webcam over the Internet, things get a tad trickier because you need to configure your network's router to allow this. Unfortunately, every router manufacturer has a different way of configuring their devices, so I can't give you the specific steps to follow. Just so you know what to do, here are the general steps:

1. **Open your router's setup pages.** You do this by entering the router's IP address into a Web browser. See your router's manual to learn the IP address to use.

2. **Set up port forwarding (sometimes called a virtual server) to the Mac that's running the Webcam.** Again, see your router manual for the specific steps required here. You usually have to specify some or all of the following:

   - **Name.** This can be anything you want, such as "Webcam."

   - **IP address.** This is the address of the Mac running the Webcam and is the address you used in the previous section, minus the :5100 at the end. For example, if you used http://192.168.0.51:5100 to access the Webcam over the network, the IP address is http://192.168.0.51.

   - **Protocol.** Select TCP here.

   - **Port.** Use 5100 for this.

3. **Determine your router's public IP address.** This is the IP address of the router's Internet connection. In your router setup pages, look for a Status page, which will tell you the current IP address of the router.

With all that done, you access the Webcam over the Internet by entering the address http://*RouterIP*:5100 into the Web browser, where *RouterIP* is the router's public IP address.

That mass of wires and cables under your desk doesn't have a name, although some of the more waggish suggestions I've heard are *corducopia*, *quagwire*, and *nerdnest*. In the end, though, it doesn't much matter because let's face it: wires are *so* last century. Wireless is the way to go, and chances are your Mac is already configured to use a wireless technology called Bluetooth. In this chapter, I cover what Bluetooth is; how to set up your Mac with Bluetooth; how to connect your Mac with various Bluetooth devices such as a mouse, keyboard, headset, and cell phone; and how to configure your Mac's Bluetooth capabilities.

Finding Your Bluetooth Connection

In the same way that your Mac must have a wireless network adapter installed to use Wi-Fi, so too must your Mac have a Bluetooth adapter installed to make Bluetooth connections. Fortunately, most modern Macs come with built-in Bluetooth, including the latest models of the iMac, Mac mini, MacBook Pro, and MacBook. Bluetooth is an optional component with the Mac Pro. Note, too, that all Macs running OS X 10.2 (Jaguar) or later can get in on the Bluetooth thing by installing a Bluetooth adapter in a free USB port.

How can you tell whether your Mac supports Bluetooth? Look for the Bluetooth status icon in the menu bar, as shown in figure 2.1.

If you don't see the icon there, click the System Preferences icon in the Dock and look for the Bluetooth icon in the Hardware section of the System Preferences window, as shown in figure 2.2.

2.1 If your Mac has built-in Bluetooth, you usually see the Bluetooth status icon (far left) in the menu bar.

2.2 If your Mac is Bluetooth-capable, you see the Bluetooth icon in the System Preferences window.

A Bit of Bluetooth Background

You're probably familiar with Wi-Fi, the standard that enables you to perform networking chores without the usual network cables. Bluetooth is similar in that it enables you to exchange data between two devices without any kind of physical connection between them. Bluetooth uses radio frequencies to set up a communications link between the devices. That link is another example of an ad hoc wireless network that you learned about in Chapter 1, only in this case the network that Bluetooth creates is called a *piconet*.

Bluetooth is a short-distance networking technology, with a maximum range of about 33 feet (10 meters). You can use your Mac's Bluetooth capabilities to make connections with a wide variety of devices, including:

- Another Bluetooth-enabled Mac
- Mouse (such as Apple's Wireless Mighty Mouse)
- Keyboard (such as Apple's Wireless Keyboard)
- Headset
- Cell phone
- Personal digital assistant
- Printer
- Digital camera

Note

The Bluetooth name comes from Harald Bluetooth, a tenth-century Danish king who united the provinces of Denmark under a single crown, the same way that, theoretically, Bluetooth will unite the world of portable wireless devices under a single standard. Why name a modern technology after an obscure Danish king? Here's a clue: two of the most important companies backing the Bluetooth standard — Ericsson and Nokia — are Scandinavian.

Adding a Bluetooth Adapter

If your Mac doesn't have built-in Bluetooth, you can still get in on the action by installing a separate Bluetooth adapter. There are only two requirements:

- Your Mac must have a free USB port, given almost all external Bluetooth adapters are USB devices.

- Your Mac must be running OS X 10.2 (Jaguar) or later. OS X 10.1 and OS 9 don't offer Bluetooth support.

Most Bluetooth adapters are small devices that look similar to the D-Link DBT-120 shown in figure 2.3.

Insert the Bluetooth adapter in a free USB port and your Mac should immediately recognize the new device and awaken the previously dormant OS X Bluetooth features. (You can confirm this by using the techniques I mentioned in the previous section.) You can now connect with other Bluetooth devices.

2.3 The D-Link DBT-120 is a typical Bluetooth adapter.

Bluetooth Adapter Buyer's Guide

Bear in mind these points when you're shopping for a Bluetooth adapter for your Mac:

- Most Bluetooth adapters are priced between $15 to $35 at online retailers such as NewEgg.com and Amazon.com, and there's really no reason to spend any more than that.

- Bluetooth data transfers aren't particularly fast, but to ensure maximum speed you need to get an adapter that supports Bluetooth 2.0, which is about three times faster than Bluetooth 1.2 or 1.1.

- There are adapters with extended ranges of up to 100 meters (330 feet), but these are usually more expensive, and it's almost always not worth the extra bucks. Bluetooth is meant for short-range connections.

- To ensure a quality product, stick with the major manufacturers, including ASUS, D-Link, GWC, IOGEAR, Linksys, Micro-Star International (MSI), SMC Networks, and TRENDnet.

Caution When you're researching Bluetooth adapters, pay close attention to the operating system support. Some adapters only work with Windows, and some Mac-friendly adapters require a later version of OS X (for example, the D-Link DBT-120 requires OS X 10.3 [Panther] or later).

Connecting Bluetooth Devices

In theory, connecting Bluetooth devices should be criminally easy: You turn on each device's Bluetooth feature — in Bluetooth jargon, you make the device *discoverable* — bring them within 33 feet of each other, and they connect without further ado. In practice, however, there's usually at least a bit of further ado (and sometimes plenty of it). This usually takes one or both of the following forms:

- **Making your device discoverable.** Unlike Wi-Fi devices that broadcast their signals constantly, most Bluetooth devices only broadcast their availability when you say so. This makes sense in many cases because you usually only want to use a Bluetooth device such as a mouse or keyboard with a single computer. By controlling when the device is discoverable, you ensure that it works only with the computer you want it to.

- **Pairing your Mac and the device.** As a security precaution, many Bluetooth devices need to be *paired* with another device before the connection is established. In most cases, the pairing is accomplished by your Mac generating an 8-digit *passkey* that you must then type into the Bluetooth device (assuming, of course, that it has some kind of keypad). In other cases, the device comes with a default passkey that you must enter into your Mac to set up the pairing. Finally, some devices set up an automatic pairing using an empty passkey.

Connecting a Bluetooth mouse or keyboard

Having a wireless mouse and keyboard is a blissful state because, with no cord to tie you down, it gives you the freedom to interact with your Mac from just about anywhere. Wi-Fi mice and keyboards are often cumbersome because they require a separate transceiver, and these tend to be large and take up a USB port. If your Mac already has Bluetooth, however, you don't need anything else to use a Bluetooth-compatible mouse or keyboard.

Follow these general steps to connect a Bluetooth mouse or keyboard:

1. **Click the Bluetooth status icon in the menu bar, and then choose Set up Bluetooth Device.** The Bluetooth Setup Assistant appears.

Note You can also choose System Preferences ➪ Bluetooth to open the Bluetooth window, and then click Set Up New Device. If the Bluetooth window shows that you already have at least one Bluetooth device set up, you start the Bluetooth Setup Assistant by clicking the + icon below the device list.

2. **Click Continue.** The Select Device Type dialog box appears.

3. **Select the option for the device you want to connect and then click Continue.** If the mouse or keyboard has an on/off switch, turn it on. If the mouse or keyboard has a separate switch or button that makes it discoverable, turn on that switch or press that button. When the Bluetooth Setup Assistant discovers the device, it displays the device name, as shown in figure 2.4.

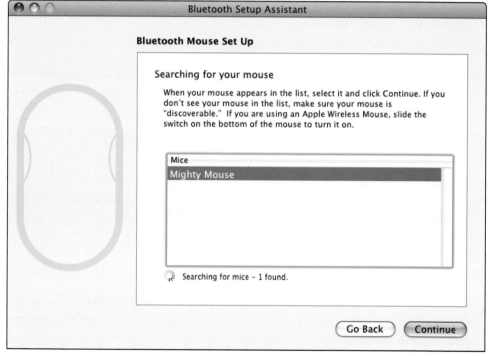

2.4 When the Bluetooth Setup Assistant discovers a Bluetooth device, it displays the device name.

4. **Click Continue.** Your Mac connects with the mouse or keyboard. When your Mac connects with the keyboard, the Bluetooth Setup Assistant displays a passkey for the pairing, as shown in figure 2.5. Using the Bluetooth keyboard, type the passkey and then press Return.

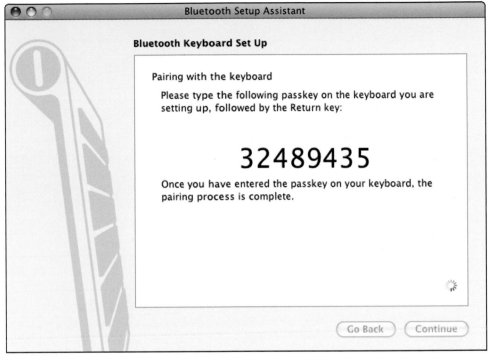

Bluetooth Setup Assistant

Bluetooth Keyboard Set Up

Pairing with the keyboard

Please type the following passkey on the keyboard you are setting up, followed by the Return key:

32489435

Once you have entered the passkey on your keyboard, the pairing process is complete.

Go Back   Continue

2.5 To establish a pairing with a Bluetooth keyboard, you need to type a passkey on the keyboard.

5. **Click Quit and you are ready to use your Bluetooth mouse or keyboard.**

Configuring your Bluetooth mouse and keyboard

When you connect a Bluetooth mouse and/or keyboard, in most cases you just go ahead and start mousing and typing. However, your Mac does give you a limited set of configuration options, and it also enables you to monitor the battery levels of these devices.

To change the configuration options, display the Keyboard & Mouse preferences by clicking the Dock's System Preferences icon, and then clicking the Keyboard & Mouse icon. From there click the Bluetooth tab, shown in figure 2.6.

Note

When your Mac wakes from sleep mode, the Bluetooth mouse doesn't always respond right away. Wait a few seconds (usually no more than about 10 seconds) to give the mouse time to re-establish itself. Sometimes clicking the mouse helps it to reconnect right away.

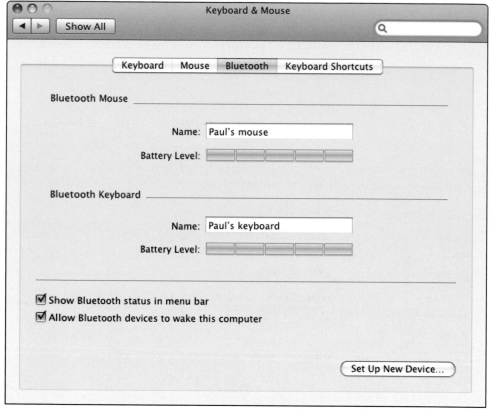

2.6 Use the Bluetooth tab to rename your device and monitor the battery level.

You can use the Name text boxes to rename the devices, if desired. Or, use the Battery Level icons to monitor the current battery level for each device. You can also decide to have your Mac wake from sleep mode by tapping the keyboard or clicking the mouse. Simply select the Allow Bluetooth devices to wake this computer check box.

Connecting a Bluetooth headset

If you want to listen to music, headphones are a great way to go because the sound is often better than with the built-in Mac speakers, and no one else around gets subjected to Led Zeppelin at top volume. Similarly, if you want to conduct a voice chat, a headset (a combination of headphones for listening and a microphone for talking) makes life easier because you don't need a separate microphone and at least one half of your conversation remains private. Add Bluetooth into the mix, and you've got an easy and wireless audio solution.

Follow these general steps to connect a Bluetooth headset:

1. **Launch the Bluetooth Setup Assistant.**

   - Click the Bluetooth status icon in the menu bar, and then choose Set up Bluetooth Device.

   - Choose System Preferences ⇨ Bluetooth to open the Bluetooth window, and then click Set Up New Device.

2. **Click Continue.** The Select Device Type dialog box appears.

3. **Select the Headset option and then click Continue.** If the headset has a separate switch or button that makes the device discoverable, turn on that switch or press that button. Wait until you see the correct headset name appear in the list.

4. **Click Continue.** Your Mac connects with the headset and the Bluetooth Setup Assistant prompts you for the headset's default passkey to establish the pairing, as shown in figure 2.7.

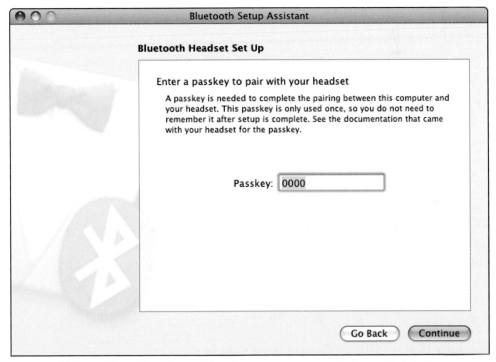

2.7 To establish a pairing with a Bluetooth headset, you need to type the headset's default passkey.

5. **See the headset document to get the passkey (it's often 0000); type the passkey and then click Continue.**

6. **Click Quit and the headset is ready to use.**

Using Bluetooth headphones for sound output

Because when you connect Bluetooth headphones, your Mac doesn't automatically use them as the default sound output device, if you want to listen to, say, your iTunes library without disturbing your neighbors, then you need to configure your Mac to use your headphones as the sound output device. Here's how:

1. **Click the System Preferences icon in the Dock.** The System Preferences window appears.

2. **Click the Sound icon.** The Sound preferences appear.

3. **Click the Output tab, and then select your Bluetooth headphones from the list, as shown in figure 2.8.**

4. **Adjust the other sound settings as desired.**

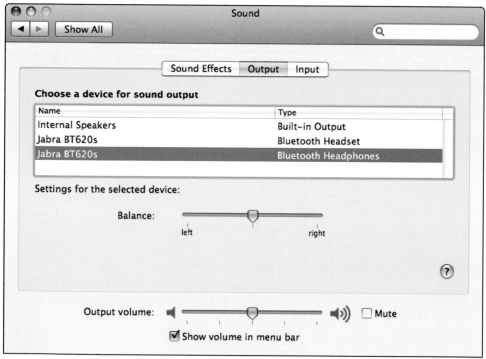

2.8 To keep your iTunes to yourself, select your Bluetooth headphones as your Mac's sound output device.

Setting up a Bluetooth headset for voice chat

If you love to chat, typing messages back and forth is a fun way to pass the time. However, if you want to take things up a notch, then you need to use iChat's voice chat capabilities, which enable you to have voice conversations with your buddies. When you connect to a Bluetooth headset, your Mac usually sets up the headset as the voice chat microphone, but it usually doesn't set up the headphones as the sound output device. Follow these steps to configure voice chat to use your Bluetooth headset:

1. **Click the Dock's iChat icon and choose iChat ⇨ Preferences from the menu that appears.**

2. **Click the Audio/Video tab.**

3. **Select your Bluetooth headset from the Microphone and Sound Output lists as shown in figure 2.9.**

Making the connection to your Bluetooth phone

Your cell phone should be, at least theoretically, an extension of your Mac given both devices store information such as contact data, appointments, tasks, and notes, and you can use both devices to store media files such as digital music and digital photos. To avoid having two different sets of data to deal with,

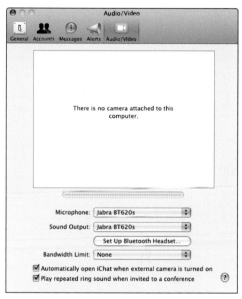

2.9 For voice chats, choose your Bluetooth headset in both the Microphone and Sound Output lists.

you'll want to synchronize your Mac and your Bluetooth cell phone. I cover doing this in Chapter 3, but for now, you just need to know how to connect your Bluetooth phone.

Follow these general steps to connect a Bluetooth phone:

1. **Click the Bluetooth status icon in the menu bar, and then choose Set up Bluetooth Device to launch the Bluetooth Setup Assistant.**

2. **Click Continue.** The Select Device Type dialog box appears.

3. **Select the Mobile phone option and then click Continue.**

Genius

If your buddies often tell you to stop shouting, even though you're using your normal voice, you'll need to make a quick volume adjustment. In the Audio chat window, you can click and drag the volume slider to the left. To set the global volume level, choose System Preferences ⇨ Sound and then click the Input tab. Click and drag the Input volume slider to the left to reduce the volume.

4. **Turn on the phone and activate the feature that makes the phone discoverable.** Wait until you see your phone's name appear in the list, as shown in figure 2.10.

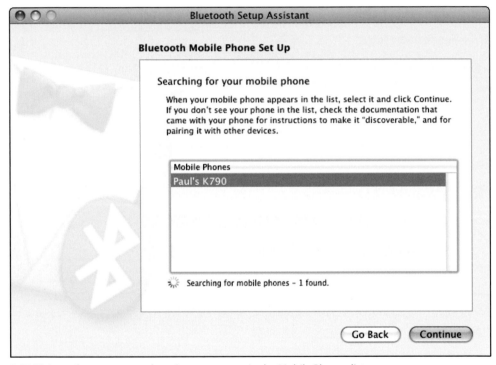

Bluetooth Setup Assistant

Bluetooth Mobile Phone Set Up

Searching for your mobile phone

When your mobile phone appears in the list, select it and click Continue. If you don't see your phone in the list, check the documentation that came with your phone for instructions to make it "discoverable," and for pairing it with other devices.

Mobile Phones
Paul's K790

Searching for mobile phones – 1 found.

Go Back   Continue

2.10 Wait until you see your phone's name appear in the Mobile Phones list.

Note

Mac OS X 10.5 (Leopard) can work with many different phones from a number of different manufacturers, particularly Motorola, Nokia, Samsung, and Sony Ericsson. For a list of compatible phones, check out www.apple.com/macosx/features/isync/index.html.

5. **Click Continue.** Your Mac connects with the phone.

6. **Click Continue.** The Bluetooth Setup Assistant displays a passkey for the pairing, as shown in figure 2.11. When your phone asks whether you want to allow the Mac to connect, accept the connection.

Note You can also choose System Preferences ⇨ Bluetooth to open the Bluetooth window, and then click Set Up New Device. If the Bluetooth window shows that you already have at least one Bluetooth device set up, you start the Bluetooth Setup Assistant by clicking the + icon below the device list.

2.11 To establish a pairing with a Bluetooth cell phone, you need to enter a passkey using the phone's keypad.

7. **Using the Bluetooth phone's keypad, enter the passkey.** Your Mac pairs with the cell phone.

8. **Choose the services you want to use with the cell phone:**

   - **Set up iSync to transfer contacts and events.** Select this check box to add the phone to iSync so you can synchronize your Mac's Address Book contacts and iCal events with the phone. See Chapter 3 for more on synching with a cell phone.

   - **Use with Address Book (OS X 10.4 only).** Select this check box to use the cell phone as your Mac Address Book's Bluetooth device.

- **Access the Internet with your phone's data connection.** Select this check box to surf the Internet on your Mac using your cell phone's Internet connection. You provide the connection information on the next screen (see figure 2.12).

- **Use device as a remote control for this computer.** Select this check box to use your phone's keypad to control your Mac. If your phone supports this feature, it should give you various remote control choices, such as a basic desktop template and a media control template.

- **Use device as a network port (OS X 10.5 only).** Select this check box to connect your Mac to another network via your phone.

9. **Click Continue.** What happens next depends on the services you selected in Step 8:

    - **Set up iSync to transfer contacts and events.** If you selected this check box, the iSync application opens to enable you to configure your phone. Again, check out Chapter 3 for the details.

    - **Access the Internet with your phone's data connection.** If you selected this option, you see the Bluetooth Mobile Phone Set Up dialog box, shown in figure 2.12. Fill in the data given to you by your cell phone service provider, and then click Continue.

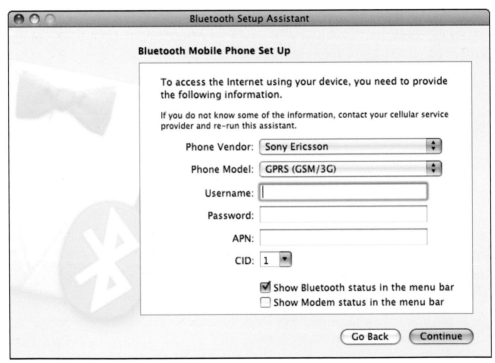

2.12 If you want to access the Internet through your cell phone, you may need to fill in your service provider's data.

- **Use device as a remote control for this computer.** If you selected this option, your phone should ask you to confirm that you want to use the phone as a remote control. Make the confirmation. Your phone may then ask if you want to start the remote control feature, which you can either start now or wait until later.

10. **Click Quit.** You can now use the cell phone.

Using your cell phone as a Bluetooth modem

As I covered in the previous section, you can configure the pairing between your Mac and a Bluetooth cell phone so that the Mac uses the cell phone's Internet connection. In this configuration, the cell phone acts as a Bluetooth modem, which can come in handy if you're on the road with your Mac notebook and there's no other Internet connection nearby. (It's also useful at home if your regular Internet connection goes down and you desperately need to access some information online. We've all been there!)

Note   If your cell phone is set up to automatically connect to the Internet, then you probably don't have to enter any information in the Bluetooth Mobile Phone Set Up dialog box.

To make the connection, turn on your cell phone, click the Bluetooth status icon in the menu bar, and then use one of the following techniques:

- **OS X 10.5 (Leopard).** Choose your Bluetooth phone, and then choose Connect to Network.

- **OS X 10.4 or earlier.** Click the Bluetooth status icon in the menu bar, and then choose Join Network on *Phone* (where *Phone* is the name of your Bluetooth phone).

In either case, when your cell phone asks you to confirm the connection, select Yes (or whatever the affirmative option is).

Using your Bluetooth phone with the Address Book

If you're running OS X 10.4 (Tiger), the Address Book application comes with built-in Bluetooth features that enable it to work hand in hand with your cell phone. (Sadly, these useful features were taken out of the Leopard Address Book.)

The Address Book comes with a Bluetooth icon in the toolbar. Click that icon to connect the Address Book and your Bluetooth phone. For this to work, you need to have configured your phone to use the Address Book.

With your Address Book and Bluetooth phone on speaking terms, the Address Book enables a few features related to outgoing and incoming calls:

● **Outgoing calls and messages.** Click and hold the name of a phone number field in an Address Book entry and you see the menu shown in figure 2.13. Click SMS Message to send a message to this person via your Bluetooth phone; click Dial with *Phone* (where *Phone* is your cell phone name) to call this person via your Bluetooth phone.

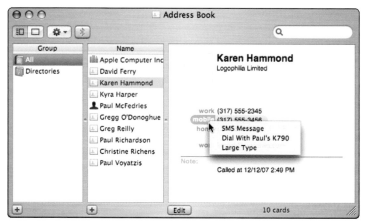

2.13 With your Address Book connected to your Bluetooth phone, you can use the phone to call someone or to send that person a text message.

● **Incoming calls.** If you receive a call on your Bluetooth phone while it's connected to your Address Book, your Mac displays an Incoming Phone Call dialog box like the one shown in figure 2.14. This usually shows as Unknown, but if the caller is in your Address Book, you see the person's name and phone num-

2.14 With your Address Book and Bluetooth phone connected, you see the Incoming Phone Call dialog box when your phone receives a call.

ber. Note, too, that if you have an Address Book entry for a caller, the Note section of that entry tells you when the person last called (as you can see in figure 2.13).

Connecting to the Palm OS PDA

Your Mac can make a connection to certain Palm OS Bluetooth devices, which enables you to exchange files and synchronize your contacts and calendar. Unfortunately, your Mac is finicky when it comes to Palm devices, so it only works with two types: the Palm Tungsten family and the Palm Zire family.

Note If you have another type of PDA, you may still be able to synchronize it with your Mac, but you need third-party software to do it. See the mark/space site at www.markspace.com/ for the Missing Sync program, which works with most PDAs.

Before making the connection, you need to configure your Palm handheld to activate Bluetooth and make the device discoverable. Follow these steps:

1. **Tap the Home icon.**

2. **Tap the Bluetooth icon.**

3. **Tap the On button.**

4. **In the Discoverable menu, tap Yes.**

5. **To customize the device name, tap inside the Device Name box and then enter the new name.**

Now that your Palm is discoverable, follow these general steps to connect a Bluetooth Palm OS PDA:

1. **Launch the Bluetooth Setup Assistant.**

   - Click the Bluetooth status icon in the menu bar, and then choose Set up Bluetooth Device.

   - Choose System Preferences ⇨ Bluetooth to open the Bluetooth window, and then click Set Up New Device.

Note If the Bluetooth window shows that you already have at least one Bluetooth device set up, you start the Bluetooth Setup Assistant by clicking the + icon below the device list.

2. **Click Continue.** The Select Device Type dialog box appears.

3. **Select the Any device option and then click Continue.**

4. **Turn on the Palm OS device.** Wait until you see your handheld's name appear in the list, as shown in figure 2.15.

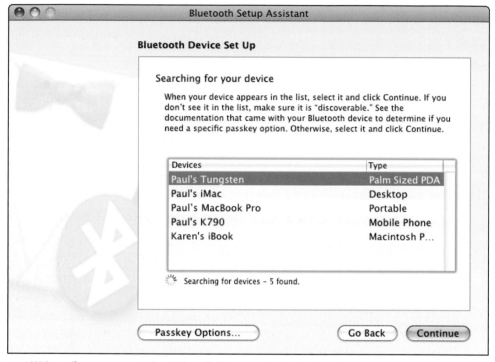

2.15 Wait until you see your Palm OS handheld appear in the Devices list.

5. **Click Continue.** Your Mac connects with the handheld.

6. **Click Continue.** The Bluetooth Setup Assistant displays a passkey for the pairing.

7. **On your Palm OS handheld, enter the passkey.** If you want your Palm OS handheld to always trust your Mac, select the Add to trusted device list check box.

8. **Click OK.** Your Mac pairs with the Palm OS device.

9. **Click Continue.**

10. **Click Quit.** Your Palm OS device is now connected to your Mac.

Exchanging Files Using Bluetooth

If you have a Bluetooth device that can work with files such as documents, music, and images, or data such as appointments and addresses, you can exchange files between your Mac and the Bluetooth device. Bear in mind, however, that this is useful only for small files. Bluetooth isn't the fastest technology out there, so these transfers can be glacially slow. Small items such as addresses and appointments transfer reasonably fast, but it can take a few minutes to transfer a single MP3 file. Still, if you have no other way to transfer data, Bluetooth will do in a pinch.

You can either transfer files from your Mac to a Bluetooth device using your Mac's Bluetooth File Exchange utility or from a Bluetooth device to your Mac by activating and configuring your Mac's Bluetooth Sharing feature.

Making sure your Mac is discoverable

If you want other Bluetooth devices to see your Mac and initiate pairings or other operations such as cell phone remote control, then you need to make sure not only that your Mac's Bluetooth power is on, but also that your Mac is discoverable. Follow these steps:

1. **Open the Bluetooth preferences.**
   - Click the Bluetooth status icon in the menu bar, and then choose Open Bluetooth Preferences.
   - Click the Dock's System Preferences icon and then click Bluetooth.

2. **Turn on the Bluetooth power.**
   - **OS X 10.5 (Leopard).** Select the Bluetooth Power check box.
   - **OS X 10.4 or earlier.** Click the Settings tab and, if the Bluetooth Power setting is currently Off, click Turn Bluetooth On.

3. **Make your Mac discoverable.**
   - **OS X 10.5 (Leopard).** Select the Discoverable check box.
   - **OS X 10.4 or earlier.** Click the Settings tab and then select the Discoverable check box.

Browsing a Bluetooth device

When you browse a Bluetooth device, you examine the contents of the device and, optionally, get one or more files from the device. You do this using the Bluetooth File Exchange utility; follow these steps:

1. **In Finder, choose Applications ⇨ Utilities ⇨ Bluetooth File Exchange.** If you see the Select File to Send dialog box, click Cancel.

2. **Choose File ⇨ Browse Device.** You can also press Shift+⌘+O. The Browse Files dialog box appears and displays a list of available Bluetooth devices, as shown in figure 2.16.

3. **Click the device you want to browse.**

4. **Click Browse.** The Browsing dialog box appears.

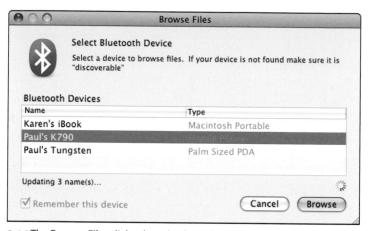

2.16 The Browse Files dialog box displays a list of nearby Bluetooth devices.

5. **Double-click the folders to get to the one you want to view.** If you want to download a file to your Mac, click the file, click Get, as shown in figure 2.17, select a location, and then click Save.

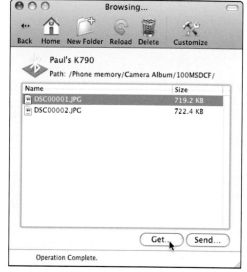

Sending files to a Bluetooth device

If you've got some data you want to share with a Bluetooth device, the Bluetooth File Exchange utility is only too happy to help you do it. Here's how it works:

1. **In Finder, choose Applications ⇨ Utilities ⇨ Bluetooth File Exchange.** If you don't see the Select File to Send dialog box right away, choose File ⇨ Send File. You can also press ⌘+O.

2.17 Use the Browsing dialog box to navigate the Bluetooth device's folders and, optionally, download a file to your Mac.

2. **Choose the file you want to upload and then click Send.** The Select Bluetooth Device dialog box appears and displays a list of waiting devices.

3. **Click the device you want to use.**

4. **Click Send.** The Bluetooth File Exchange attempts to connect with the device. Use the device interface to accept the incoming file.

Activating Bluetooth sharing

The Bluetooth File Exchange utility is great for browsing and sending stuff to a Bluetooth device or to another Bluetoothed Mac, but what about the other way around? That is, what about getting a Bluetooth device to send things to your Mac? If the Bluetooth device is another Mac then, of course, you can crank up Bluetooth File Exchange on that computer and use the techniques from the previous two sections. For cell phones, PDAs, and other file-friendly devices, connect them to your Mac and initiate the browsing or sending from there.

You must activate and configure your Mac's Bluetooth Sharing feature. This feature enables other Bluetooth devices to connect to your Mac, specifies what those devices can see and do, and also determines whether pairing is required to browse or send files to your Mac. How you do all this is completely new in Leopard, so I cover the Leopard and pre-Leopard steps separately.

The Leopard steps required to activate and configure Bluetooth Sharing are as follows:

1. **Click the Dock's System Preferences icon and then click Sharing.**

2. **Select the Bluetooth Sharing check box to turn on the Bluetooth Sharing feature, as shown in figure 2.18.**

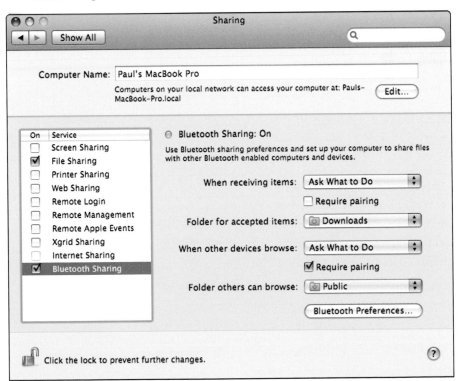

2.18 Select the Bluetooth Sharing check box and then use the other controls to configure this feature.

3. **Configure your Mac to receive files.**

   - **When receiving items.** Use this list to determine what your Mac does when a Bluetooth device attempts to send a file. It's usually best to choose Ask What to Do so you always have control over the transfer. If you never want files sent to your Mac, choose Never Allow instead.

   - **Require pairing.** If you select this check box, your Mac won't allow a Bluetooth device to initiate a file transfer unless the two devices have been paired.

   - **Folder for accepted items.** Use this list to choose the folder where files sent to your Mac get stored.

4. **Configure your Mac for browsing.**

   - **When other devices browse.** Use this list to determine what your Mac does when a Bluetooth device attempts to browse the Mac's file. Again, it's best to choose Ask What to Do so you always have control over the browsing. If browsing isn't a problem for you, you can avoid being pestered by choosing Always Allow instead. If you never want Bluetooth devices to browse your Mac, choose Never Allow.

   - **Require pairing.** This check box is selected by default, which means your Mac won't allow a Bluetooth device to browse unless the two devices have been paired.

   - **Folder others can browse.** Use this list to choose the folder that Bluetooth devices can browse.

The OS X 10.4 or earlier steps required to activate and configure Bluetooth Sharing are as follows:

1. **Click the Dock's System Preferences icon and then click Bluetooth.**

2. **Click the Sharing tab, shown in figure 2.19.**

3. **Choose Bluetooth File Transfer in the list of services.**

4. **Configure your Mac for browsing.**

   - **Start.** Click this button to start the Bluetooth File Transfer service. (You can also select the On check box beside Bluetooth File Transfer in the list of services.)

   - **Folder other devices can browse.** Use this list to choose the folder that Bluetooth devices can browse.

   - **Require pairing for security.** Select this check box to allow a Bluetooth device to browse your Mac only when the two devices have been paired.

5. **Choose Bluetooth File Exchange in the list of services.**

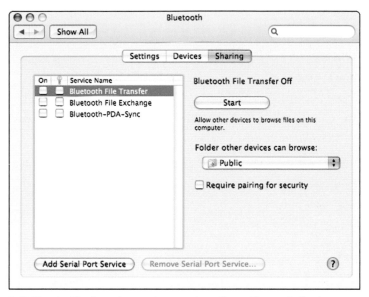

2.19 Use the Sharing tab to activate and configure Bluetooth Sharing.

6. **Configure your Mac to receive files.**

- **When receiving items.** Use this list to determine what your Mac does when a Bluetooth device attempts to send a file. It's usually best to choose Prompt for each file so you always have control over the transfer. If you never want files sent to your Mac, choose Refuse all instead.

- **When PIM items are accepted.** Use this list to determine what your Mac does when you accept incoming personal information management items such as contacts.

- **When other items are accepted.** Use this list to determine what your Mac does when you accept other files.

- **Folder for accepted items.** Use this list to choose the folder where files sent to your Mac get stored.

- **Require pairing for security.** If you select this check box, your Mac won't allow a Bluetooth device to initiate a file transfer unless the two devices have been paired.

My Mac with Other Devices?

Your Mac is a big part of your life, but it's not your whole life. You've got music, photos, podcasts, calendars, and addresses on your iPod; you've got contacts and appointments on your cell phone or PDA; and you've got files, bookmarks, mail accounts, calendars, contacts and more on your MobileMe account. That's a lot to keep track of, so how do you keep up? The secret is *synchronization*: ensuring that the data on your Mac is the same as the data on your other devices. Fortunately, your Mac has some great tools that make it easy to keep your Mac and your life in sync.

Synchronizing with an iPod

Long gone are the days when the only thing you could fill up your iPods with was music. With modern iPods and the latest version of iTunes, you can cram your players not only with your favorite tunes but also with music videos, audiobooks, movies, TV shows, podcasts, photos, contacts, calendars, and even games. Suddenly those once massive 80GB iPods don't look so big anymore. Whatever your iPod's hard drive size, if you find yourself running out of space, the alternative isn't (necessarily) to go out and buy a bigger player. Instead, iTunes gives you lots of options for controlling what gets added to (and removed from) your iPod when you sync.

Genius

If iTunes doesn't fire up automatically when you connect your iPod, you can force it to do so. In iTunes, click your iPod in the Devices list, click the Summary tab, and then select the Open iTunes when this iPod is connected check box. Click Apply to put the setting into effect.

Synchronizing music and videos

iPods are digital music players at heart, so most of you load up your devices with lots of audio content and, depending on the version of iPod you have, lots of music videos, too. To get the most out of your iPod's music and video capabilities, you need to know all the different ways you can synchronize these items. For example, if you'll be using your iPod primarily as a music player and it has far more disk capacity than you need for all of your digital audio, feel free to throw all your music onto the player. On the other hand, you may have an iPod with a limited capacity, or you may only want certain songs and videos on the player to make it easier to navigate. In such cases, you need to configure the iPod to sync only those songs and videos you want to play.

You can easily tell iTunes to toss every last song and video onto your iPod or just selected playlists. Follow these steps:

1. **In iTunes, click your iPod in the Devices list.**

2. **Click the Music tab.**

3. **Select the Sync music check box.** From this point, the options you select determine what is actually synchronized.

   - Select the Selected playlists option to choose specific playlists to be included as shown in figure 3.1. If there are videos in any of the selected playlists you do not want synced, deselect the Include music videos checkbox.

- Select the Include music videos check box to include all music videos.

- Select the Display album artwork on your iPod if you want to see this artwork on your iPod.

4. **Click Apply.** iTunes syncs the iPod using the new settings.

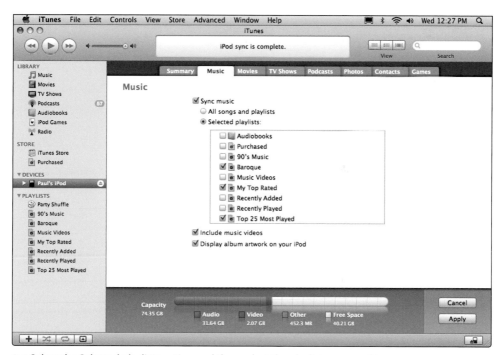

3.1 Select the Selected playlists option and then select the playlists you want to sync.

Genius

If space is tight on your iPod, you can skip syncing the album artwork by deselecting the Display album artwork on your iPod check box. You only see this check box if your iPod supports displaying color pictures.

If you want to control the individual tracks that get synced to your iPod, then you can manage your music and videos by hand. One way to do this is to use the check boxes that appear beside each track in your iTunes Music library.

Here's how you do it:

1. **In iTunes, click your iPod in the Devices list.**

2. **Click the Summary tab.**

3. **Select the Sync only checked songs and videos check box.**

4. **Click Apply.** If iTunes starts syncing your iPod, click the Cancel button, as shown in figure 3.2.

5. **Click Music from your Library list.** If a track's check box is selected, iTunes syncs the track with your iPod. If a track's check box is deselected, iTunes doesn't sync the track with your iPod. If the track is already on your iPod, iTunes removes the track.

Click to cancel sync

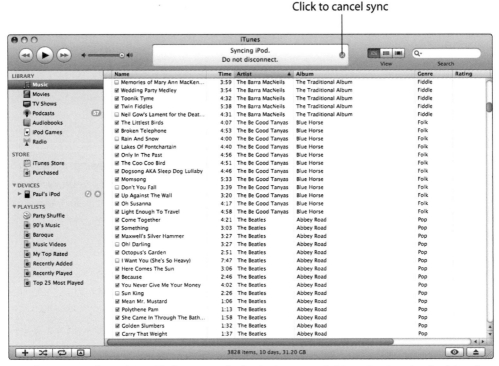

3.2 When you configured your iPod to sync only checked songs and videos, deselect the check box for each track you don't want to sync.

6. **In iTunes, click your iPod in the Devices list.**

7. **Click the Summary tab.**

8. **Click Sync.** iTunes syncs just the checked tracks.

An alternative method is to drag tracks from the Music library and drop them on your iPod. Here's how this works:

1. **In iTunes, click your iPod in the Devices list.**

2. **Click the Summary tab and select the Manually manage music and videos check box.** iTunes asks you to confirm.

3. **Click OK, then Apply, then Music.**

4. **Select the tracks you want to sync.** For non-contiguous tracks, ⌘+click each track. For contiguous groups, Shift+click the first track, hold down Shift, and then click the last track.

5. **Click and drag the selected tracks to the iPod icon that appears in the Devices list and drop the selected tracks on the iPod icon.** iTunes syncs the selected tracks.

Genius

For maximum control over manual syncing, you can configure your iPod for syncing checked tracks *and* tracks that you drag and drop. In the Summary tab, select the Sync only checked songs and videos check box before you select the Manually manage music and videos check box.

Synchronizing movies

It wasn't all that long ago when technology prognosticators and pundits laughed at the idea of people watching movies on a 2.5-inch screen. Who could stand to watch even a music video on such a tiny screen? The pundits were wrong, of course, because nowadays it's not at all unusual for people to use their iPods to watch not only music videos, but also short films, animated shorts, and even full-length movies.

The major problem with movies is that their file size tends to be quite large — even short films lasting just a few minutes weigh in at dozens of megabytes, and full-length movies are gigabytes. Clearly there's a compelling need to manage your movies to avoid filling up your iPod and leaving no room for the latest album from your favorite band. If you have a video-friendly iPod, follow these steps to configure and run the movie synchronization:

1. **In iTunes, click your iPod in the Devices list.**

2. **Click the Movies tab.**

3. **Select the Sync movies check box.**

4. **Select one of these options.**

   - **All movies.** Select this option to sync all your movies with your iPod.

● **Unwatched movies.** Select this option to sync only movies you haven't yet viewed. Use the list to choose how many unwatched movies you want synced: All; 1 most recent; 3 most recent; 5 most recent; or 10 most recent.

Note

A movie is unwatched if you haven't yet viewed it either in iTunes or on your iPod. If you watch it on your iPod, the player sends this information to iTunes when you next sync. This is one of the rare examples of information that gets sent to iTunes when you sync an iPod.

● **Selected.** Select this option to pick out the specific items you want to sync. Choose either movies or playlists in the list, and then select the check boxes for the items you want to sync, as shown in figure 3.3. A blue bullet indicates the movie has not been viewed yet.

5. **Click Apply.** iTunes syncs the iPod using your new movie settings.

3.3 To sync specific movies, choose the Selected movies option and then select the check boxes for each movie you want synced.

Genius

What happens if you watch a movie but you want to leave it on the iPod during the next sync? You need to mark the movie as new (that is, unwatched). In iTunes, choose the Movies library, Ctrl+click (or right-click) the movie, and then choose Mark as New.

Synchronizing TV show episodes

If the average video iPod is at some risk of being filled up by a few large movie files, it probably is at grave risk of being overwhelmed by a large number of TV show episodes. A single half-hour episode will eat up approximately 250MB, so even a modest collection of shows will consume multiple gigabytes of precious iPod disk space.

This means it's crucial to monitor your collection of TV show episodes and keep your iPod synced with only the episodes you need. Fortunately, iTunes gives you a decent set of tools to handle this:

1. **In iTunes, click your iPod in the Devices list.**

2. **Click the TV Shows tab.**

3. **Select the Sync check box and choose an option from the drop-down menu.**

   - **All.** Choose this item to sync every TV show episode.

   - **1 Most Recent.** Choose this item to sync the most recent episode.

   - **3 Most Recent.** Choose this item to sync the three most recent episodes.

   - **5 Most Recent.** Choose this item to sync the five most recent episodes.

   - **10 Most Recent.** Choose this item to sync the ten most recent episodes.

   - **All unwatched.** Choose this item to sync all the episodes you haven't yet viewed.

Genius

If you download a music video from the Web and then import it into iTunes (by choosing File ➪ Import), iTunes will add the video to its Movies library. To display it in the Music library instead, open the Movies library, Ctrl+click (or right-click) the music video, and then click Get Info. Click the Video tab and then use the Kind list to choose Music Video. Click OK. iTunes moves the music video to the Music folder.

- **1 Most Recent Unwatched.** Choose this item to sync the most recent episode that you haven't yet viewed.

- **3 Most Recent Unwatched.** Choose this item to sync the three most recent episodes that you haven't yet viewed.

- **5 Most Recent Unwatched.** Choose this item to sync the five most recent episodes that you haven't yet viewed.

- **10 Most Recent Unwatched.** Choose this item to sync the ten most recent episodes that you haven't yet viewed.

- **1 Least Recent Unwatched.** Choose this item to sync the oldest episode that you haven't yet viewed.

- **3 Least Recent Unwatched.** Choose this item to sync the three oldest episodes that you haven't yet viewed.

- **5 Least Recent Unwatched.** Choose this item to sync the five oldest episodes that you haven't yet viewed.

- **10 Least Recent Unwatched.** Choose this item to sync the ten oldest episodes that you haven't yet viewed.

Note

As with movies, a TV episode is unwatched if you haven't yet viewed it either in iTunes or your iPod. If you watch an episode on your iPod, the player sends this information to iTunes when you next sync.

4. **Select one of these options.**

   - **All TV shows.** Select this option to sync all your TV shows with your iPod.

   - **Selected.** Select this option to sync specific TV shows with your iPod. Choose either TV shows or Playlists in the list, and then select the check boxes for the items you want to sync, as shown in figure 3.4.

5. **Click Apply.** iTunes syncs the iPod using your new TV show settings.

Genius

To mark a TV episode as unwatched, in iTunes choose the TV Shows library, Ctrl+click (or right-click) the episode, and then choose Mark as New.

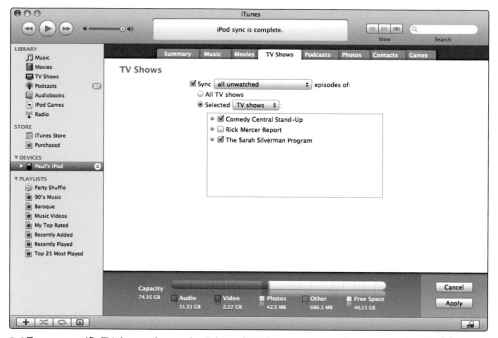

3.4 To sync specific TV shows, choose the Selected TV shows option and then select the check boxes for each show you want synced.

Synchronizing podcasts

In many ways, podcasts are the most problematic of the various media you can sync with your iPod. Not that the podcasts themselves pose any concern. Quite the contrary: They're so addictive that it's not unusual to collect them by the dozens. Why is that a problem? Because most professional podcasts are at least a few megabytes in size, and many are tens of megabytes. A large enough collection can put a serious dent in your iPod's remaining storage space.

All the more reason, then, to take control of the podcast syncing process. Here's how you do it:

1. **In iTunes, click your iPod in the Devices list.**

2. **Click the Podcasts tab.**

3. **Select the Sync check box and choose an option from the drop-down menu.**

   - **All** Choose this item to sync every podcast.

   - **1 Most Recent** Choose this item to sync the most recent podcast.

- **3 Most Recent** Choose this item to sync the three most recent podcasts.

- **5 Most Recent** Choose this item to sync the five most recent podcasts.

- **10 Most Recent** Choose this item to sync the ten most recent podcasts.

- **All Unplayed** Choose this item to sync all the podcasts you haven't yet played.

- **1 Most Recent Unplayed** Choose this item to sync the most recent podcast that you haven't yet played.

- **3 Most Recent Unplayed** Choose this item to sync the three most recent podcasts that you haven't yet played.

- **5 Most Recent Unplayed** Choose this item to sync the five most recent podcasts that you haven't yet played.

- **10 Most Recent Unplayed** Choose this item to sync the ten most recent podcasts that you haven't yet played.

- **1 Least Recent Unplayed** Choose this item to sync the oldest podcast that you haven't yet played.

- **3 Least Recent Unplayed** Choose this item to sync the three oldest podcasts that you haven't yet played.

- **5 Least Recent Unplayed** Choose this item to sync the five oldest podcasts that you haven't yet played.

- **10 Least Recent Unplayed** Choose this item to sync the ten oldest podcasts that you haven't yet played.

- **All New** Choose this item to sync all the podcasts published since the last sync.

- **1 Most Recent New** Choose this item to sync the most recent podcast published since the last sync.

- **3 Most Recent New** Choose this item to sync the three most recent podcasts published since the last sync.

- **5 Most Recent New** Choose this item to sync the five most recent podcasts published since the last sync.

- **10 Most Recent New** Choose this item to sync the ten most recent podcasts published since the last sync.

- **1 Least Recent New** Choose this item to sync the oldest podcast published since the last sync.

- **3 Least Recent New** Choose this item to sync the three oldest podcasts published since the last sync.

- **5 Least Recent New** Choose this item to sync the five oldest podcasts published since the last sync.

- **10 Least Recent New** Choose this item to sync the ten oldest podcasts published since the last sync.

4. **Select one of these options.**

   - **All podcasts.** Select this option to sync all your podcasts with your iPod.

   - **Selected podcasts.** Select this option to sync specific podcasts with your iPod. Select the check boxes for the items you want to sync, as shown in figure 3.5.

5. **Click Apply.** iTunes syncs the iPod using your new podcast settings.

Note

A podcast episode is unplayed if you haven't yet played at least part of the episode either in iTunes or your iPod. If you play an episode on your iPod, the player sends this information to iTunes when you next sync. Even better, your iPod also lets iTunes know if you paused in the middle of an episode; when you play that episode in iTunes, it starts at the point where you left off.

3.5 To sync specific podcasts, choose the Selected podcasts option and then select the check boxes for each podcast you want synced.

Synchronizing photos

If your iPod can display photos (and all new iPods can), then you can use iTunes to synchronize photos between your iPod and either your Pictures folder or iPhoto. Note that Apple supports a number of image file types — the usual TIFF and JPEG that you normally use for your photos as well as BMP, GIF, JPG2000 or JP2, PICT, PNG, PSD, and SGI.

If you use your Mac to process lots of photos, and you want to take copies of some or all of those photos with you on your iPod, then you need to follow these steps to get synced:

1. **In iTunes, click your iPod in the Devices list.**

2. **Click the Photos tab.**

3. **Select the Sync photos from check box and choose an option from the drop-down menu.**

   - **Pictures.** Choose this item to sync the images in your Pictures folder.

   - **Choose folder.** Choose this command to sync the images contained in some other folder.

   - **iPhoto.** Choose this item to sync the photos, albums, and events you've set up in iPhoto.

4. **Select the photos you want to sync.** The controls you see depend on what you chose in Step 3:

   - **If you chose either Pictures or the Choose folder.** In this case, select either the All photos option or the Selected folders option. If you select the latter, select the check box beside each subfolder you want to sync, as shown in figure 3.6.

   - **If you chose iPhoto.** In this case, you get three further options: Select the All photos and albums option to sync your entire iPhoto library; select the X events option, where X is one of the following values that determines the number of iPhoto events that get synced: All, 1 most recent, 3 most recent, 5 most recent, 10 most recent, or 20 most recent; select the Selected albums option and then select the check box beside each album you want to sync.

5. **If you selected either the Selected folders option or the Selected albums option, use your mouse to click and drag the folders or albums to set the order you prefer.**

6. **Click Apply.** iTunes syncs the iPod using your new photo settings.

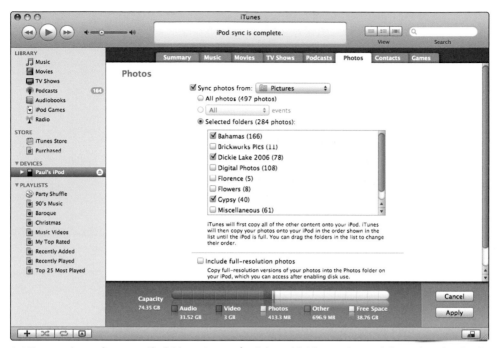

3.6 To sync photos from specific folders, choose the Selected folders option and then select the check boxes for each folder you want synced.

Note iTunes doesn't sync exact copies of your photos to the iPod. Instead, it creates what Apple calls TV-quality versions of each image. These are copies of the images that have been reduced in size to match the iPod's screen size. This not only makes the sync go faster, but it also means the photos take up much less room on your iPod.

Synchronizing your address book and calendars

I don't know too many people who use their iPod as a PDA (personal digital assistant), and I'd bet not many people even know about the iPod's PDA features. I'm talking, of course, about the iPod's ability to display contact information — for each contact, you see the person's name, job title, company, work phone number, street address, and e-mail address, and optionally the contact's picture — and calendar data, including both events and to-do lists.

Still, if you're traveling with your iPod and you need to look up a phone number or get reminded of some important event, then why not embrace the technology? This is especially true when you can sync your iPod with contact data from your Mac's Address Book application, and calendar data from your Mac's iCal application.

Follow these steps to sync this data with your iPod:

1. **In iTunes, click your iPod in the Devices list.**

2. **Click the Contacts tab.**

3. **Select the Sync Address Book contacts check box and select an option.**

   - **All contacts.** Select this option to sync all your Address Book contacts.

   - **Selected groups.** Select this option to sync only those groups that have their check box selected.

4. **Select the Include contacts' photos check box if you have photos for some or all of your contacts.**

5. **Select the Sync iCal calendars check box and select an option to add the calendar data as well.** If you want to bypass synching calendars, deselect the Sync iCal calendars check box and click Apply.

   - **All calendars.** Select this option to sync all your iCal calendars.

   - **Selected calendars.** Select this option to sync only those calendars that have their check box selected (see figure 3.7).

6. **Click Apply.** iTunes syncs the iPod using your new contacts and calendars settings.

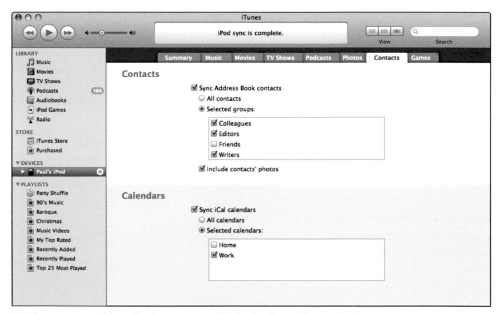

3.7 You can sync Address Book contacts and iCal calendars with your iPod.

Synchronizing games

Listening to tunes is a great way to pass the time, but if you find yourself in a long lineup or other-wise delayed without a book in sight, perhaps a rousing game of Tetris would help keep you occu-pied. Fortunately, that's a lot easier to do now that the iTunes Store is selling quite a few games designed for the iPod screen. You can get old favorites such as Pac-Man, Sonic the Hedgehog, Solitaire, Mahjong, and, yes, Tetris, as well as newer pastimes such as Sudoku, Lost, and Brain Challenge.

After you purchase a game or three from the iTunes Store, follow these steps to sync them to your iPod:

1. **In iTunes, click your iPod in the Devices list.**

2. **Click the Games tab.**

3. **Select the Sync games check box and select an option.**

   - **All games.** Select this option to sync all your games.

   - **Selected games.** Select this option to sync only specific games. Click those you want to sync (a check box appears) as shown in figure 3.8.

4. **Click Apply.** iTunes syncs the iPod using your new games settings.

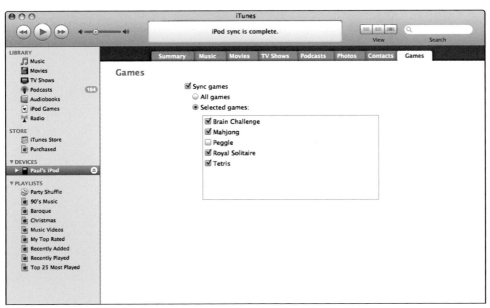

3.8 To sync specified games, select the Selected games option and then select the check boxes for each game you want synced.

Synchronizing with a Cell Phone or Palm PDA

You can use iTunes to sync Address Book contacts and iCal calendars with your iPod. There's nothing wrong with having this kind of information on your music player, but a more useful place for it is a device more suited to such data: a cell phone or PDA. iTunes can't work with these types of devices, but another Mac application sure can: iSync. This program can work with many different types of cell phones, as well as some Palm OS PDAs. With iSync, you can send some or all of your Mac's contact data and calendar data to the device. However, unlike with iTunes and your iPod, you can also bring new information on the cell phone or PDA to your Mac. This is great if you add new data to the device or change existing data on the device, because it adds this update information to your Mac, resulting in true synchronization.

Note For a list of phones and PDAs that are compatible with iSync, go to www.apple.com/macosx/features/isync/index.html.

Adding a cellphone to iSync

Before you can sync a cell phone, you must make sure it is added to iSync. Launch iSync by opening Finder and then choosing Applications ⇨ iSync.

There are two ways to proceed depending on the phone:

- **Bluetooth phone.** Connect the phone as I describe in Chapter 2. When the Bluetooth Setup Wizard displays the list of services available for the phone, be sure to select the Set up iSync to transfer contacts and events check box.

- **Another type of phone.** Turn on the phone and connect it to your Mac, if necessary. In iSync, select Devices ⇨ Add Device, and then double-click your phone when it appears in the Add Devices window.

Adding a Palm PDA to iSync

Your Palm must be added to iSync before you can sync it. And, the process has three main steps: installing Palm Desktop; setting up iSync to recognize Palm OS devices; and finally configuring your Palm PDA to use iSync.

Begin by downloading and installing Palm Desktop:

1. **Go to www.palm.com and search for *palm desktop Mac*.**

2. **Launch the installer and in the first dialog box, click Next.**

3. **Select Create new user, click Next.**

4. **Type a user name in the Name text box, and then click Next.**

5. **Click Done and then restart your Mac when prompted.** You have now downloaded and installed Palm Desktop.

You must now configure iSync to work with Palm OS devices:

1. **Open Finder and then choose Applications ⇨ iSync.**

2. **Choose Devices ⇨ Enable Palm OS Syncing.** The Enable Palm Syncing dialog box appears.

3. **Click Continue.** iSync may display some conduits that need to be disabled.

4. **Click Continue.** iSync disables the conduits and enables Palm OS device syncing.

5. **Click OK.** Palm OS will now work with Palm OS devices.

Note A *conduit* is a communications channel that Palm Desktop establishes between your Mac and your Pal OS PDA.

You now need to configure the Palm Desktop's HotSync Manager program to use the iSync HotSync Conduit:

1. **In Finder, choose Applications ⇨ Palm ⇨ HotSync Manager.**

2. **Choose HotSync ⇨ Conduit Settings (or press ⌘+J).** The Conduit Settings dialog box appears.

3. **Double-click the iSync Conduit.**

4. **Select the Enable iSync for this Palm device check box, as shown in figure 3.9 and click OK.** Finally, your Palm OS device is ready to work with iSync.

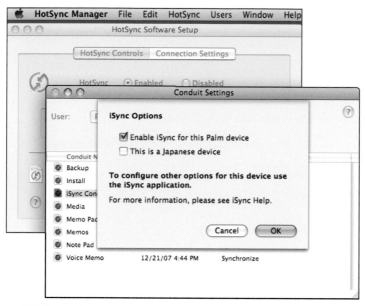

3.9 Tell the HotSync Manager to use the iSync Conduit for the synchronization.

The next time you start the program, you'll see an icon for the device, as shown in figure 3.10. (The icon on the right is the Palm OS device icon; the icon on the left is for a cell phone.)

3.10 iSync connected to two devices: a cell phone (left) and a Palm OS PDA (right).

Configuring sync settings for the device

Before starting in on the syncing fun, you might want to configure a few settings that control what gets synced and how it's done. The settings you see depend on whether you're syncing a phone or Palm OS PDA.

Genius Are you stuck if you want to synchronize your Mac with other devices, such as Pocket PCs and Windows Mobile devices? Not at all. A company called Mark/Space (www.markspace.com) sells a product called the Missing Sync that enables you to synchronize with these and many other devices.

First start with a cell phone. In iSync, click the icon for your connected cell phone. iSync displays the settings shown in figure 3.11.

Here's what you see:

- **For first sync.** You see this list if you've never used iSync to sync with the device. (After you run the first sync, this area shows the data and time of the most recent sync.) You get two choices.

  - **Merge data on computer and device.** This option adds your Mac data to the device and your device data to your Mac. Choose this option if you have data on the device that you want to preserve.

  - **Erase data on device then sync.** This option wipes out all the contact and calendar data on the device and then adds your Mac data.

3.11 The iSync settings for a connected cell phone.

- **Turn on (your device) synchronization.** Select this check box to enable synchronization for your device.

- **Contacts.** Select this check box to include your Address Book contacts in the synchronization. You can then use the Synchronize list to select which contacts get synchronized. Choose either All Contacts or a specific contact group.

- **Calendars:** Select this check box to include your iCal calendars in the synchronization. You can then select either the All option to sync all your calendars, or the Selected option to sync on this calendars with selected check boxes.

- **Put events created on phone into.** Use this list to choose which iCal calendar will store those events you create on the phone.

Genius

If you don't see the For first sync list and you'd like to start your syncing fresh, choose Devices ⇨ Reset Device and when iSync asks you to confirm, click Reset.

- **More Options.** Click this button to display the following settings (click OK when you're done).

  - **Synchronize only contacts with phone numbers.** Choose this check box to avoid syncing contacts that don't have phone numbers.

  - **Don't synchronize events prior to.** Use this list to control how far into the past you want events synced. If you rarely view past events, then choosing a shorter time frame (such as Today) can save space on your phone.

  - **Don't synchronize events after.** Use this list to control how far into the future you want events synced. Again, if you don't have any need to view far off events, choosing a shorter time frame (such as One week) can save space.

  - **Synchronize alarms.** Select this check box to have your cell phone alert you when an event or to-do item is due.

  - **Synchronize all-day events.** Select this check box to include all-day events in the sync.

To change the settings for a Palm, click the icon for your connected Palm device. The settings for a Palm OS device are similar to the phone's settings, as you can see in figure 3.12.

Note that the Palm iSync has a few additional options on the main screen and no additional options.

- **Force slow synchronization.** Select this check box if iSync has trouble syncing with the Palm device.

- **Ignore Palm events older than.** If you are syncing calendar information, you can choose to control how far into the past you want events on your Palm to be synced.

- **Set.** If you are syncing calendar information, you can click this button to change the time zone used for the calendar.

3.12 The iSync settings for a connected Palm OS device.

Synchronizing the device

You're now ready to do some actual syncing (insert a round of applause here). Fortunately, iSync makes this part as easy as can be:

1. **Connect your device to your Mac.**

2. **In iSync, click Sync Devices.** You can also press ⌘+T or choose Devices ⇨ Sync Devices.

3. **Okay the sync on your device.**

   - Your cell phone will probably ask if it's okay for your Mac to access the phone's data. Select Yes (or OK or whatever affirmative option your phone gives you).

   - On your Palm OS device, press the HotSync button or tap the HotSync icon to initiate the sync.

Synchronizing with MobileMe

If you need to transfer important data back and forth between your Mac and your MobileMe account, the MobileMe synchronization feature is for you. You can synchronize some or all of the following items:

- **Bookmarks.** The bookmarks you've saved in Safari.

- **Calendars.** Your iCal calendars, including all your events and to-do items.

- **Contacts.** Your Address Book contacts.

- **Dashboard widgets.** The widgets on your Mac's Dashboard.

- **Dock items.** The icons you currently display in your Mac's Dock.

- **Keychains.** Your saved passwords.

- **Mail accounts.** The details of the e-mail accounts you've set up in Mail.

- **Mail rules, signatures, and smart mailboxes.** The message rules, account signatures, and smart mailboxes that you've created in Mail.

- **Notes.** The notes that you created in Mail.

- **Preferences.** The options, settings, and other data that you've configured using System Preferences.

Besides these items, some third-party programs add their own stuff that you can sync. For example, if you use Entourage, you can synchronize your Entourage Notes with MobileMe.

Why sync? The main reason is to maintain a backup copy of your data. If, say, your Address Book becomes messed up (perhaps because of a bad sync with a cell phone or PDA), then you can grab the data from MobileMe. Another good reason to sync is to get access to items such as your contacts, bookmarks, and mail accounts over the Web. By logging on to your MobileMe account, you can access your Mac data from any location using any computer.

Note

If you have a MobileMe account, you'll learn lots of great things you can do with that account in Chapter 5.

Synchronizing your Mac and MobileMe

You have to configure your Mac to specify what information you want synchronized with your MobileMe account. Follow these steps to set your preferences:

1. **Click the System Preferences icon in the Dock.**

2. **In the Internet & Network section, click the MobileMe icon.**

3. **Click the Sync tab.**

4. **Select the Synchronize with MobileMe check box.** Your Mac enables the check boxes beside the various items you can sync, as shown in figure 3.13.

3.13 Select the Synchronize with MobileMe check box, and then select the items you want to sync.

5. **Use the Synchronize with MobileMe list to select the sync frequency you prefer.**

   ● **Automatically.** Your Mac syncs with your MobileMe account every time you change any of the data you select for syncing. This is the item to choose if you make near-constant changes to your Mac data because it ensures that you'll never lose any information.

   ● **Every Hour.** Your Mac syncs with your MobileMe account every 60 minutes. Choose this item if you make frequent changes to the data you select for syncing.

   ● **Every Day.** Your Mac syncs with MobileMe daily. Choose this item if you don't make changes to the data you select for syncing all that often, but you add or edit the data at least once each day.

   ● **Every Week.** Your Mac syncs with MobileMe weekly. Choose this item if you only make occasional changes to the data you select for syncing.

   ● **Manually.** You must sync your Mac with your MobileMe account by hand. Choose this item if you want to control when the synchronization happens.

6. **Select the check box beside each data item you want to sync with your MobileMe account.**

7. **Select the Show status in menu bar check box to keep an eye on your sync status.** Figure 3.14 shows the status icon and an example of the status info that appears when you click it.

3.14 Adding the sync status icon to the menu bar gives you easy access to the current sync status.

If you elected to sync your Mac and your MobileMe account manually, then you have two choices for performing the sync:

   ◉ **In the MobileMe preferences pane, click the Sync tab and then click Sync Now.**

   ◉ **If you displayed the sync status icon in the menu bar, click that icon, and then choose Sync Now.**

Using MobileMe to keep two or more Macs in sync

Syncing your Mac's data with your MobileMe account provides the peace of mind of an easily accessed backup copy of your data, and it also gives you quick access to that data from anywhere on the Web. However, this sync business becomes even more useful when you add a second (or, even a third) Mac into the mix. Let's say you have a desktop Mac and a portable Mac. There's a good chance you'll want to use the same bookmarks, Mail accounts and settings, calendars, and contacts on both machines, but sharing all this data can be tough. However, if you bring in MobileMe as a kind of digital middleman, sharing this data between the two machines suddenly becomes as easy as clicking a few buttons.

You need to already have one Mac synced with your MobileMe account. Then, you need to sign up your second Mac with the same MobileMe account:

1. **Click the System Preferences icon in the Dock.**

2. **In the Internet & Network section, click the MobileMe icon.**

3. **If you're already signed in using a different MobileMe account, click Sign Out and, when your Mac asks you to confirm, click Sign Out.**

4. **Type the member name and password of the MobileMe account you used for syncing the first Mac earlier.**

5. **Click Sign In.**

After you've done this, click the Sync tab, set up which items you want synced, and then click Sync Now. The first time you run the sync, you see the MobileMe Sync Alert dialog box, shown in figure 3.15. The Select an action list gives you three choices:

- **Merge all data.** Choose this item to bring the existing MobileMe data to your Mac and to send your Mac data to MobileMe.

- **Replace data on computer.** Choose this item to only bring the existing MobileMe data to your Mac.

- **Replace all data on MobileMe.** Choose this item to only send your Mac data to MobileMe.

For more control, click More Options to see a list of each type of data to be synced. For each type, you can choose one of the previous three options.

3.15 You may see this dialog box if you already have data synced to your MobileMe account.

Stopping a Mac from syncing with MobileMe

What happens if you no longer want to sync a particular Mac with your MobileMe account? For example, if you want to give your Mac to someone else, you probably don't want the Mac to continue syncing with your data. Similarly, you may be syncing two Macs with the same MobileMe account and want to change your sync settings (the ones shown in figure 3.15). For these sorts of situations, you need to stop the Mac from syncing with the MobileMe account, a process called *unregistering* the Mac. Here's how you do it:

1. **Using any Mac that syncs with a MobileMe account, click the System Preferences icon in the Dock.**

2. **In the Internet & Network section, click the MobileMe icon.**

3. **Click the Sync tab.**

4. **Click Advanced.** You see a list of the Macs that are being synchronized with the MobileMe account, as shown in figure 3.16.

3.16 Click Advanced in the Sync tab to see a list of Macs registered to sync with the MobileMe account.

5. **Click the computer you want to stop syncing.**

6. **Click Unregister.** The Mac asks you to confirm.

7. **Click Unregister again.** The Mac unregisters the computer.

8. **Click Done.**

Resolving sync conflicts

In most cases, you'll change your synced data in only one place: either on your Mac or through your MobileMe account. However, it's possible that you might change a particular item in both places. If

the changes are different, then you end up with a *sync conflict*. (This is more likely to happen when you're syncing two Macs with a single MobileMe account, because it wouldn't be hard to make changes to a particular item on both Macs.) To fix this, your Mac brings on the Conflict Resolver. This program shows you the conflicting data, as you can see in the example conflict shown in figure 3.17 where two nearly identical entries appear (St. Johns versus St. John's). Your Mac asks you to choose which one is correct. You click the correct information, and then click Done to resolve the conflict.

3.17 Use the Conflict Resolver to fix sync conflicts.

How Can I Get More Out of the Web?

One of the most popular Mac pastimes is Web surfing, and like most Mac users you probably perform these surfin' safaris using, appropriately enough, the Safari browser that comes with OS X. Safari is one of the world's best browsers, and out of the box it's easy to use and intuitive. However, Safari is loaded with options and features, many of which are hidden in obscure nooks and crannies of the program. If you think your surfing activities could be faster, more efficient, more productive, or more private, Safari has tons of features that can help.

Making Site Navigation Easier

Surfing the Web is all about navigating from one site to another to find what you need, check out intriguing links, and explore the vastness of the Web. To get the most out of your online excursions, it helps to know a few navigation techniques beyond just clicking links and entering URLs into Safari's address bar.

Opening a site in a new tab

For efficient Web browsing, it's tough to beat Safari's slick tabs feature, which lets you use a single Safari window to display a bunch of Web pages by opening each page in its own tab. You probably know that you create a new tab by choosing File ⇨ New Tab or by pressing ⌘+T. However, Safari offers a number of other useful techniques for opening sites in their own tab.

For example, when you click a link, Safari opens the new page in the same tab. However, if you ⌘+click the link (that is, you hold down ⌘ when clicking), Safari opens the page in a new tab. (If you have a two-button mouse, you can also right-click the link and then click Open in New Tab.)

By default, Safari opens the new page in the background, which is great if you want to keep reading the current page. What if you want to start reading the new page right away, instead? To avoid the extra click required to display the new tab, select the link with Shift+⌘+click.

You may find that most of the time you prefer to switch to the new tab right away. Rather than always using the slightly awkward Shift+⌘+click method each time, you can configure Safari to always switch to new tabs that you open. Follow these steps:

1. **Choose Safari ⇨ Preferences to display the Preferences dialog box.** You can also Press ⌘+, (comma).

2. **Click the Tabs pane.**

3. **Select the Select tabs and windows as they are created option, as shown in figure 4.1.**

Safari also lets you open a site in a new tab from the address bar. Type the URL of the new site and then use either of these techniques:

- Press ⌘+Return to open the new site in a background tab.
- Press Shift+⌘+Return to open the new site in a foreground tab.

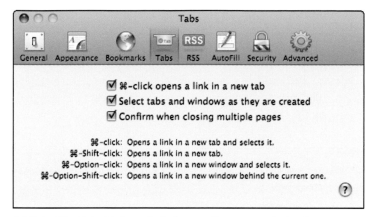

4.1 Select the Select tabs and windows as they are created option.

Finally, if you have a site saved as a bookmark, you can open it in a new tab from the Bookmarks Bar or the Bookmarks menu:

- ⌘+click the bookmark to open the site in a background tab.
- Shift+⌘+click the bookmark to open the site in a foreground tab.

Opening a Site in a New Window

You can use similar techniques to open a site in a new window instead of a new tab:

Press	To
Option+⌘+click	Opens a link or bookmark in a background window
Shift+Option+⌘+click	Opens a link or bookmark in a foreground window
Option+⌘+Return	Opens the address bar URL in a background window
Shift+Option+⌘+Return	Opens the address bar URL in a foreground window

Genius

One common scenario is when you only want to keep a single tab open and close all the rest. That's not hard to accomplish when you only have two or three tabs going, but if you're sitting there with a half dozen or a dozen tabs in front of you, you might think you're better off shutting down and restarting Safari. Not so! Instead, select the tab you want to keep open, then Option+click that tab's Close This Tab icon. Safari leaves the current tab open, and shuts down all the others.

Using Back and Next to navigate your history

As you navigate from one page to the next in a Safari session, you can retrace your steps by clicking Safari's Back button (or by pressing ⌘+[) and, having done that, you can traverse your history in the opposite direction by clicking the Next button (or by pressing ⌘+]). This is fine if you just want to go back (or forward) a few sites, but if you need to go back a long way, constantly clicking the Back or Next button can get old in a hurry.

To solve that problem, you need to know that the Back and Next buttons also come with hidden history lists. For example, the Back button stores a list of all the sites in the current session that you've been to prior to the current site. To get at those lists, click and hold down the mouse button over the Back or Next button. As shown in figure 4.2, Safari pops up the corresponding history list, and you then click the page you want to jump to.

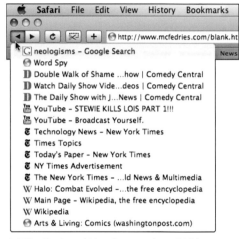

4.2 The Back and Next buttons have hidden history lists.

Using the title bar to navigate a site

When a link takes you to a site, you don't always end up on the home page. Instead, you may "deep link" to a page that's buried several layers down in the site's folder hierarchy. That's fine, but if the page you end up on is interesting or entertaining, it's natural to wonder if the site has similar pages. If the site's navigation links don't help, a good strategy is to dis-

4.3 ⌘+click the site title to see the folder hierarchy associated with the current page.

play the contents of whatever folder contains the current page. You could delete the filename portion of the URL in the address bar, but Safari gives you an easier way: ⌘+click the site title in Safari's title bar. (If you have a two-button mouse, you can also right-click the site title.) Safari displays a list that includes the current page, its parent folder, the folder above that, and so on all the way up to the site's root folder. Figure 4.3 shows a simple example. From there, you click the folder you want to investigate.

Selecting the address bar text quickly

If you want to navigate to a new site by typing the site's URL into Safari's address bar, you know that you first need to delete the existing URL. For a short address, it's bad enough to have to click past the end of the address and then press Delete until the address is gone. For a long address that doesn't fit entirely in the address bar, you have to first click inside the address bar and then press Ctrl+end to move the cursor to the end.

All of that's just way too much work. It's much easier to select the entire address bar text in one swoop, which you can do using either of these techniques:

Genius

If you need to use the current site's address in another program (such as an e-mail message), the quickest way to do that is to select the address bar text as described in this section, press ⌘+C to copy the address, switch to the other program, and then press ⌘+V to paste the address.

- Click the site icon that appears by the left edge of the address bar (see figure 4.4).
- Press ⌘+L.

4.4 Click the site icon to select the entire address bar text.

Searching for a word or phrase instantly

Safari's Google search box is super handy for performing quick searches without having to first head over to the Google site. A search scenario that's typical to the curious among you is to come across a word or phrase in a Web page and run a Google search on that text to learn more about it. You might think the quickest way to do this is to copy and paste the text into the Google search box. Think again! Here's a better method that requires just two easy steps:

1. **Select the page text.**
2. **Press Shift+⌘+L.** Safari automatically adds the text to the Google search box and runs the search without further ado.

Making Safari appear to be another browser

Some primitive or poorly coded Web sites may not show up properly because they don't recognize Safari. There's not much you can do directly to combat this browser discrimination, but you can fight back indirectly at least. You do that by taking advantage of the fact that the site is probably deciding which browsers are legitimate by using code to examine a string called the *user agent* that all browsers provide as a kind of identification. It's possible to configure Safari to provide a *different* user agent string (such as Internet Explorer), thus fooling the site into letting you in.

To perform this trick, you must first configure Safari to display its normally hidden Debug menu. Here's how you do that:

1. **Shut down Safari.**

2. **Open the Terminal utility.**

   - In the Dock, click Finder.

   - In Finder, choose Applications ⇨ Utilities ⇨ Terminal.

3. **At the Terminal prompt, type** defaults write com.apple.Safari IncludeDebugMenu 1 **and press Return.**

Caution

The Terminal command is case-sensitive, so make sure you type the characters exactly as they appear in the previous set of steps.

Exit Terminal and restart Safari. You see a new Debug menu, which contains lots of commands of great interest to programmers. For your purposes, you need to choose Debug ⇨ User Agent to see a list of user agent strings, as shown in figure 4.5. Choose the string you want to use and then try accessing the site. If you still don't get in, keep trying different user agents.

When you're done with the site, choose Debug ⇨ User Agent ⇨ Automatically Chosen to rein-

4.5 With the Debug menu in place, the User Agent command presents a list of user agent strings you can use to fool a site into letting Safari in.

state the default user agent setting. To get rid of the Debug menu, exit Safari, start a new Terminal session, and then type this command: **defaults write com.apple.Safari IncludeDebugMenu 0**.

Shutting off Safari's quit prompt

One of the most annoying things about Safari is when you quit the program with two or more tabs open, Safari throws up a dialog box to ask if you're sure you want to quit. If you're tired of being treated like a child, configure Safari to stop this useless prompt:

1. **Shut down Safari.**

2. **Open the Terminal utility.**

   - In the Dock, click Finder.
   - In Finder, choose Applications ⇨ Utilities ⇨ Terminal.

3. **At the Terminal prompt, type** defaults write com.apple.Safari ConfirmClosingMultiplePages 0 **and press Return.** Remember that the command you type is case-sensitive.

Exit Terminal and restart Safari. The next time you quit with multiple tabs going, Safari shuts down without a fuss.

Getting More Out of Bookmarks

The unfathomable size of the Web means that if you stumble upon a site today, finding that site again a month from now (when the site no longer appears in Safari's history) is just about impossible. That's why if you like a site or find it useful, you should create a bookmark for it.

Bookmarks are an essential part of a modern Web surfer's toolkit, but there's more to bookmarks than adding them and clicking them. Safari offers a number of options and techniques that let you get the most out of this useful feature.

Genius

By default, Safari keeps pages in the history list for a month. If you often find yourself trying to locate a previously visited (and non-bookmarked) site after more than a month, consider extending Safari's "memory." Choose Safari ⇨ Preferences ⇨ General, use the Remove history items list to select either the After one year item or the Manually item. Note that if you choose Manually, pages stay in the history indefinitely (that is, until you delete them by hand).

Importing Internet Explorer bookmarks

If you're switching from Windows to Mac, you might be wondering if you have to give up all your hard-earned Internet Explorer favorites as part of the deal. No way! As long as you still have access to your Windows machine, you can export your favorites from Internet Explorer and import them as bookmarks into Safari.

First, follow these steps to export your Internet Explorer favorites to a file:

1. **On your Windows PC, launch Internet Explorer.**

2. **Start the Import/Export Wizard.**

   ● In Internet Explorer 7, click the Add to Favorites icon (or press Alt+Z) and then click Import and Export.

   ● In all versions of Internet Explorer, choose File ⇨ Import and Export. (To see the menu bar in Internet Explorer 7, press Alt.)

3. **Click Next.** The Import/Export Selection dialog box appears.

4. **Click Export Favorites, and then click Next.** The Export Favorites Source Folder dialog box appears.

5. **Click the Favorites folder (see figure 4.6), and then click Next.** The Export Favorites Destination dialog box appears.

4.6 Select the Favorites folder to export all your Internet Explorer favorites.

6. **Choose a location for the export file.**

   ● If your Windows PC and your Mac are on the same network, save the favorites file in a folder that's shared on the network.

   ● If your Windows PC and Mac aren't on the same network, insert a USB flash drive into the Windows PC and then save the favorites file to the flash drive.

7. **Click Next.** Internet Explorer exports the favorites to a file.

8. **Click Finish.**

Now you're ready to import your Internet Explorer favorites into Safari by following these steps:

1. **In Safari, choose File ⇨ Import Bookmarks.** The Import Bookmarks dialog box appears.

2. **Open the folder that contains the favorites file you exported earlier from Internet Explorer.**

   - If your Windows PC and your Mac are on the same network, open the shared network folder that contains the favorites file.

   - If your Windows PC and Mac aren't on the same network, insert the USB flash drive that contains the favorites file.

3. **Click the favorites file.** In most cases, the file is named bookmark.htm, as shown in figure 4.7.

4. **Click Import.** Safari adds the Internet Explorer favorites as bookmarks.

4.7 Use the Import Bookmarks dialog box to select the file that contains your exported Internet Explorer favorites.

Note

If you're using an older Mac that has Internet Explorer for the Mac installed, you may want to import the local favorites. In Safari, choose File ⇨ Import Bookmarks to open the Import Bookmarks dialog box. Choose your user folder, and then choose Library ⇨ Preferences ⇨ Explorer. Click the Favorites.html file, and then click Import.

Creating a Safari startup folder

Do you have several sites you like to fire up first thing in the morning when you launch Safari? If so, it's a shame that Safari doesn't give you any way to define multiple home pages that would all open automatically at startup. The next best thing is to create a new folder on the Bookmarks Bar, use the new folder to store bookmarks for all your startup sites, and then open the folder's sites right after you launch Safari.

Creating a new folder on the Bookmarks Bar is easy:

1. **Ctrl+click (or right-click) the Bookmark Bar and then click New Folder.** Safari asks for the name of the new folder.

2. **Type the folder name.** For example, you might name the new folder Startup.

3. **Click OK.**

Now you use the following steps to populate the folder with site bookmarks:

1. **Navigate to the site you want to save as a bookmark.**

2. **Display the Add Bookmark dialog box in one of two ways.**
   - Choose Bookmarks ⇨ Add Bookmark.
   - Press ⌘+D.

3. **Adjust the site name, if you feel like it.**

4. **In the list of folders, select the folder you created earlier.** In figure 4.8, I've selected a folder I created named Startup.

5. **Click Add.** Safari adds the bookmark to the folder.

6. **Repeat Steps 2, 3, and 5 to add more bookmarks to the folder.** You don't need to repeat Step 4 because Safari automatically selects your most recent folder.

4.8 When you add your bookmark, be sure to store it in the folder you just created.

Note   If you don't need to adjust the site titles when adding your bookmarks, you can reduce Step 6 to a quick keyboard sequence: Press ⌘+D, and then press Return.

Opening a folder's sites with a single click

You can stuff a new folder full of sites to launch after you start Safari, and you can open all those sites at once by clicking the folder, and then clicking Open in Tabs, as shown in figure 4.9.

However, an even faster way to open all the sites in the folder is to ⌘+click the folder name. Still not fast enough for you? Okay, you can take out the ⌘ key and launch the folder's sites with just a click by following these steps:

4.9 To open a folder's sites, click the folder and then click Open in Tabs.

1. **Display the Bookmarks.**

   - Choose Bookmarks ⇨ Show All Bookmarks.
   - Click the Show All Bookmarks icon on the left side of the Bookmarks Bar (see figure 4.10).
   - Press Option+⌘+B.

2. **In the Collections pane, click Bookmarks Bar.**

3. **Select the Auto-Click option beside the folder you want to open with just a click.** Figure 4.10 shows the Auto-Click option selected for a folder named Startup.

Genius

Did you know that you can open the first nine pages on your Bookmarks Bar via the keyboard? Press ⌘+1 to open the first page, ⌘+2 to open the second page, and so on.

Show/Hide Bookmarks

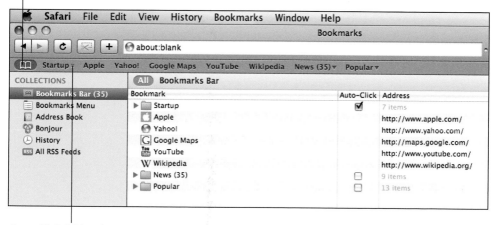

Auto-Click folder shows a square instead of an arrow

4.10 To open a folder with a click, select the folder's Auto-Click option.

Now you can open the folder's sites with just a single click on the folder name. Note that Safari helps you remember that Auto-Click is turned on for a folder by changing the usual folder drop-down arrow to a square, as I show in figure 4.10.

Caution

After you have activated Auto-Click for a folder, don't forget that it's turned on. Otherwise, you might try to display the folder's contents by clicking it and end up with all your sites loaded into tabs. If that happens, you can quickly fix the problem by clicking Safari's Back button. To see the contents of an Auto-Click folder, Option+click the folder name.

Loading sites automatically at startup

Earlier I mentioned that it's too bad Safari has no way of defining multiple startup pages (the way Internet Explorer 7 does). If you have several sites that you always open at the beginning of each Safari session, you can create a folder of startup sites and launch that folder with a click. That's handy, but it would be better if you could get Safari to open those sites automatically.

You cannot configure Safari to do that, but you can use the Automator program to do it. You use Automator to create a script that implements a *workflow*: a series of actions where the data returned by one action is passed along to the next. In this case, the workflow is just two steps: get the addresses of the Web sites to open, and then launch Safari and open those addresses.

First, I assume you want Safari to open the startup sites in separate tabs. To ensure this happens, you need to configure Safari to open application links in tabs as follows:

1. **Start Safari.**
2. **Select Safari ⇨ Preferences ⇨ General.**
3. **In the Open links from application section, select the in a new tab in the current window option.**

Close Safari and then open Automator by clicking Finder in the Dock and then selecting Applications ⇨ Automator. In the dialog box that Automator displays at startup, click Custom, and then click Choose. You can now follow these steps to build your workflow:

1. **In the Library list, click Internet.** Automator displays a list of Internet-related actions.
2. **Double-click the Get Specified URLs action.** Automator adds the Get Specified URLs action to the workflow pane on the right side of the window.
3. **Click Add to add a new URL.**

4. **In the new URL, double-click the URL name text, type the name of the site, and then press Tab to select the text in the Address column.**

5. **Type the address of the site and then press Return.**

6. **Repeat Steps 3, 4, and 5 to add all the sites you want to display when you launch Safari.**

7. **Double-click the Display Webpages action.** Automator adds the Display Webpages action to the workflow pane, as shown in figure 4.11. This action takes the addresses in the Get Specified URLs action and displays them in Safari.

4.11 Automator passes the Get Specified URLs addresses to Display Webpages to open the sites in Safari.

8. **In the Automator Library, click Utilities.**

9. **Double+click the Launch Application action.** This action ensures that Safari becomes the active window when you run the workflow.

10. **Select File ⇨ Save, type a name in the Save As box, and then click Save.** Automator saves your workflow file.

Running the workflow

To run the workflow, you have two choices:

- In Automator, click the Run button or press ⌘+R.

- Locate the workflow file in Finder, Ctrl+click or right-click the file, click Open With, and then click Automator Runner.

These methods are simple enough, but they're not very convenient because they either require you to have Automator running or they require the use of the Automator Runner utility. It would be much better to simply double-click a file to run the workflow. Here's how to set this up:

1. **In Automator, open your workflow file.**

2. **Select File ⇨ Save As.**

3. **In the File Format list, choose Application.**

4. **Click Save.** Automator saves the file as an application that you can double-click to launch.

Replacing the Safari dock icon

In the previous section, you learned how to create an Automator application to launch Safari and automatically open several Web pages. To make this project as convenient as possible, you should replace the default Safari icon with an icon for your new Automator workflow application.

The first thing you should do is apply the Safari icon to your workflow application so that you have a visual way of identifying the icon. Follow these steps:

1. **Choose Finder ⇨ Applications.** The Applications folder opens.

2. **Control- or right-click Safari, and then click Get Info.**

3. **Copy the Safari icon.** Click the Safari icon, press ⌘+C, and close the Safari Info window.

4. **Use Finder to locate your Automator workflow application.**

5. **Control+click or right-click the application, and then click Get Info.**

6. **Paste the Safari icon.** Click the Automator icon and press ⌘+V (see figure 4.12).

7. **Close the Info window.**

Now you're ready to replace the default Safari Dock icon with the icon for your Automator workflow application:

1. **Click-and-drag the icon for the Automator workflow application from Finder and drop it on the Dock.**

2. **Control+click or right-click the default Safari icon.**

3. **Click Remove from Dock.**

Saving bookmarks as a Web page

The more you use Safari's bookmarks, the more indispensible they become as a tool for organizing, categorizing, memorizing, and just plain making sense of those parts of the Web that you've surfed. Unfortunately, your bookmarks won't be there for you in the following situations:

- Using another computer on your network

- Using a computer at work (or at home, if your Safari bookmarks are on a work Mac)

- Using a computer in an Internet café

- Using a computer at another person's home or office

- Using a mobile browser, such as a cell phone or PDA

4.12 Copy the Safari icon and paste in over the icon for your Automator workflow application.

One solution to this problem is to synchronize your Safari bookmarks with your MobileMe account, if you have one. (To learn how to do this, see Chapter 3.) If you don't have a MobileMe account (or even if you do), a second solution is to save your bookmarks as a Web page file. You can then save that page in a shared network folder or you can upload the page to your Web site hosting provider, which lets you access your bookmarks from anywhere in the world.

Follow these steps to save your bookmarks as a Web page:

1. **Choose File ➪ Export Bookmarks.**
   Safari opens the Export Bookmarks dialog box, shown in figure 4.13.

2. **Use the Save As text box to edit the**
   name of the file. If you're going to
   upload the file to the Web, remove any
   spaces from the file name.

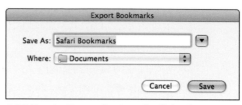

4.13 Use the Export Bookmarks dialog box to
save your bookmarks as a Web page.

3. **Use the Where list to select a different location, if necessary.**

4. **Click Save.** Safari saves the bookmarks to an HTML file.

Synchronizing bookmarks with another computer

Each MobileMe account has a Bookmarks feature, and you can synchronize that feature and your
Safari bookmarks. This also enables you to synchronize your bookmarks with any other computer
that can access your MobileMe account. What if you don't have a MobileMe account? Fortunately,
it's still possible to synchronize your bookmarks with another computer by using the Automator
application.

The basic idea is that you first synchronize your bookmarks to a shared network folder, and then
other computers synchronize bookmarks by copying them from that shared folder.

Follow these steps to set up an Automator workflow to synchronize your bookmarks to a shared
network folder:

1. **Make a connection to the shared network folder and save the logon data to your key-**
   chain. The *keychain* is your Mac's master list of passwords.

2. **In Finder, select Applications ➪ Automator.**

3. **Click Custom, and then click Choose.**

4. **In the Library, click Files & Folders and then double-click the Get Specified Finder**
   Items action. Automator adds the Get Specified Finder Items action to the workflow pane.

5. **To add your bookmarks to the Get Specified Finder Items action, click Add and navi-**
   gate to your user account's Library ➪ Safari folder.

6. **Click the Bookmarks.plist file and click Add.** Automator adds the bookmarks file to the
   Get Specified Finder Items action.

7. **In the Library, click Files & Folders and then double-click the Copy Finder Items action.** Automator adds the Copy Finder Items action to the workflow pane.

8. **To add the shared network folder to the Copy Finder Items action, open the To list and click Other.**

9. **Navigate to and select the shared network folder, and then click Open.** The shared network folder appears in the Copy Finder Items action, as shown in figure 4.14.

10. **Select File ⇨ Save, type a name in the Save As box, and then click Save.** Automator saves your workflow file.

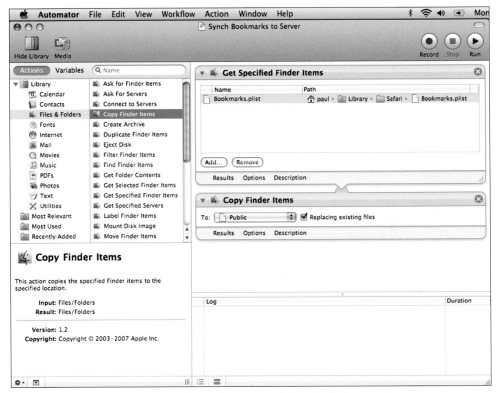

4.14 In Automator, use the Get Specified Finder Items and Copy Finder Items actions to copy your bookmarks to a shared network folder.

Now, on the other computer, you need to create an Automator workflow that brings the book-marks file from the shared network folder to that computer. Follow these steps:

1. **Make a connection to the shared network folder and save the logon data to your keychain.**

2. **In Finder, select Applications ⇨ Automator.**

3. **Click Custom, and then click Choose.**

4. **In the Library, click Files & Folders and then double-click the Get Specified Finder Items action.** Automator adds the Get Specified Finder Items action to the workflow pane.

5. **To add the shared network folder to the Get Specified Finder Items action, click Add.**

6. **Navigate to and select the shared network folder, and then click Add.** The shared network folder appears in the Get Specified Finder Items action.

7. **In the Library, click Files & Folders and then double-click the Get Folder Contents action.** Automator adds the Get Folder Contents action to the workflow pane.

8. **In the Library, click Files & Folders and then double-click the Filter Finder Items action.** Automator adds the Filter Finder Items action to the workflow pane.

9. **Complete the Filter Finder Items action.**

   - In the first list, choose Name.

   - In the second list, choose contains.

   - In the text box, type Bookmarks.

10. **In the Library, click Files & Folders and then double-click the Copy Finder Items action.** Automator adds the Copy Finder Items action to the workflow pane.

11. **To add your Safari folder to the Copy Finder Items action, open the To list and click Other.**

12. **Navigate to your user account's Library ⇨ Safari folder and click Open.** Automator adds the Safari folder to the Copy Finder Items action. Figure 4.15 shows the completed workflow.

13. **Select File ⇨ Save, type a name in the Save As box, and then click Save.** Automator saves your workflow file.

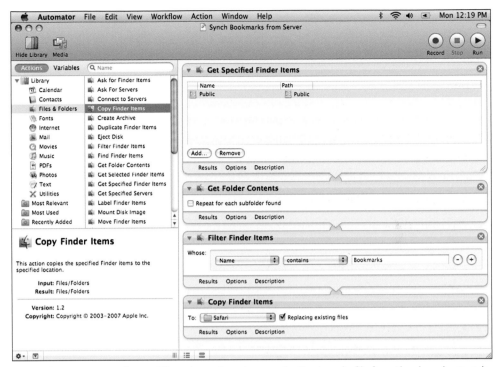

4.15 In Automator, use the workflow shown here to copy the Bookmarks file from the shared network folder to your computer.

Saving Pages for Later Use

Bookmarking pages is useful if you want to return to a site later to see what's new or to visit other parts of it. However, it's common to want to use all or part of a page in some way. If you're doing research, for example, you might want to copy some page data into your notes. Safari offers a number of ways to copy various data from a Web page:

- **Page text.** Select the text with your mouse and then press ⌘+C.
- **An image.** Ctrl+click (or right-click) the image, and then click Copy Image.
- **A text link address.** Ctrl+click (or right-click) the link, and then click Copy Link.
- **An image link address.** Ctrl+click (or right-click) the image, and then click Copy Image Address.

After you copy the data, switch to your notes (or wherever you want to paste the information), and then press ⌘+V to paste the data. Besides these basic techniques, Safari also gives you a few more advanced techniques for saving page data.

E-mailing a page

If you come across a particularly interesting, useful, or funny page, you might want to share it with other people. However, rather than telling people where the page is located and asking them to surf there themselves, you can save them the trip by including the entire page inside an e-mail message. You can also send the page to yourself, which is a handy way to remind yourself about a site.

Many sites offer some sort of Email This Page link that you can use. In the absence of such a link, you can e-mail the page. To do this, follow these steps:

1. **From the Web page you want to e-mail, choose File ⇨ Mail Contents of This Page.** Mail creates a new message and inserts the page into the body of the message, as shown in figure 4.16. You can also load the current page into a message by pressing ⌘+I.

2. **Type the recipient's address in the To text box.** To share your find with multiple people, type their addresses in either To or Cc, separated by commas.

3. **Edit the Subject line, if necessary.** The default Subject line is the page title.

4. **Click Send.** Mail sends the message to the recipients.

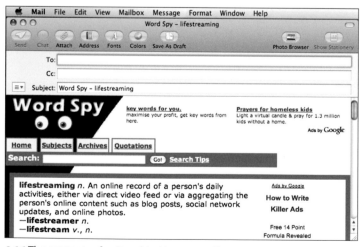

4.16 The contents of a site added to an e-mail message

Genius

What if you want to just e-mail the *address* of the current page instead of the page itself? Not a problem. Choose File ⇨ Mail Link to This page, or press Shift+⌘+ I. The Mail program fires up a new message and pastes the address into the body of the message. If you only want to send part of the address, select what you need in the address bar and then choose Safari ⇨ Services ⇨ Mail ⇨ Send Selection.

Adding part of a Web page to the Dashboard

What do you do if you come across a chunk of a Web page that you want to save for later use? For example, you find a compelling YouTube video, an engaging Flickr photo, an important craigslist ad, a funny cartoon, or a useful list of links. Saving bits of Web pages for easy reuse has never been easy, but Safari offers a method that makes saved Web page parts just a click or two away.

The feature that accomplishes this is Safari's Open in Dashboard feature, which can save part of a Web page to the Dashboard's Web Clip widget. You can then access the page piece at any time just by opening the Dashboard. This is a new feature in Leopard (OS X 10.5), so you need to be running at least that version of OS X to use it.

First, here are the steps to follow to add part of a Web page to the Dashboard's Web Clip widget:

1. **From the Web page with the content you want to save, choose File ⇨ Open in Dashboard.** Safari grays out all of the page except for a small selection window.

2. **Click the part of the page that contains the content you want to save.**

   - To save an image, click the image and Safari automatically selects the entire image.
   - To save a video, click the video playback window and Safari automatically selects the window.
   - To save any other content, click anywhere within the content.

3. **Use the handles that appear around the clip to adjust the size and shape of the clip, if necessary.**

4. **Click Add.** Safari opens the Dashboard and loads the clip. Figure 4.17 shows a YouTube video loaded as a Web clip in the Dashboard.

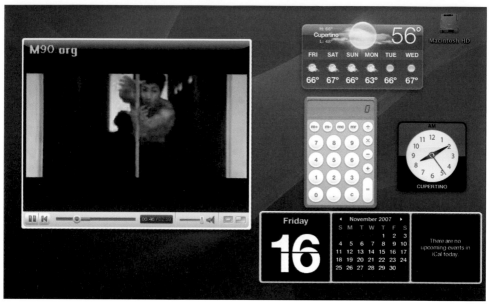

4.17 You can save Web page text, images, and even videos to the Dashboard's Web Clip widget.

Archiving a Web page

One of the key characteristics of the Web is that it's always changing. On the one hand, that's a good thing because it means there's always fresh content to check out. On the other hand, it's often a bad thing because some good content that was available last week might not be around this week. This can happen because a Web author edits or deletes the page, or because a site moves or goes dark for some reason.

If you come across a page that has content that's important to you, you can tell Safari to save a copy of the current version of the page. This is called *archiving* the page, and it works like this:

1. **From the Web page that you want to save as a Web archive, choose File ⇨ Save As.** Safari displays the Save As dialog box.

2. **Use the Export As text box to name the archive.**

3. **Make sure the Format list shows Web Archive, as shown in figure 4.18.**

4. **Click Save.** Safari saves the page and its contents as an archive.

To open a Web archive later on, run Safari, choose File ⇨ Open File (or press ⌘+O), click the Web archive file, and then click Open. Alternatively, use Finder to locate the Web archive file, click and drag the file to the Dock, and then drop it on the Safari icon.

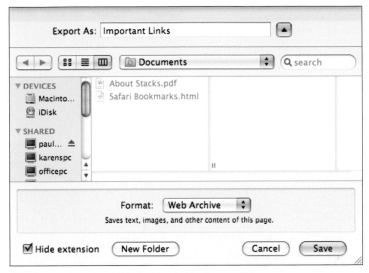

4.18 Be sure to select Web Archive in the Format list.

Enhancing Safari Privacy

The sites you visit on your own time are nobody else's business but your own, of course. However, in the interest of convenience, Safari keeps careful track of the sites you've visited and the pages within those sites that you've loaded. This information is stored in various Safari areas, particularly the history, but also in cookies and the Downloads window. If you're worried about other people seeing where you've been browsing, then you need to remove some or all of this data.

Deleting a site from your history

It's distressingly easy to take a wrong turn on the Web and end up in a bad part of town. Click an apparently innocuous link in a Web page or an e-mail message, and you can land on a page that contains pornography, spam links, phishing code, or even malware. Of course you make tracks to a safer neighborhood right away, but that site still lurks in your browser history. To ensure that no one sees the site in your history, and to prevent you or someone else from accidentally revisiting the site, you should delete it from the history. Follow these steps:

1. **Choose History ➪ Show All History to display the History collection.** You can also click the Show All Bookmarks icon on the left side of the Bookmarks Bar (see figure 4.10, earlier) and then click History in the Collections pane.

2. **Ctrl+click or right-click the page you want to remove.**

3. **Click Delete, as shown in figure 4.19.** Safari removes the page from the history.

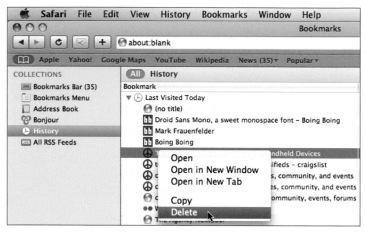

4.19 Ctrl+click or right-click a history item and then click Delete.

If you don't want *any* sites of pages to appear in your history, you can clear out the whole thing by choosing History ⇨ Clear History.

Erasing all your browser tracks

Clearing the browser history is all well and good, but you're just fooling yourself if you think that your browsing activities are now safe from prying eyes. Even a moderately skilled snoop could still find out all about where you've been by checking your cookies, the Downloads window, Google search entries, and, most importantly, the browser's cache of saved site files. You're a wide open book, my friend.

If you want to close that book, then you need to take things a step farther and clear everything. Safari calls this *resetting* the program, and you do it with just a few steps:

1. **Choose Safari ⇨ Reset Safari.** The Reset Safari dialog box appears, as shown in figure 4.20. Note that this is the Safari 3.0 version of the dialog box. The dialog box you see may be different.

4.20 Use the Reset Safari dialog box to erase all your browsing tracks.

2. **Select the options that you do not want Safari to reset.** For maximum privacy, you should select all the options. However, you might want to deselect the Close all Safari windows option if you plan to continue using the program.

3. **Click Reset.** Safari resets the items you selected.

Activating private browsing

If you find yourself constantly resetting Safari, you can save yourself a bit of time by configuring Safari to reset itself automatically. This is called *private browsing* and it means that Safari doesn't save any data as you browse:

⊙ Sites aren't added to the history (although the Back and Forward buttons still work for navigating sites that you've visited in the current session).

⊙ Files aren't added to the Downloads window.

⊙ Search text isn't saved with the Google search box.

⊙ AutoFill text isn't saved.

To activate private browsing, choose Safari ⇨ Private Browsing and click OK when Safari asks if you're sure you want to turn on private browsing. Safari activates the private browsing feature. That's how easy it is.

Macs have never been about just the technology. Yes, they look stylish and they just work, but Mac users usually don't know or care about things such as the speed of the machine's CPU or even how much memory they have installed. These things don't matter all that much because Macs have always been about helping you get things done and helping you make your life better, more creative, and more efficient. And as you see in this chapter, your Mac can also go a long way toward making your life — particularly your contacts, appointments, and to-do lists — more organized.

Managing Your Contacts

One of the paradoxes of modern life is that as your contact information becomes more important, you store less and less of that information in the easiest database system of them all — your memory. That is, instead of memorizing phone numbers like you used to, you now store your contact info electronically. When you think about it, this isn't exactly surprising because it's not just a land-line number that you have to remember for each person; it might also be a cell number, an instant messaging handle, an e-mail address, a Web site address, a physical address, and more. That's a lot to remember, so most of you have gone electronic. And for most Mac users, "electronic" means the Address Book application, which seems simple enough, but it's actually loaded with useful features that can help you organize and get the most out of the contact management side of your life.

Saving a person's contact information

Entering a person's contact data by hand into a new Address Book card is a tedious bit of business at the best of times, so it helps if you can find a faster way to do it. If you can cajole a contact into sending her contact data electronically, then you can add that data with just a couple of mouse moves. What do I mean when I talk about sending contact data electronically? The world's contact management gurus long ago came up with a standard file format for contact data: the *vCard*. It's a kind of digital business card that exists as a separate file. People can pass this data along by attaching their (or someone else's) card to an e-mail message. (You learn how to do this for your own contact data in the next section.)

If you get a message with contact data, you see an icon for the .vcf file, as shown in figure 5.1.

You now have two ways to get this data into your Address Book:

- Ctrl+click (or right-click) the vCard file icon, and then choose Open With ⇨ Address Book.

- Click Address Book in the Dock, click and drag the vCard file icon, and then drop it inside either the Name column or anywhere within the currently displayed card, as shown in figure 5.2.

When Address Book asks you to confirm the new card, click Add.

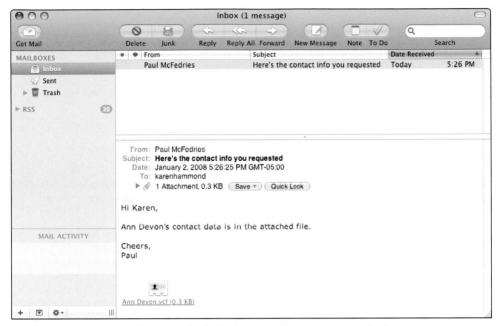

5.1 If you get a message with an attached vCard, an icon for the file appears in the message.

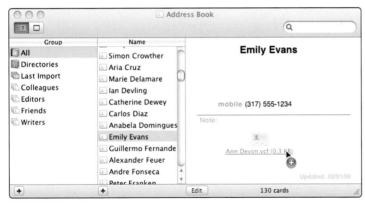

5.2 You can click and drag the vCard attachment and drop it inside the Address Book window.

Sending your contact information

The easiest way to get someone's contact info into your Address Book is to use that person's vCard, typically sent to you as an e-mail attachment. So why not turn things around and offer the same convenience to your colleagues, friends, and others? That is, why not create your own vCard and fire it off to whoever you think wants it?

A card should have been added automatically when you set up your user account, so look for a card under your username. (If for some reason you don't have a card, choose File ⇨ New Card, or press ⌘+N, and then fill in the fields.) Make sure that Address Book knows this is your card by choosing the card and then choosing Card ⇨ Make This My Card. This changes the standard card icon to a silhouette of a head shot, as shown in figure 5.3.

Note

One of the main advantages to designating your own card is that you can easily navigate to it by choosing Address Book's Card ⇨ Go to My Card command.

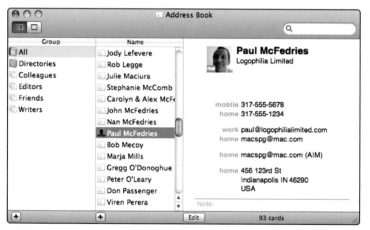

5.3 When you specify a card as your own, Address Book changes the icon to the silhouette of a head shot.

Now you're ready to create your own vCard. Follow these steps:

1. **Make sure your Address Book card contains all the data you want to include in your vCard and that the data is accurate.**

2. **Choose your card.**

3. **Choose File ⇨ Export ⇨ Export vCard.** You can also Ctrl+click or right-click the card and then click Export vCard. Address Book prompts you for a name and location for the new vCard file.

4. **Use the Save As text box to change the filename.** Ideally, the vCard filename should be the same as your name.

5. **Use the Where list to choose a location to store the file.** It's usually best to store the vCard in your Documents folder for easiest access.

6. **Click Save.** Address Book exports your vCard file.

Before sending your card, note that Address Book doesn't include your card's picture by default. If you'd like to add your picture to your vCard, choose Address Book ⇨ Preferences, click the vCard tab, and then select the Export photos in vCards check box.

With your vCard good to go, you can now use Mail to ship it. In any e-mail message, run the Attach File command and then select your vCard file to attach it to the message.

Note

Some corporate mail servers may block vCard attachments because of some security concerns from a few years back, so your attachment might not make it through.

Sending messages to a group of contacts

Choosing recipients one by one is fine if your list of recipients changes each time, or if you only e-mail a particular collection of recipients every once in a while. However, these days it's fairly common to send messages to the same bunch of recipients frequently. It could be the other people in your department, colleagues on a particular project, your family members, your club members, or whatever. In each case, selecting all those addresses one at a time gets old quickly. Fortunately, the Address Book can help you eliminate the drudgery from addressing these messages. How? By enabling you to place a particular collection of recipients in their own group. After the group is set up, you just send your message to that group, and each member of the group gets a copy. What could be simpler?

To create a new group, open Address Book and follow these steps:

1. **Choose some or all of the contacts you want to include in your new group.**

2. **Choose File ⇨ New Group From Selection.** Address Book adds a new group and places the group name in a text box so you can edit it.

3. **Type a name for the new group and then press Return.**

4. **To add another contact to the new group, click the All group, click and drag the contact, and then drop it on the new group.**

A really useful variation on the group theme is the *smart group*. This is a group where each member has something in common. For example, consider the following scenarios:

● If everyone is employed by the same company, then the Company field is the same for each contact.

- If everyone works in the same department, then the Department field is identical for each contact.

- If everyone lives in the same city, then the City field for each contact is the same.

In other words, there's a specific field in each contact's card that contains the same data. A smart group is a group where you specify not only the field on which to base the group, but also the value of the field that each contact must have in common. For example, if you want a group that consists of all your contacts who live in Schenectady, then you need to set up the group so that it only includes those cards where the City field equals Schenectady.

So why is such a group smart? Because Address Book monitors your contacts. For example, consider a smart group of contacts in Schenectady:

- If it sees that you've added a new card where the City fields equals Schenectady, then Address Book automatically adds that contact to your smart group.

- If you edit an existing contact to change its City field to Schenectady, Address Book dutifully adds the edited contact to the smart group.

- If you delete a card that had Schenectady in the City field, Address Book removes the card from the smart group.

Now *that* is smart! Follow these steps to create a smart group:

1. **Choose File ⇨ New Smart Group.** You can also press Option+⌘+N. Address Book displays a dialog box so you can define your smart group.

2. **Use the Smart Group Name text box to type a name for the new group.**

3. **Use the dropdown list on the left to choose the field you want to use as the basis for your smart group.**

4. **Use the middle drop-down list to select an operator.** The operators you see depend on the field type. Here are the operators for most text fields:

   - **contains.** A contact is included in the smart group if the field in the contact's card you specified in Step 3 is partially or exactly the same as the value you specify in Step 5.

   - **does not contain.** A contact is included in the smart group if the field in the contact's card you specified in Step 3 isn't partially or exactly the same as the value you specify in Step 5.

   - **is.** A contact is included in the smart group if the field in the contact's card you specified in Step 3 is exactly the same as the value you specify in Step 5.

- **is not.** A contact is included in the smart group if the field in the contact's card you specified in Step 3 is different from the value you specify in Step 5.

- **begins with.** A contact is included in the smart group if the field in the contact's card you specified in Step 3 starts with the value you specify in Step 5.

- **ends with.** A contact is included in the smart group if the field in the contact's card you specified in Step 3 ends with the value you specify in Step 5.

- **is set.** A contact is included in the smart group if the field in the contact's card you specified in Step 3 contains any value. If you choose this operator, the text box disappears because it's not required.

- **is not set.** A contact is included in the smart group if the field in the contact's card you specified in Step 3 is empty. If you choose this operator, the text box disappears.

5. **Use the right text box to type the value you want contacts to match to qualify for membership in the group.** Figure 5.4 shows a filled in dialog box that defines a smart group.

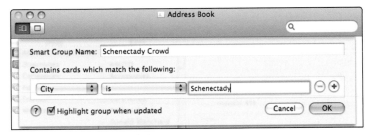

5.4 Use this dialog box to define your smart group.

6. **Click OK.** Address Book adds the smart group to the Group column.

With your regular group or smart group defined, you can now blast out e-mail messages to the group in two ways:

- **In Mail.** Start a new message and then either type the group name in the To text box, or click Address, click the group name in the Addresses window, and then click To:.

- **In Address Book.** Click the group you want to use, Ctrl+click or right-click the group, and then click Send Email to "*Group*," where *Group* is the name of the group.

Note

If you don't see your most recently added group in the Addresses window, shut down and then restart Mail.

Keeping track of birthdays

Do you have trouble remembering birthdays? If so, then I feel your pain because I, too, used to be pathetically bad at keeping birthdays straight in my head. And no wonder: these days you not only have to keep track of birthdays for your family and friends, but increasingly often you have to remember birthdays for staff, colleagues, and clients, too. It's too much! My secret was that I simply gave up and outsourced the job to Address Book, which has a hidden Birthday field that you can use to store birth dates.

To add the Birthday field to a card, choose the card and then choose Card ➪ Add Field ➪ Birthday. As you can see in figure 5.5, Address Book adds the Birthday field, and you then enter the month, day, and year, either by typing the values in each section or by clicking the up and down arrows on the right. Click Edit when you're done.

5.5 Add the Birthday field to those contacts whose birthdays you want to track.

Genius

If you want to track the birthdays for lots of people, don't add the Birthday field by hand for each contact. Instead, add the Birthday field to *all* contacts by customizing the card template to include the Birthday field. Choose Card ➪ Add Field ➪ Edit Template, use the Add Field list to choose Birthday, and then click the dialog box.

Creating a smart group that shows upcoming birthdays

If you start tracking birthdays in Address Book, you still have the problem of remembering when someone's birthday occurs. To avoid the embarrassment of sending belated birthday greetings, you can get Address Book to remind you when one or more birthdays are on the horizon.

You do this by setting up a smart group that only contains contacts whose birthdays are upcoming — for example, within the next seven days. Here's how it's done:

1. **Choose File ⇨ New Smart Group.** You can also press Option+⌘+N. Address Book displays a dialog box so you can define your smart group.

2. **Use the Smart Group Name text box to type a name for the new group.** For example, you could name the group Upcoming Birthdays.

3. **Use the drop-down list on the left to choose the Birthday field.**

4. **Use the middle drop-down list to select the *is in the next* operator.**

5. **Use the text box next to the middle drop-down list to specify the number of days within which you want the birthdays to fall in order for a contact to be added to this smart group.**

6. **Make sure that you choose days from the drop-down list on the right.** Figure 5.6 shows a filled in dialog box for a smart group that looks for contacts with birthdays in the next seven days.

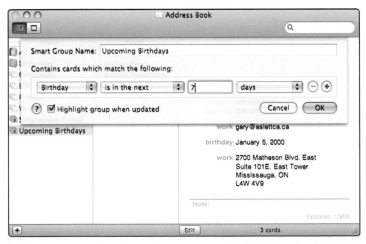

5.6 A smart group that shows those contacts with birthdays that fall within the next week.

7. **Make sure you select the Highlight group when updated check box.**

8. **Click OK.** Address Book adds the smart group to the Group column.

The key here is that when Address Book detects a contact whose birthday falls within the time-frame specified by the group, it displays the group name in a bold purple font, as shown in figure 5.7. When you see the font change, click the smart group to see which contact has an upcoming birthday.

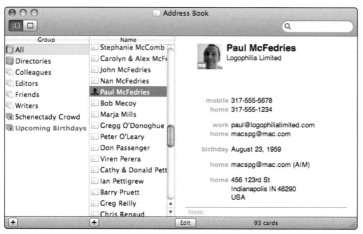

5.7 When the smart group detects a contact with an upcoming birthday, the group name appears in a bold purple font.

Sending yourself an e-mail birthday reminder

Although you can create a birthday smart group, which is useful, you might prefer a more direct reminder. You can build an Automator workflow that looks for those contacts that have a birthday next week and then sends you an e-mail message to remind you of those upcoming birthdays. Here are the steps to follow:

1. **Choose Finder ⇨ Applications ⇨ Automator.** The Automator application appears.

2. **In the Library branch, choose Contacts.**

3. **Double-click the Find People with Birthdays action to add it to the workflow pane.**

4. **In the Find people whose birthday is drop-down list, choose Next Week.**

5. **Double-click the Get Contact Information action to add it to the workflow pane.**

6. **Select the check boxes to select which information you want to include in the e-mail message.** At the very least you should include the contact's name and birthday. Figure 5.8 shows an example.

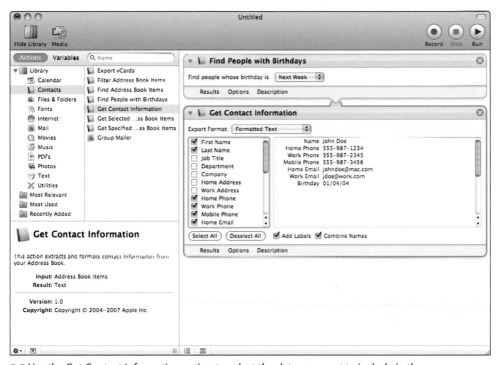

5.8 Use the Get Contact Information action to select the data you want to include in the message.

7. **In the Library branch, choose Mail.**

8. **Double-click the New Mail Message action to add it to the workflow pane.**

9. **Fill in the To field and the Subject field.** The results of the Get Contact Information action will be automatically added to the Message field.

10. **Double-click the Send Outgoing Messages action to add it to the workflow pane.** This action tells Automator to automatically send the e-mail message. Figure 5.9 shows the workflow with the New Mail Message and Send Outgoing Messages actions added.

11. **Save the workflow by choosing File ➪ Save.**

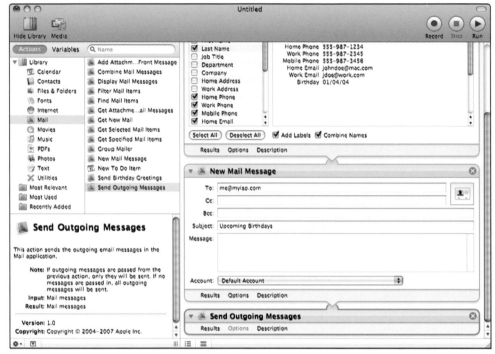

5.9 The New Mail Message and Send Outgoing Messages actions create and send the birthday reminder message.

Be sure to run the workflow at the end of each week so you know whether there are any upcoming birthdays you need to remember. To run a workflow, open Automator, choose File ⇨ Open to open the workflow file, and then click Run.

Importing contacts from Microsoft Outlook

If you've recently made the switch to Mac from Windows, you may have left behind a large collection of contact data in Microsoft Outlook. Don't worry, you don't have to enter all that data by hand into Address Book. Instead, you can export the data from Outlook and then import it into Address Book.

First, follow these steps to export your Outlook data:

1. **In Outlook, choose the Contacts folder.**

2. **Choose File ⇨ Import and Export.** The Import and Export Wizard appears.

3. **Choose Export to a file, and then click Next.**

4. **Choose Comma Separated Values (Windows), and then click Next.**

Automatically Send Birthday Greetings

When someone you know has a birthday today, you can send that person a quick e-mail to wish him a happy birthday. (I'm excluding family and good friends who, of course, you'll call.) Sending out an e-mail is no big deal, of course, but your Mac does give you a way to automate this task, so let's check it out, just for fun:

1. **Choose Finder ⇨ Applications ⇨ Automator.** The Automator application appears.

2. **In the Library branch, choose Contacts.**

3. **Double-click the Find People with Birthdays action to add it to the workflow pane.**

4. **In the Find people whose birthday is list, choose Today.**

5. **In the Library branch, choose Mail.**

6. **Double-click the Send Birthday Greetings action to add it to the workflow pane.** This action enables you to specify a message and an image to include with the message.

7. **Type a birthday message and click the image you want to use.** You can also vary the images by selecting the Random Image For Each Recipient check box.

8. **Save the workflow.** Be sure to run the workflow each day.

5. **Make sure the Contacts folder is selected, and then click Next.**

6. **Select a name and location for the file, and then click Next.** For best results, save the file to a network location that you can access with your Mac. If your Mac and your Windows machine aren't on the same network, save the file anywhere you like and then e-mail it to your Mac account as an attachment.

7. **Click Finish.** Outlook exports the contact data to a text file.

Now you can import the contacts into Address Book:

1. **In Address Book, choose File ⇨ Import ⇨ Text File.** Address Book displays the Select text file to import dialog box.

2. **Choose the text file that you exported earlier from Outlook, and then click Open.** The Text File Import dialog box appears, as shown in figure 5.10.

5.10 Use the Text File Import dialog box to map the Outlook fields to the Address Book fields.

3. **Check to make sure the Address Book fields correspond with the correct fields in the text file.** If an Address Book field doesn't match, click the field and then click the correct Address Book field in the list.

4. **Click OK.** Address Book imports the contact data.

Note

If nothing happens when you click OK, it likely means that there's one or more corrupted entries in the exported text file. Open the file in a text editor and look for lines that don't begin or end with a quotation mark, or for contact data that appears on two or more lines.

Merging duplicate contacts into a single card

Despite your best organizational efforts, you might end up with duplicate contacts in your Address Book. This is particularly prone to happen when you import contacts from some other program. Not to worry, though: Address Book has a handy feature that not only seeks out duplicate contacts, but also enables you to merge them into a single card. Here's how it's done:

1. **In Address Book, choose Card ⇨ Look for Duplicates.** Address Book examines the cards to see if it can find two with the same name. If it finds two such cards, it displays the dialog box shown in figure 5.11.

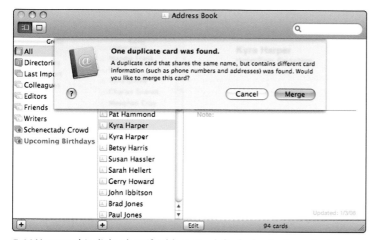

5.11 You see this dialog box if Address Book finds duplicate contacts.

2. **Click Merge.** Address Book combines the data from both cards.

Sharing your Address Book via MobileMe

If you have contacts that other people might need to use, you can share your Address Book with selected people on MobileMe. By default those people can only view your Address Book, but it's also possible to allow them to edit your contacts, if you trust them.

Before you get the ball rolling, it's important to know that your Mac will only share your contact data with people who are in your Address Book. So, for each person you want to share your data with, you need to create an Address Book contact for that person, and you need to include that person's MobileMe e-mail address (as well as any other data you want to store).

Now follow these steps to share your Address Book:

1. **In Address Book, choose Address Book ⇨ Preferences.**

2. **Click the Sharing tab.**

3. **Select the Share your address book check box.** Address Book takes a few moments to configure the data for sharing.

4. **Click the plus sign (+) in the bottom-left corner of the Sharing window.** Address Book displays a list of your contacts.

5. **Choose a contact (other than yourself) with a MobileMe address.**

121

6. **Click OK.** Address Book adds the contact to the Sharing tab, as shown in figure 5.12.

7. **If you want the person to be able to modify your Address Book, select the Allow Editing check box.**

8. **If you want to tell the person about your shared address book, click Send Invitation.** Mail opens and creates a new message addressed to the MobileMe member. The message includes a link that enables the person to subscribe to your Address Book.

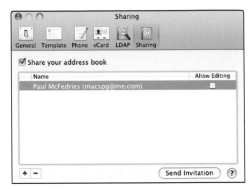

5.12 You can share your Address Book with one or more MobileMe members.

Now the other person needs to subscribe to your Address Book. If you sent the person an invitation message, he or she only needs to click the link in the message.

If you want to subscribe to another user's Address Book, but that user did not send an invitation, follow these steps:

1. **In Address Book, choose File ⇨ Subscribe to Address Book.** Address Book prompts for the sharer's MobileMe address.

2. **Type the sharer's MobileMe address.**

3. **Click OK.** Address Book connects to the shared address book and adds it to the Group column, as shown in figure 5.13.

5.13 When you subscribe to a shared Address Book, it appears in your own Address Book in the Group column.

Printing an envelope for a contact

You're probably so used to e-mailing and instant messaging people these days, that it comes as something of a shock when you find you — gasp! — have to send something by postal mail. If you're just dashing off an informal note, then a handwritten envelope will do the trick. However, for more formal correspondence, you should send the envelope through your printer to make the address look more official.

Happily, Address Book knows envelopes, and it offers all kinds of envelope-related bells and whistles to give you complete control over the look and configuration of both the recipient's address and your return address.

Follow these steps to print an envelope for an Address Book contact:

1. **Navigate to the contact you want to create the envelope for.**

2. **Choose File ⇨ Print.** You can also press ⌘+P. The Print dialog box appears.

3. **Choose the printer you want to use from the Printer list.**

4. **Click the arrow next to the Printer list to expand the Print dialog box.**

5. **From the Style list, choose Envelopes, as shown in figure 5.14.**

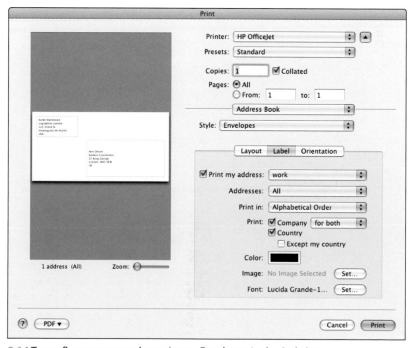

5.14 To configure your envelope, choose Envelopes in the Style list.

6. **Use the controls in the Label tab to configure the return address and contact address labels.**

7. **In the Layout tab, use the Layout list to select the type of envelope you're using.**

8. **Insert the envelope into your printer according to the printer's instructions.**

9. **Click Print.** Address Book prints the envelope.

Note

If you're sending the envelope out of the country, you need to include the country in the recipient's address. To do this, select the Layout tab's Country check box. If this is business correspondence, then you should also select the Company check box, and choose the *for both* option in the list.

Printing mailing labels for contacts

If you're working on your Christmas card list, a print newsletter, or a direct mail marketing campaign, you eventually have to mail out a bunch of pieces. You can make this tedious chore quite a bit easier by printing a mailing label for each recipient. If you have all your recipients in your Address Book — ideally, they should be set up as a group — then you print those mailing labels right from the friendly confines of Address Book itself.

Follow these steps to print mailing labels for your Address Book contacts:

1. **Select the contacts you want to create the mailing labels for.**

2. **Choose File ⇨ Print.** You can also press ⌘+P. The Print dialog box appears.

3. **Use the Printer list to choose the printer you want to use.**

4. **Click the arrow next to the Printer list to expand the Print dialog box.**

5. **In the Style list, choose Mailing Labels, as shown in figure 5.15.**

6. **Use the controls in the Label tab to configure the contact address labels.**

7. **In the Layout tab, use the two Page lists to select the type of mailing labels you're using.**

8. **Insert the mailing labels into your printer according to the printer's instructions.**

9. **Click Print.** Address Book prints the mailing labels.

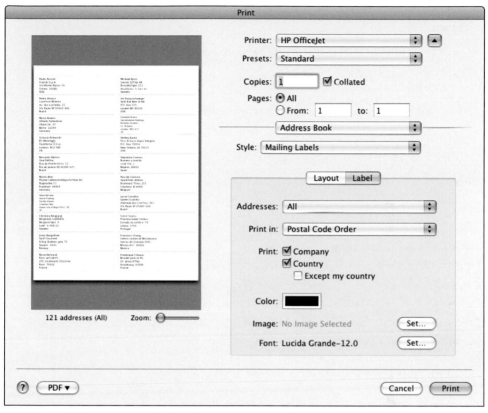

5.15 Choose Mailing Labels in the Style list to configure your labels.

Managing Your Appointments

When you meet someone and ask "How are you?", the most common reply these days is a short one: "Busy!" We're all as busy as can be these days, and that places-to-go-people-to-see feeling is everywhere. All the more reason to keep your affairs in order, and that includes your appointments. Your Mac comes with a program called iCal that you can use to create items, called *events*, which represent your appointments. iCal acts as a kind of electronic personal assistant, leaving your brain free to concentrate on more important things.

Setting up a meeting with a contact

If you want to add a meeting to iCal, you could set it up the usual way by displaying the date, double-clicking the meeting time, and then typing a title for the new event. From there, you can double-click the new event and specify the attendees.

However, if the meeting is with one or more people in your Address Book, there's an easier way to add the meeting to iCal:

1. **In iCal, make sure the day of the meeting is visible.**

2. **In Address Book, select the contact or contacts you're having the meeting with.**

3. **Click and drag the selected contacts and drop then inside iCal at the hour the meeting is to occur.** iCal creates a new event named Meeting with *Contact* (where *Contact* is the name of the first contact in your selection).

4. **Double-click the new event's time (the top half of the event).** As you can see in figure 5.16, iCal automatically added each contact to the attendees list.

Note
For the technique in this section to work, each contact you select must have at least one e-mail address defined. Before proceeding, this is a good time to check that each contact you want to meet with has an e-mail address and to include addresses for those contacts who don't.

5.16 When you drag contacts from Address Book and drop them on a calendar, iCal sets up a meeting with the contacts as attendees.

5. **Adjust the other event settings, as needed.**

6. **Click Send.** iCal sends a meeting invitation to each attendee.

Genius

If you forget to include a contact in the original drag-and-drop, you can still add that person to the meeting. Double-click the event time in iCal to open the event, then click and drag the contact from Address Book and drop it inside the attendees list.

Adding an alarm to an event

One of the truly useful secrets of stress-free productivity in the modern world is what I call the set-it-and-forget-it school of appointments. That is, you set up an appointment electronically, and then get the same technology to remind you when the appointment occurs. That way, your mind doesn't have to waste energy fretting about missing the appointment because you know your technology has your back.

On your Mac, the technology of choice for doing this is iCal and its alarm feature. When you add an alarm to an event, iCal automatically displays a reminder of the event. This reminder can be a message that pops up on the screen or an e-mail sent to your address. You also get to choose when the alarm triggers (such as a specified number of minutes, hours, or days before the event), and you can even set up multiple alarms, just to be on the safe side.

Follow these steps to add an alarm to an event:

1. **If you want to add the alarm to a new event, display the date, click the time, and then choose File ⇨ New Event, or press ⌘+N.** Fill in the other event details as needed.

2. **Double-click the event and then click Edit.**

3. **Click the alarm list and then click the type of alarm you want:**

   - **Message.** Displays a pop-up message with the event particulars.

   - **Message with sound.** Displays a pop-up message accompanied by a sound effect that you choose.

   - **Email.** Sends a message with the event particulars to the e-mail address specified in your Address Book card. (If you have multiple addresses, you get to choose the one you prefer to use for the alarm.)

   - **Open file.** Opens a file or program that you specify.

   - **Run script.** Runs a script file that you specify.

Genius If you have a cell phone or PDA that can receive e-mail, be sure to add the mobile device's e-mail address to your Address Book card (use the Other e-mail address field). This way, if you choose Email as the alarm type, you can then choose your mobile device address, which enables you to get the reminder while you're on the go.

4. **If the alarm requires more data (such as choosing a sound file, e-mail address, file, or script), use the list provided to make your choice.**

5. **Choose the reminder unit (such as minutes before or days before) and then set the number of units.** Figure 5.17 shows a completed example of an alarm.

5.17 An event with a defined alarm.

6. **Using the new alarm list that appears below the alarm you just created, follow Steps 3 to 5 to set up another alarm for the same event, if needed.**

7. **Click Done.**

Stopping automatic calendar additions

When you receive an e-mail message that includes an invitation to an iCal event, Mail automatically adds the event to your default calendar. This is one of Mail's more annoying tendencies, because I think most of us would rather add an invitation manually (by clicking the link in the invite message) and then either accepting or declining the invitation (by double-clicking the event in iCal and then clicking either Accept or Decline).

Follow these steps to stop Mail from automatically adding event invitations to your calendar:

1. **In Mail, select Mail ➪ Preferences.**

2. **Click the General tab.**

3. **In the Add invitations to iCal list, choose Never, as shown in figure 5.18.**

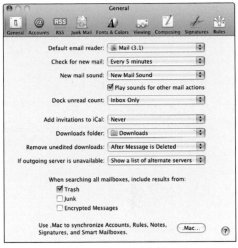

5.18 In the Add invitations to iCal list, choose Never to prevent pesky automatic calendar additions.

Setting up a custom repeat interval

One of iCal's truly great timesavers is the event repeat feature, which enables you to set up a single event and then get iCal to automatically repeat the same event at a regular interval. By default you can repeat an event every day, week, month, or year, and you can continue the events indefinitely or end them after a specific number of times or on a specific date.

You can make this great feature even better by coming up with a custom repeat interval. For example, if you have an event that always occurs on the last Friday of every month, there's no way to schedule that using the regular repeat intervals. With a custom interval, however, it takes just a few mouse clicks.

Follow these general steps to set up a custom repeat interval:

1. **Create the event you want to repeat.** If you want to modify an existing event, instead, double-click the event, and then click Edit.

2. **Click the repeat list, and then click Custom.**

3. **Use the Frequency list to select the base interval.** You have four choices:

   - **Daily.** This choice changes the dialog box to the one shown in figure 5.19. Use the text box to set the number of days you want to use for the interval.

129

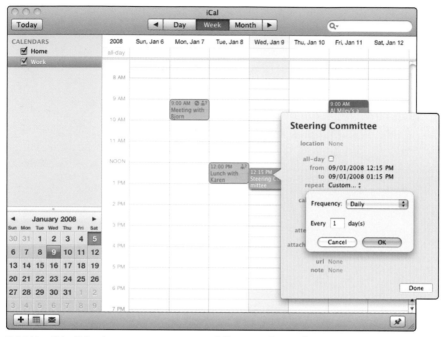

5.19 Use this dialog box to create a custom daily repeat interval.

- **Weekly.** This choice changes the dialog box to the one shown in figure 5.20. Use the text box to set the number of weeks you want to use for the interval, and click the day of the week on which you want the events to fall.

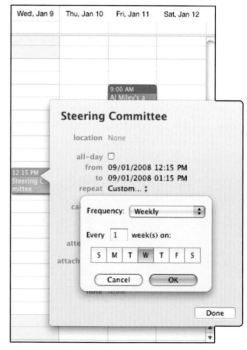

5.20 Use this dialog box to create a custom weekly repeat interval.

- **Monthly.** This choice changes the dialog box to the one shown in figure 5.21. Use the text box to set the number of months you want to use for the interval. You can then either select Each and click the day of the month on which you want the events to fall, or select On the and choose a generic day on which you want the events to fall (such as the second Wednesday of the month).

- **Yearly.** This choice changes the dialog box to the one shown in figure 5.22. Use the text box to set the number of years you want to use for the interval, and then click the month in which you want the events to fall. You can also select the On the check box and then choose a generic day on which you want the events to fall (such as the last Friday of the year).

4. **Click OK.**

5. **Click Done.**

5.21 Use this dialog box to create a custom monthly repeat interval.

5.22 Use this dialog box to create a custom yearly repeat interval.

Creating a calendar of people's birthdays

Earlier in this chapter I covered how to add the Birthday field to your Address Book cards to keep track of this special day for your friends, family, and even colleagues. However, you may find that you spend more time in iCal than in Address Book, so it would be nice to also add all those birthdays to your calendar. You might groan at the thought of setting up a bunch of repeating, all-day events, but you don't have to! With just a few mouse clicks, you can get iCal to do the heavy lifting for you. Here's how:

1. **Choose iCal ⇨ Preferences.**

2. **Click the General tab.**

3. **Select the Show Birthdays calendar check box, as shown in figure 5.23.**

iCal sets up a Subscriptions section in the Calendar List and adds a calendar named Birthdays, as shown in figure 5.24.

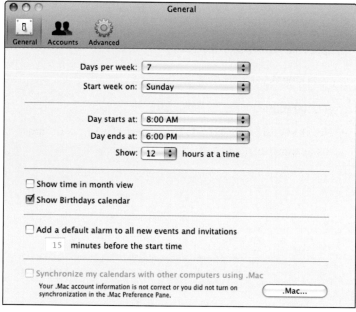

5.23 Select the Show Birthdays calendar check box to see Address Book birthdays in iCal.

Importing a calendar from Microsoft Outlook

If you're a reformed Microsoft Outlook user who has switched to iCal to manage your schedule, you may not relish the idea of adding all your pending appointments and events to iCal by hand. Fortunately, if you still have access to your Outlook data, you can export Outlook's Calendar data and then import it into iCal.

5.24 The Address Book birthdays appear in the Birthdays calendar.

To start off, you need to export your Outlook Calendar data:

1. **In Outlook, choose the Calendar folder.**

2. **In the Navigation pane, click the Send a Calendar via E-mail link.** The Send a Calendar via E-mail dialog box appears, as shown in figure 5.25.

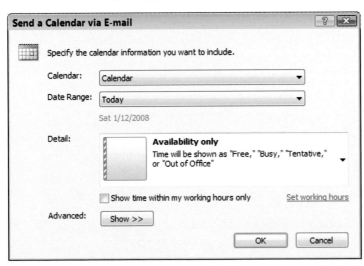

5.25 Use the Send a Calendar via E-mail dialog box to export your Outlook calendar.

Caution
If you have a large number of appointments in the past, exporting the whole calendar can take quite a while. To speed things up, use the Date Range list to choose Specify dates, and then specify the dates you want using the Start and End calendar controls.

3. **If you have more than one calendar, use the Calendar list to choose the one you want to export.**

4. **Use the Date Range list to choose Whole calendar.**

5. **In the Detail list, choose Full details.**

6. **Click the Show button to expand the dialog box.**

7. **If you have any private items in the calendar, select the Include details of items marked private to export those items.**

8. **In the E-mail Layout list, choose List of events.** The e-mail layout isn't important, and choosing the List of events value is much better than choosing the Daily schedule value because it greatly reduces the amount of time Outlook spends composing the e-mail message.

9. **Click OK.**

10. **Outlook asks you to confirm that you want to send the whole calendar.**

11. **Click Yes.** Outlook gathers the calendar data, starts a new e-mail message, and attaches an iCalendar file that includes the data.

12. **You have two ways to proceed from here:**

   ● If your Windows PC and your Mac are on the same network, right-click the attached iCalendar file, click Copy, open a shared network folder that you can access with your Mac, and then press Ctrl+V to paste the file into that folder.

   ● Use the To text box to type your MobileMe address (or whatever e-mail address you use with your Mac), and then click Send. When you receive the iCalendar file, open the message, click and drag the attachment icon, and then drop the file on your desktop or in some other folder.

13. **Click Finish.** Outlook exports the contact data to a text file.

With that out of the way, you can now import the calendar into iCal:

1. **In iCal, choose File ⇨ Import.** iCal displays the Import dialog box, shown in figure 5.26.

2. **Select the Import an iCal file option.** An iCal file uses the same format as an iCalendar file.

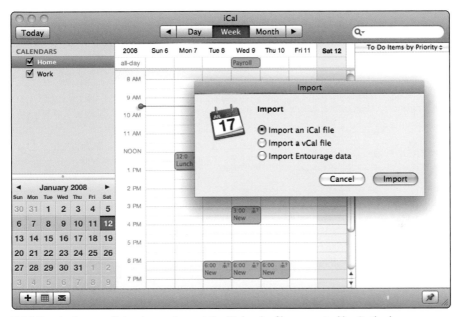

5.26 Use the Import dialog box to import the iCalendar file generated by Outlook.

3. **Click Import.** The iCal Import dialog box appears.

4. **Navigate to the folder containing the iCalendar file, click the file, and then click Import.** The Add events dialog box appears.

5. **Choose the iCal calendar you want to use to import the Outlook events.** You can also choose New Calendar to import the events into a separate calendar.

6. **Click OK.** iCal imports the calendar data.

What happens if there are existing appointments that are the same as the ones you're importing? In that case, iCal simply overwrites the existing appointments.

Publishing a calendar to MobileMe

There may be times when you want people to know what you're up to. For example, knowing when you have appointments scheduled helps other folks to schedule their own appointments or events. If you publish your calendar to MobileMe, this enables your friends to either view your calendar online using a Web browser, or it enables them to subscribe to your calendar (see the next section for the specifics) and, so, keep tabs on you via iCal.

Follow these steps to publish a calendar to MobileMe:

1. **In iCal, choose the calendar you want to publish.**

2. **Choose Calendar ⇨ Publish.** The Publish calendar dialog box appears, as shown in figure 5.27.

3. **Use the Publish calendar as text box to type the name under which you want your calendar published.**

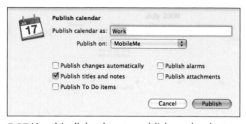

5.27 Use this dialog box to publish a calendar to MobileMe.

4. **Make sure that MobileMe appears in the Publish on list.**

5. **Select the calendar options you want to publish.**

6. **Click Publish.** iCal publishes the calendar to MobileMe.

7. **iCal displays a dialog box with these three buttons:**

   - **Visit Page.** Click this button to display your online calendar in Safari.

   - **Send Mail.** Click this button to create an e-mail message that you can use to tell people about your online calendar.

   - **OK.** Click this button to complete the operation.

Subscribing to a published calendar

If you know of someone who has published a calendar, you might want to keep track of that calendar within your version of iCal. You can do that by subscribing to the published calendar. iCal sets up the published calendar as a separate item in the Calendars section, so you can easily switch between your own calendar and the published calendar.

To pull this off, you need to know the address of the published calendar. This address usually takes the following form: webcal://*server*.com/*calendar*.ics.

Here, *server*.com is the address of the calendar server, and *calendar*.ics is the name of the iCalendar file (almost always preceded by a folder location). For calendars published to MobileMe, the address always looks like this: webcal://ical.me.com/*member*/*calendar*.ics.

Here, *member* is the MobileMe member name of the person who published the calendar.

Follow these steps to subscribe to a published calendar:

1. **In iCal, choose Calendar ⇨ Subscribe.** The Subscribe to calendar dialog box appears.

5.28 Type the address of the published calendar.

2. **Use the Calendar URL text box to type the address of the published calendar.** Figure 5.28 shows an example.

3. **Click Subscribe.** iCal locates the published calendar and begins downloading the data. The "Calendar" Info dialog box appears, as shown in figure 5.29.

4. **Type a new name for the calendar, if desired, and choose a calendar color.**

5. **Type a description of the calendar if you feel like it.**

5.29 Use the "Calendar" Info dialog box to configure your calendar subscription.

6. **Deselect the check boxes beside the calendar items you want to keep: Alarms, Attachments, or To Do items.**

7. **Choose a refresh interval from the Auto-refresh list if you want iCal to automatically refresh the calendar.** The options are Every 5 minutes, Every 15 minutes, Every hour, Every day, Every week, or No. Select No if you don't want iCal to automatically refresh.

8. **Click OK.** iCal creates a Subscriptions section and adds the calendar to that section.

Genius

To refresh the calendar by hand, Ctrl+click or right-click the calendar, and then click Refresh.

How Do I Use My Mac to Organize My Online Life?

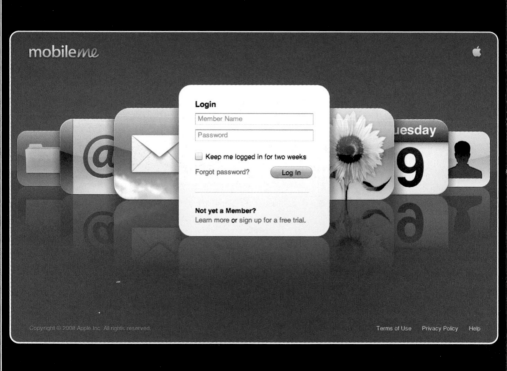

When you go online, you take your life along with you, of course, so your online world becomes a natural extension of your real world. However, just because it's online that doesn't mean the digital version of your life is any less busy, chaotic, or complex than the rest of your life. You'll get the most out of your online presence with a few useful techniques for MobileMe and iWeb — your Mac's main online life tools.

Getting More Out of MobileMe

These days, the primary source of online chaos and confusion is the ongoing proliferation of services and sites that demand your time and attention. What started with Web-based e-mail has grown to a Web site, a blog, a photo-sharing site, online bookmarks, and perhaps a few social networking sites, just to consume those last few precious moments of leisure time. You might be sitting in a chair, but you're getting run ragged anyway!

A great way to simplify your online life is to get a MobileMe account. For a Basic Membership fee ($99 per year currently), or a Family Pack membership, which consists of one main account plus four sub-accounts ($149 per year currently), you get a one-stop Web shop that includes e-mail, an address book, a calendar, a Web Gallery for sharing photos, and online file storage. The price is, admittedly, a bit steep, but it really is convenient to have so much of your online life in one place.

Genius

If you don't want to commit any bucks before taking the MobileMe plunge, you can sign up for a 60-day trial that's free and offers most of the features of a regular account. Go to www.me.com and click the sign up for a free trial link.

After you've got your account up and running, you get the MobileMe login screen by going to www.me.com.

Accessing any e-mail account online

Your MobileMe account is a convenient place to work with messages associated with your MobileMe e-mail address, but you can also extend that convenience to another e-mail account. That is, you can configure MobileMe to also check messages from some other account, even if it's not a MobileMe address. Note, however, that you can only check messages for this account; you can't send messages.

Note

To check another e-mail account with MobileMe, that account must support the Post Office Protocol (POP). Most e-mail accounts support POP, but not all. (For example, MobileMe accounts use Internet Message Access Protocol [IMAP], instead of POP.)

Follow these steps to add an external e-mail account to your MobileMe inbox:

1. **On any MobileMe page, click Mail.** The MobileMe Mail page appears.

2. **Click Preferences.** The Preferences window appears.

3. **Click the Other tab.**

4. **Select the Check mail from an external POP account check box.** The window expands to display the controls for specifying the account particulars.

5. **Fill in the following controls (see figure 6.1 for an example).**

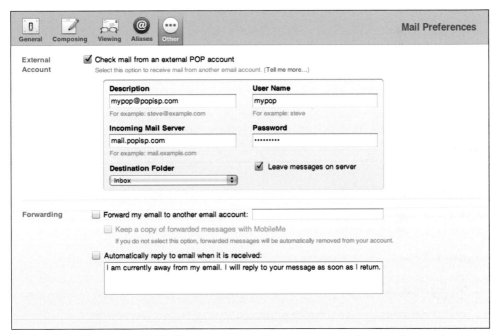

6.1 You can configure your MobileMe account to check messages on another e-mail account.

- **Description.** A short description for the account, such as the account address.

- **Incoming mail server.** The name of the server your provider uses for incoming mail. It usually takes the form mail.*provider*.com or pop.*provider*.com, where *provider*.com is the domain name of your e-mail provider (such as your ISP).

- **User name.** The name you use to log in to the account. This is most often your username, but some providers require your e-mail address.

- **Password.** The password you use to log in to the account.

- **Destination Folder.** Use this list to choose where you want the account's messages stored.

- **Leave messages on server.** If you leave this check box selected, MobileMe leaves a copy of each message on the mail server. This is a good idea because it enables you to also download the messages to your regular e-mail program. If you never do that, you should deselect this check box to avoid messages piling up on the server.

6. **Click Save.**

Forwarding MobileMe messages to another account

If you've got a bunch of e-mail addresses, chances are you've got them all set up in your Mac's Mail application or some other e-mail program because it's convenient to have all your messages in one spot. However, when you set up a MobileMe account, your life becomes a tad less convenient because now your MobileMe messages reside only online. To fix this, you can forward your MobileMe messages automatically to one of your existing accounts. That way, the messages come to your e-mail program via that account, and all your messages can once again be together.

Follow these steps to forward your MobileMe messages to another e-mail address:

1. **On any MobileMe page, click Mail.** The MobileMe Mail page appears.

2. **Click the Actions icon, and then Preferences.** The Preferences window appears.

3. **Click the Other tab.**

4. **Select the Forward my email to check box.**

5. **Use the Forward my email to text box to type the address where you want the MobileMe messages forwarded.** See figure 6.2 for an example.

6. **If you don't want to save a copy of each message in your MobileMe inbox, deselect the Keep a copy of forwarded messages check box.**

7. **Click Save.**

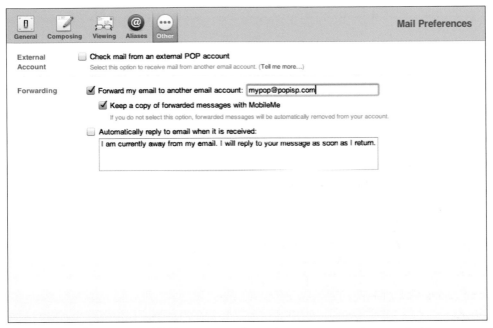

6.2 You can configure your MobileMe account to forward messages to another e-mail address.

Storing files online

Most of the info stored on your MobileMe account — e-mail messages, address book con-tacts, appointments, photos, and so on — is readily available online even if you're not using your Mac. For example, if you're at work, at a friend's house, or at an Internet café, you can still access your MobileMe stuff by logging in to your account using whatever Web browser is handy.

The same can't be said for important files on your Mac, because when you leave your Mac behind, you leave your files behind, as well. Fortunately, MobileMe can help here, too. Each MobileMe account has access to an iDisk, a bit of online storage real estate that you can use to store whatever pictures, videos, documents, or whatever you think you might want to access from anywhere online. MobileMe also uses your iDisk to store any Web sites you set up and any backups you make to iDisk.

To access your iDisk, you have two choices:

- If you're logged in to your MobileMe account, click the iDisk icon in the toolbar. Figure 6.3 shows the iDisk window that appears.

- Open Finder and click the iDisk icon. Figure 6.4 shows the iDisk folder that appears.

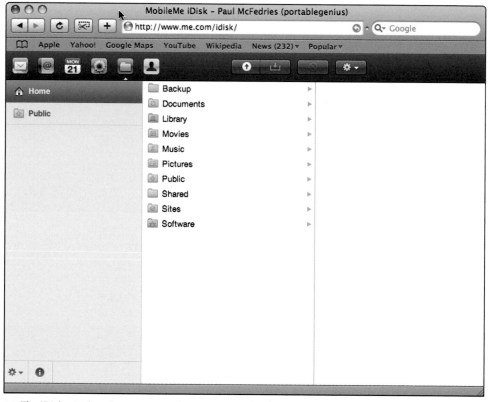

6.3 The iDisk window that appears when you access iDisk via your MobileMe account.

Genius

If you also have a Windows computer at home or at work, you can use it to access your iDisk. Open a Web browser and enter the address http://idisk.mac.com/*username*/, where *username* is your MobileMe member name. When Windows asks you to log on, type your MobileMe member name and password, and then click OK. To access your iDisk Public (which doesn't require a login), enter the address http://idisk.mac. com/*username*-Public/.

144

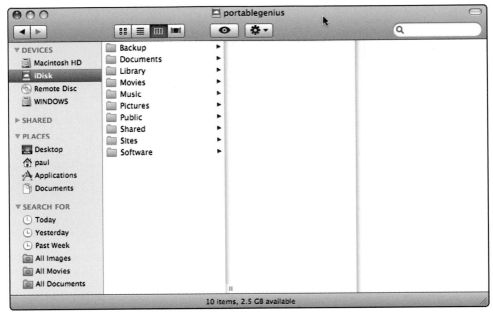

6.4 The iDisk folder that appears when you access iDisk via Finder.

iDisk provides you with a collection of folders, some of which you can use to store files from your Mac. Here's a summary:

- **Backup.** MobileMe uses this folder to store data files created by its Backup feature.

- **Documents.** You can use this folder to store miscellaneous files.

- **Library.** MobileMe uses this folder to store items such as contacts and bookmarks that you've synced with your Mac (see Chapter 3 for more on syncing with MobileMe).

- **Movies.** You can use this folder to store digital video files. If you create Web pages with MobileMe, you can embed these movies in your pages.

- **Music.** You can use this folder to store digital audio files and music playlists.

- **Pictures.** You can use this folder to store digital image files. You can add these images to your MobileMe Web pages and iCards.

● **Public.** You can use this folder to share files with other people over the Web. Other people need only enter the address http://idiskMobileMe.com/*username*-Public/, where *username* is your MobileMe member name. No password is required, so others can easily work with these files. See the next section to learn how to create a custom page for the Public folder.

Caution

The Public folder doesn't require a password, so don't use it to store files that contain confidential or sensitive data. If you want to share such data with other people, you can assign a password to the Public folder. Open System Preferences and click the MobileMe icon. Click the iDisk tab and then select the Password-protect your public folder check box. Type your password in the Password and Confirm text boxes, and then click OK.

● **Shared.** You only see this folder if you signed up for a MobileMe Family Pack. You use this folder to share files with other accounts in your Family Pack.

● **Sites.** MobileMe uses this folder to store pages you created using the now defunct HomePage feature.

● **Software.** MobileMe uses this folder to store applications and other files that are made available solely to MobileMe members.

● **Web.** You only see this folder after you've used iWeb to publish a Web site to your MobileMe account.

To get files from your Mac to iDisk, you have two choices:

● **Using Finder.** First open the iDisk folder you want to use to store the files. Click and drag the file or files you want to upload, and then drop them inside the iDisk folder.

● **Using MobileMe.** In the iDisk window, open the folder you want to use to store the files. Click Upload, click Choose File, choose the file, and then click Upload.

Genius

By default, MobileMe allocates half your storage space (5GB) to MobileMe Mail and half to iDisk. This is dumb because it's extremely unlikely you'll ever need so much space for e-mail messages. To fix this, access iDisk, click Storage Settings, and log in when prompted. In the Storage Settings window, choose a smaller value in the MobileMe Mail list (for example, 700MB). MobileMe automatically allocates the rest of the storage to iDisk. Click Save.

Backing up your data online

Earlier in this chapter I discussed uploading files from your Mac to your MobileMe iDisk. I didn't mention it, but iDisk doubles as a quick-and-dirty backup destination for important files. Backing up your files online is an excellent practice for two reasons:

- **Your backups are always available if you ever need them.** If you lose data, you can restore your files as long as you have an Internet connection.

- **Your backups are safer.** If you back up by making a copy of a file on your Mac hard drive, you're toast if your hard drive dies. Similarly, backing up to a second hard drive or to discs won't help you if a fire or other catastrophe should strike and cause you to lose everything. If your backups are online, however, they're safe from these sorts of mishaps.

You can back up files by hand using iDisk, but MobileMe provides an easier way: the Backup program. This program offers a number of backup scenarios, but the one I'm focusing on here backs up the personal data on your Mac — your Address Book contacts, iCal calendars, Safari preferences, keychain data, and Stickies — to your MobileMe iDisk every day.

To install this program, click the iDisk icon, click Software, click Backup for Mac OS X 10.4.2 or later or 10.5, click Backup_3.1.2.dmg, and then click Download. After you've done that, follow these steps to set up the Personal Data & Settings backup:

1. **In Finder, choose Applications ⇨ Backup.**

2. **If your Mac warns you that Backup wants to access your keychain, click Always Allow.** The first time you run Backup, you see the Welcome to Backup dialog box.

3. **Select the check box beside Personal Data & Settings, as shown in figure 6.5.**

4. **Click Continue.**

5. **If you want to run the backup now, click Personal Data & Settings in the Backup window and then click Back Up.** Backup backs up your data and settings to the iDisk Backups folder.

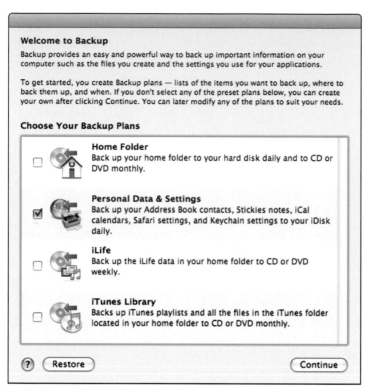

Welcome to Backup

Backup provides an easy and powerful way to back up important information on your computer such as the files you create and the settings you use for your applications.

To get started, you create Backup plans — lists of the items you want to back up, where to back them up, and when. If you don't select any of the preset plans below, you can create your own after clicking Continue. You can later modify any of the plans to suit your needs.

Choose Your Backup Plans

Home Folder
Back up your home folder to your hard disk daily and to CD or DVD monthly.

☑ **Personal Data & Settings**
Back up your Address Book contacts, Stickies notes, iCal calendars, Safari settings, and Keychain settings to your iDisk daily.

iLife
Back up the iLife data in your home folder to CD or DVD weekly.

iTunes Library
Backs up iTunes playlists and all the files in the iTunes folder located in your home folder to CD or DVD monthly.

(?)　(Restore)　　　　　　　　　　　　　　(Continue)

6.5 The Personal Data & Settings backup sends contacts, calendars, and settings to your MobileMe iDisk daily.

Backing up your contacts, calendars, and settings is certainly a good thing, but there's more to your Mac than just those tidbits of data. Chances are you have way too much data on your Mac to fit on your iDisk, but that shouldn't stop you from backing up a few really important files or folders to iDisk. To do that, you need to construct a custom backup plan. Here's how to do it:

1. **In the Backup window, click plus (+).** The Choose a Plan Template dialog box appears.

2. **Click Custom.**

3. **Click Choose Plan.** The Untitled dialog box appears.

4. **In the Backup Items section, click plus (+).** The Choose Items to Back Up dialog box appears.

5. **Use the following tabs to choose what you want to back up.**

   • **QuickPicks.** This tab displays a number of data types, including application preferences, GarageBand projects, and mail messages and settings. Select the check box beside each data type you want to include in the backup.

- **Files & Folders.** Click a file or folder you want to back up and then select the Include this file or the Include this folder option. Repeat for each file and folder you want to add to the backup.

- **Spotlight.** Use this tab to run a spotlight search for items you want to add to the backup. Click a file or folder in the search results and then select the Include this file or the Include this folder option.

6. **Click Done.**

7. **In the Destination and Schedule section, click plus (+).** The Choose a Destination and Schedule dialog box appears.

8. **In the Destination list, choose iDisk, as shown in figure 6.6.**

6.6 Be sure to choose iDisk in the Destination list.

 Note After you select the data to be backed up, the Backup program calculates the total size of the files. Make sure the size doesn't exceed the free space you have in your iDisk. To check iDisk free space, open System Preferences, click MobileMe, and then click the iDisk tab.

9. **Choose the schedule you want to use for the backup.** Select the interval, the date if applicable to your interval selection, and the time.

10. **Click OK.**

11. **Choose Plan ➪ Rename Plan, type a name for the backup plan, and then press Return.**

12. **If you want to run the backup right away, click Back Up Now.**

Accessing your Mac remotely

Having a few important files in your MobileMe iDisk can bail you out of a jam if you forget one of those files when you leave the house or office. Of course, a variation on Murphy's Law states that whatever file you need when you're away from your Mac will be a file that you didn't upload to iDisk.

Besides missing a particular file, another problem you may run into when you're on the road is missing a particular application. For example, suppose you have Microsoft Word on your iMac but not on your MacBook Pro. If you need to create a Word document or check a Word setting while you're away, you're out of luck.

You can solve both types of problems by accessing your Mac from a remote location. For this to work, you need two Macs set up as follows:

- A local Mac that's running Leopard (OS X 10.5) signed in to a MobileMe account that's a full member with a broadband connection to the Internet.

- A remote Mac that's running Leopard (OS X 10.5) signed in to the same MobileMe account as the local Mac with a broadband connection to the Internet.

Note

Your local Mac also needs to connect to the network using a router that supports Universal Plug and Play (UPnP). Most modern routers support UPnP, so this shouldn't be a problem, but check your router manual to see how to ensure that UPnP is enabled. If you're using an AirPort Extreme or AirPort Express base station, choose Finder ➪ Applications ➪ Utilities ➪ AirPort Utility, click Internet, and then select the Enable NAT Port Mapping Protocol check box.

If you have two such Macs, you're good to go. You can use the MobileMe Back to My Mac feature, which enables you to use the remote Mac to connect to the local Mac via the MobileMe account that they have in common. To configure Back to My Mac, you need to follow these steps on both Macs:

1. **Click System Preferences in the Dock.**

2. **Click the MobileMe icon.** The MobileMe dialog box appears.

3. **In the Account tab, sign in to the same MobileMe account on both Macs.**

4. **Click the Back to My Mac tab.**

5. **If the Back to My Mac setting is Off, click Start to change the setting to On, as shown in figure 6.7.**

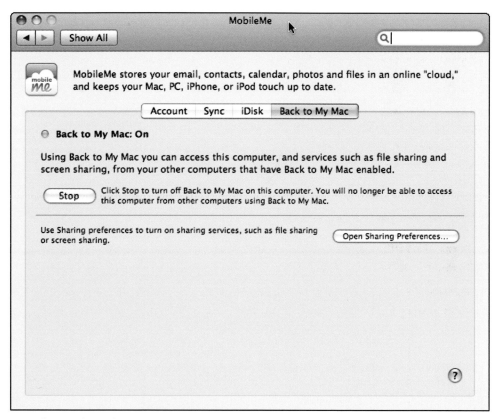

6.7 Make sure the Back to My Mac setting is On.

The rest of the steps you only need to perform on the local Mac:

1. **Click Open Sharing Preferences.** The Sharing dialog box appears.

2. **Select the Screen Sharing check box.** Screen sharing enables you to control the local Mac as though you were sitting in front of it.

3. **Select the Only these users option, click your username, and then click Select.** The user name appears in the list, as shown in figure 6.8.

4. **Select the File Sharing check box.** File Sharing gives you remote access to the local Mac's drives and folders.

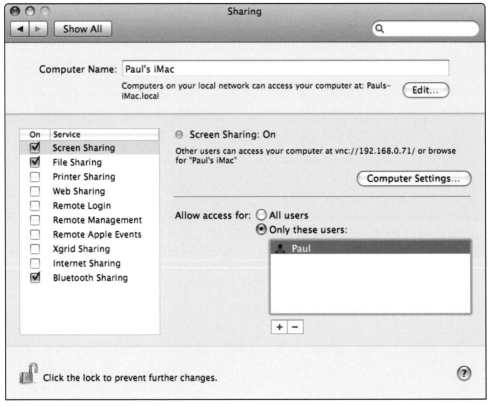

6.8 For added security, select Only these users and then add your Mac user account.

Note   Make sure the Mac you'll be using for remote access has a user account set up with the same name as the account you picked in Step 3.

You're now ready to make the remote connection. In the Finder Sidebar of the remote Mac, you see an icon for the local Mac under the Shared section. Click that icon to connect to the local Mac via the shared MobileMe account. Figure 6.9 shows a File Sharing connection. If you want to switch to a Screen Sharing connection, click the Share Screen button.

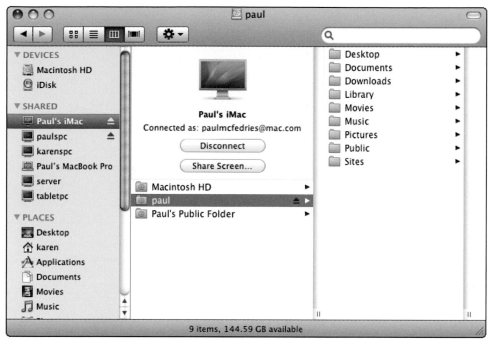

6.9 An icon for the local Mac appears in the Shared section of the sidebar on the remote Mac. Click the icon — Paul's iMac, in this example — to make the connection via MobileMe.

Creating Your Own Web Site

Your Mac comes with the iWeb application, which offers a rich set of page-creation tools. For example, you get a wider range of page templates, eight page types (Welcome, Blog, About Me, Photos, and so on) for each template, and a decent collection of objects that you can add to the page, including text boxes, shapes, MobileMe gallery items, and Google AdSense ads. You can also adjust fonts and colors; add media such as photos, movies, and sounds; insert links; and even add custom HTML code.

Fortunately, despite the extra sophistication of iWeb's page-building features, the process itself isn't insanely complex. In fact, the basic procedure is easily summed with just a few steps:

1. **In iWeb (click the iWeb icon in the Dock), choose File ⇨ New Site (or press Shift+⌘+N) to start a new Web site.** iWeb asks you to choose a template for the first page in the site, as shown in figure 6.10.

153

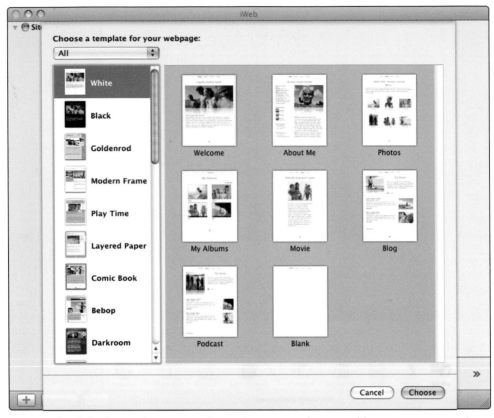

6.10 Use this dialog box to choose a template and page type when you add a new page to your site.

Note When you start iWeb, your Mac might ask if you want to give iWeb access to your MobileMe keychain data. Be sure to click Always Allow, which gives iWeb access to your MobileMe galleries and to publish the site to iDisk.

2. **In the list of templates on the left, click the template you want to use.**

3. **In the list of page types on the right, click the type of page you want to build.**

4. **Click Choose.** iWeb creates the page, complete with placeholder images and text.

5. **For each text placeholder, double-click the placeholder and then type the text you want to display on the page.**

6. **For each image placeholder, click and drag a replacement image and drop it on the image placeholder.**

7. **Use the Insert menu to add more objects to the page.**

8. **Use the Format menu to apply formatting styles to the text and other objects.**

9. **Add more pages by choosing File ⇨ New page (or pressing ⌘+N) and then repeating Steps 2 through 8.**

10. **Publish your site to MobileMe.** I discuss this step in more detail later in this chapter.

The next few sections embellish these steps by showing you how to add more complex objects to your pages, including Google Maps and AdSense ads, My iTunes widgets, YouTube videos, and more. Note that you need to be using at least iWeb '08 to have access to these features.

Inserting a Google Map

If you're slapping up a page for a store, party, wedding, or anything else where your visitors will need to know where you are (or your event is) located, and how to get there, you could spend tons of time constructing your own map by hand. Of course, *nobody* does that anymore! Nowadays you go to Google Maps and get them to do the hard work for you. But how do you get the map on your page, and how can you let people interact with the map (zoom in and out, get directions, and so on)?

The answer is to let iWeb '08 handle everything for you. iWeb '08's Google Map widget not only embeds a map that points out the location of any address you specify, but it also lets you include the Google Map zoom controls and links that enable each visitor to get directions to your address from anywhere they specify. Best of all, it's really easy to add:

1. **Choose (or create) the page on which you want the map to appear.**

2. **Choose Insert ⇨ Google Map.** You can also click the Web Widgets button and then click Google Map. The Google Map window appears.

3. **Use the address text box to type the address of your location.**

4. **Click Apply.** The widget contacts Google Maps and downloads a map for your location, as shown in figure 6.11.

5. **Use the following check boxes to determine the features included with the map.**

   - **Zoom controls.** Leave this check box selected to include the controls that enable your site visitors to zoom in and out of the map to pan the map left, right, up, and down.

   - **Address bubble.** Leave this check box activated to display the bubble that shows the address of your location and includes links to enable visitors to get directions to (and from) the location.

6.11 Type the address of your location and then click Apply to get the map from Google.

6. **Click and drag the map to set its position within the page.**

7. **Click and drag the handles that appear on the map's sides and corners to size the map.**

Placing ads on your site

If your site contains some interesting content on a particular subject, you may soon find that you're attracting quite a few visitors. In that case, you might want to try and get a bit of payback for all your hard work by getting your pages to generate some cash for you. How? By placing ads on your pages using Google's AdSense program. The AdSense server automatically examines the content of your page and generates one or more ads that are related in some way to that content. The idea is that if someone is interested in your content, they may also be interested in a related ad. If the visitor follows through on his interest by clicking an ad, you earn a few cents from Google.

Before you can place ads on your site, you need to set up a Google AdSense account. You have two choices here depending on whether you have an AdSense account set up:

● **You don't currently have an AdSense account.** In iWeb, choose File ➪ Set Up Google AdSense, type an e-mail address (such as your MobileMe address), and click Submit. When iWeb tells you the account has been created, click OK.

- **You already have an AdSense account.** In iWeb, choose File ⇨ Set Up Google AdSense, and then click I Already Have An Account. Type the e-mail address associated with your AdSense account, as well as your postal code or the last five digits of your phone number, and then click Submit. When your account is confirmed, click OK.

Before inserting any ads, you should understand the different ad types you can use:

- **Text ad.** This ad includes only text and a link to the advertiser's site. It is by far the most common type of AdSense ad.
- **Text and Image ad.** This ad includes both text and an image related to the advertised product, service, or company.
- **Text links.** This ad consists of just links to the sites of several advertisers.

Note, too, that each type of ad comes in multiple sizes. For example, a banner ad is 468 pixels wide and 60 pixels high, making it suitable for the very top (or, more rarely, the very bottom) of a page. Similarly, a skyscraper ad is 120 pixels wide and 600 pixels high, making it suitable for the left or right side of a page.

You're now ready to plunk an ad on your site. Here are the steps to follow in iWeb '08.

1. **Choose Insert ⇨ Google AdSense Ad.** You can also click the Web Widgets button and then click Google AdSense Ad. The Google AdSense Ad window appears.
2. **Use the Select ad format list to select the ad type and size you want to insert.**
3. **Use the Select ad color list to select the color or colors you want to use for the ad.** Figure 6.12 shows a banner ad using the Blue & White color scheme.
4. **Click and drag the ad to set its position within the page.**

6.12 Use the Google AdSense Ad window to choose the ad type, size, and color.

Adding your own HTML to a page

The iWeb page-creation tools are certainly quite advanced, but there are still lots of page goodies that iWeb can't do. For example, it doesn't let you create a table, set up a form, add a bulleted or numbered list, define an image map, and so on.

Fortunately, you can still add all of these features yourself if you're conversant with HTML (Hypertext Markup Language), which is the set of codes that defines most of what you see on the Web. iWeb lets you insert a snippet of HTML that you write yourself anywhere on a page. Here's how:

1. **Choose Insert ⇨ HTML Snippet.** You can also click the Web Widgets button and then click HTML Snippet. The HTML Snippet window appears.

2. **Use the large text box to enter your HTML code.**

3. **Click Apply.** iWeb renders the HTML code, as shown in figure 6.13.

4. **Click and drag the snippet to set its position within the page.**

5. **Click and drag the handles that appear on the snippet's sides and corners to size the snippet.**

6.13 Use the HTML Snippet window to enter the HTML code that you want to add to your page.

Placing a My iTunes widget on a page

If your site is music-related, or even if you just love music, you can spice up a page on your site by adding My iTunes. This is an iWeb '08 Web widget that accesses your iTunes Music Store data and displays information about your favorite bands and recently purchased music.

It's a fun way to let people know what you're up to musically, and it takes only a few steps to add:

1. **In iTunes, choose Store ⇨ Sign In.**

2. **Type your Apple ID (MobileMe e-mail address) and your password, and then click Sign In.**

3. **Choose Store ⇨ View My Account.**

4. **Type your password and click View Account.** The Apple Account Information screen appears.

5. **Click the Enable My iTunes button, shown in figure 6.14.**

6. **Select the check box to say that you agree to allow Apple to access your account info, and then click Continue.**

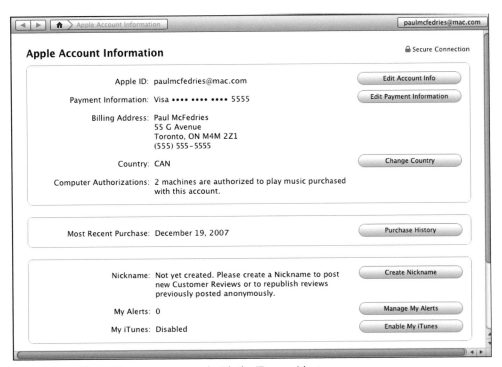

6.14 Click Enable My iTunes to get started with the iTunes widget.

159

7. **Select the check box for each widget you want to use.** As you can see in figure 6.15, iTunes adds a Get HTML Code button beside each widget.

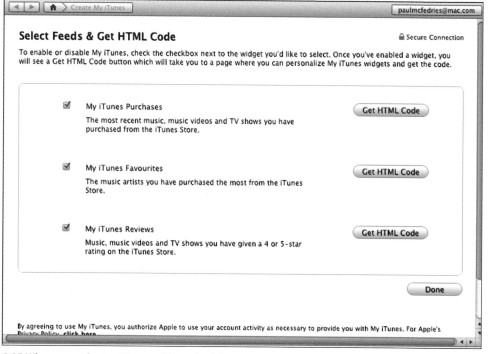

6.15 When you select an iTunes widget check box, you see a Get HTML Code button for the widget.

8. **For one of the widgets, click Get HTML Code.** iTunes displays a Web page with options for the widget.

9. **Choose the size and style of the widget and then click Copy Code.**

10. **In iWeb, create an HTML Snippet (as described in the previous section), click the text box in the HTML Snippet window, and then choose Edit ⇨ Paste (or press ⌘+V).**

11. **Click Apply.** The My iTunes widget appears in your page, as shown in figure 6.16.

12. **Repeat Steps 8 through 11 for the other widgets you want to add.**

Note

To get more widgets later on or to turn off My iTunes, display the Apple Account Information screen and then click Manage My iTunes.

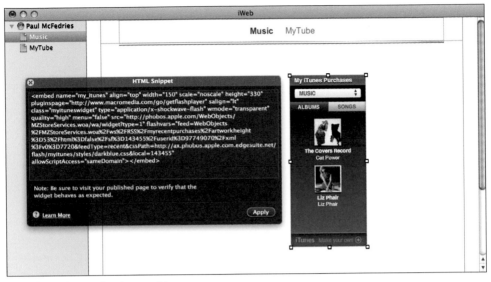

6.16 The My iTunes Purchases widget.

Adding YouTube videos to your site

YouTube is one of the most popular sites on the Web, and no wonder: With thousands upon thousands of videos to view, it's one of the world's great timewasters. If you've found a video that's particularly relevant to some of the content on your site, or if you just want to share a video that had you rolling on the floor with laughter, iWeb '08 is only too happy to comply.

Follow these steps to embed a YouTube video on a page:

1. **In Safari, go to YouTube (www.youtube.com) and find the video you want to embed on your page.**

2. **Click the customize link to the right of the video window.** YouTube displays some controls that you can use to configure the video, as shown in figure 6.17.

3. **Select the Don't include related videos option if you don't want to see related videos.**

6.17 Click the customize link to see some options for embedding the YouTube video.

161

4. **Click the color scheme you want to use.**

5. **Select the Show Border check box if you want to add a border around the window.**

6. **Click inside the Embed text box.** Safari automatically selects all the text, which is the code you use to embed the video.

7. **Choose Edit ⇨ Copy (or press ⌘+C) to copy the code.**

8. **In iWeb, create an HTML Snippet (as described earlier in this chapter), click the text box in the HTML Snippet window, and then choose Edit ⇨ Paste (or press ⌘+V).**

9. **Click Apply.** The video appears in your page, as shown in figure 6.18.

6.18 A YouTube video embedded in an iWeb page.

Genius

The http://web.me.com/*username* address displays the content of the site that's listed first in the iWeb window. If you have more than one site, decide which one you want to appear when a visitor uses the main address. If that site isn't at the top of the site list, click and drag the site and drop it at the top of the list.

Publishing your Web site to MobileMe

When some or all of your site is ready for its Web debut, you need to publish the site to your MobileMe account. iWeb sends your Web files to your MobileMe iDisk, and stores everything in the Web folder's Sites subfolder. The address of your main site is http://web.me.com/*username*, where *username* is your MobileMe member name, and each site is a subfolder of the main site. For example, if you have a site named Personal, its address will be http://web.me.com/*username*/Personal.

Follow these steps to publish your site to MobileMe:

1. **Choose File ⇨ Publish to MobileMe.** iWeb tells you to make sure you own or have permission to use your site content.

2. **Click Continue.** iWeb logs in to your MobileMe account and begins publishing the site and tells you not to quit the application until it's done.

3. **Click OK.** When the publish procedure is done, iWeb displays a dialog box to let you know.

4. **You have three choices:**

   - **Announce.** Click this button to create an e-mail message that you can use to tell people about your site.

   - **Visit Site Now.** Click this button to display your site in Safari.

   - **OK.** Click this button to complete the operation.

Publishing your Web site using your own domain name

If you already have your own domain name, you might prefer that folks access your iWeb site using that domain rather than the web.me.com domain. Not a problem! MobileMe is happy to host your domain for you, and it won't charge you anything extra for the privilege.

Your first order of business is to adjust your domain name settings to point it to MobileMe. Go to the registrar of your domain name and access the domain's settings. Choose the option to modify the Domain Name System (DNS) servers, open the CNAME (also called Domain Alias) entries, and then change the www entry so that it points to web.me.com. Figure 6.19 shows an example where I'm pointing www.paulmcfedries.com to web.me.com.

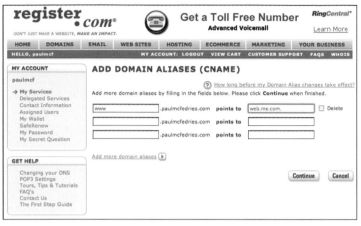

6.19 You need to point your domain's www domain alias to web.me.com.

With that done, you can now set up MobileMe to host your domain name. Here are the steps to follow:

1. **In iWeb, choose File ⇨ Set Up Personal Domain.**

2. **Log in to your MobileMe account when prompted.** The Account Settings page appears.

3. **Click Personal Domain.** The Domain Settings page appears.

4. **Click Add Domain.**

5. **Type your domain name in the two text boxes and then click Continue.** MobileMe asks you to make the CNAME change, which you've already done.

6. **Click Continue.** MobileMe adds the domain and returns you to the Account Settings page.

Now you need to wait until the CNAME changes you made propagate through the Internet. This might take as little as a few minutes, but it usually takes about 24 hours.

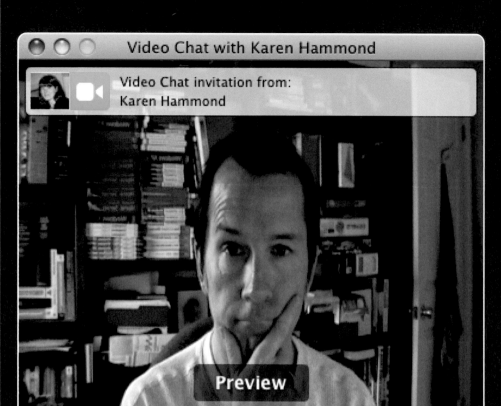

Video Chat with Karen Hammond

Video Chat invitation from:
Karen Hammond

Preview

Text Reply · Decline · Accept

You might think your Mac is all about data — creating documents, processing photos, making movies, researching stuff on the Internet, those kinds of things. Well, sure, your Mac helps you do all that, and it helps you do them with style and aplomb. But a strong case can be made that your Mac is really all about communication. After all, you probably spend great chunks of face time with your Mac sending e-mail, reading and responding to incoming messages, chatting with your buddies, and sending text messages. It's a veritable communications frenzy, but as you'll see in this chapter, your Mac can help you get more out of this part of your life.

Improving Your E-mail Life

E-mail has been called the "killer app" of the Internet, and it certainly deserves that title. Yes, chat and instant messaging are popular, social networks such as MySpace, Facebook, and LinkedIn get lots of press, and microblogging sites such as Twitter appeal to a certain type of person. However, not everyone uses these services, but it's safe to say that *everyone* uses e-mail. And if you're like the rest of us, you probably use e-mail all day long, which means that learning a few useful and efficient e-mail techniques can make your day a bit easier and save you time for more important pursuits.

Configuring Mail to not show images in messages

Lots of messages nowadays come not just as plain text, but also with fonts, colors, images, and other flourishes. This fancy formatting, either *rich text* or *HTML*, makes for a more pleasant e-mail experience, particularly for images, because who doesn't like a bit of eye candy to brighten their day?

Note

HTML stands for Hypertext Markup Language and is a set of codes that folks use to put together Web pages.

Unfortunately, however, not all images are benign. A *Web bug* is an image that resides on a remote server and is added to an HTML-formatted e-mail message by referencing an address on the remote server. (Images and other objects that reside on a remote server and are not embedded in the message are called *external content*.) When you open the message, Mail uses the address to download the image for display within the message. That sounds harmless enough, but if the message is junk e-mail, it's likely that the address also contains either your e-mail address or a code that points to your e-mail address.

When the remote server gets a request for the URL, it knows not only that you've opened the message, but also that your e-mail address is legitimate. So, not surprisingly, spammers use Web bugs all the time because, for them, valid e-mail addresses are a form of gold.

Unfortunately, the Mail application isn't entirely hip to the Web bug menace. On the positive side, if it detects that a message is spam, it blocks remote images from that message, as shown in figure 7.1. If the message is actually legitimate, you can click Load Images to see whatever pictures the message has to offer.

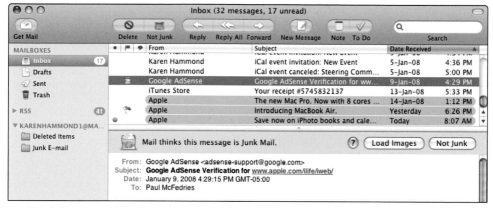

7.1 If Mail detects a junk mail message, it prevents the message from loading any remote images.

On the negative side, Mail shows remote images in any message that it doesn't think is spam. Mail's junk mail filtering feature works well, but it doesn't catch every single spam message that comes your way. This means that it could show remote images from any piece of junk mail that it misses.

To prevent that, you can configure Mail not to show remote images in any HTML or rich text message:

1. **Choose Mail ➪ Preferences.**

2. **Click the Viewing icon.**

3. **Deselect the Display remote images in HTML messages check box, as shown in figure 7.2.**

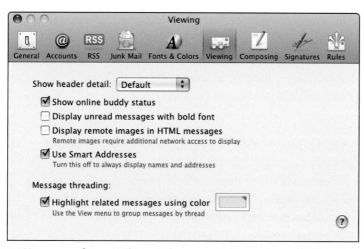

7.2 You can configure Mail to not show remote images in any HTML or rich text message.

Now if you get a non-spam message that contains remote images, you see the header shown in figure 7.3. Click Load Images to see the remote pictures.

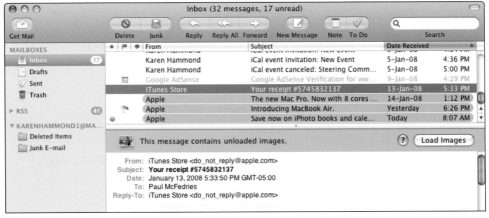

7.3 Mail now blocks remote images in non-junk messages; click Load Images to see the images.

Moving junk messages to the Junk folder

It's sad to say that there are no longer any spam-free zones. If you have an Internet-based e-mail account, then you get spam, end of story. And if you're like most people, you don't get just one or two spams a day, but more like one or two dozen (or, shudder, one or two hundred, which is, scarily, no longer an unusually high amount). That's not surprising because spam now accounts for the majority of the billions of messages sent every day, and on some days, it even accounts for 90 percent of all sent messages!

Avoiding Spam

It is no longer possible to avoid spam, but there are some things you can do to minimize how much of it you have to wade through each day:

- **Never use your actual e-mail address in a forum or newsgroup account.** The most common method that spammers use to gather addresses is to harvest them from online posts. One common tactic you can use is to alter your e-mail address by adding text that invalidates the address, but is still obvious for other people to figure out. Here's an example: yourname@yourisp.remove-this-to-email-me.com.

- **When you sign up for something online, use a fake address if possible.** If you need or want to receive e-mail from the company and must use your real address, make sure you deactivate any options that ask if you want to receive promotional offers. Alternatively, use an address from a free Web-based account (such as a Yahoo! account), so that any spam you receive goes there instead of to your main address.

- **Never open suspected spam messages or display them in the preview pane.** Doing so can sometimes notify the spammer that you've opened the message, which confirms your address is legitimate.

- **If you see a message in your Inbox that you're sure is spam, don't click it.** Clicking it displays the message in the preview pane. Instead, Ctrl+click or right-click the message and then choose Delete.

- **Never, I repeat, *never*, respond to spam.** Don't respond even to an address within the spam that claims to be a "removal" address. By responding to the spam, you prove that your address is legitimate, so you'll just end up getting more spam.

If you do get spam despite taking precautions, Mail's Junk Mail feature is your next line of defense. It's a spam filter that examines each message you receive to look for telltale signs of spamminess (as antispam types call it). If Mail determines that a message is spam, it displays the message details in a light brown text, and when you click the message, Mail displays the header shown in figure 7.4.

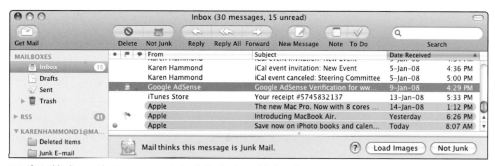

7.4 If Mail believes that a message is junk, it displays this header.

This is all well and good, but it does mean you end up with junk mail mixed in with your legitimate messages, which, given the explicit nature of so many spam subject lines these days, isn't a desirable state of affairs. It would be much better if Mail just shuffled all suspected spam to the Junk mailbox. Here's how to configure Mail to do just that:

1. **If you have any spam in your Inbox that isn't marked as junk mail, for each such message, Ctrl+click or right-click the message and then choose Mark ⇨ As Junk Mail.**

2. **Choose Mail ⇨ Preferences.**

3. **Click the Junk Mail icon.**

4. **In the When junk mail arrives section, select the Move it to the Junk mailbox option (see figure 7.5).** Mail asks if you want to move all the messages currently marked as junk to the Junk mailbox.

5. **Click Move.**

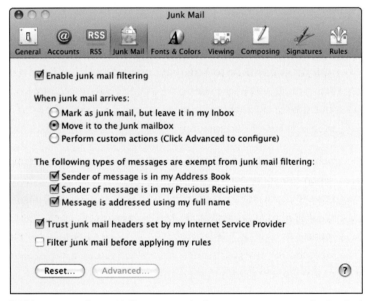

7.5 You can configure Mail to automatically move messages marked as junk to the Junk mailbox.

Be sure to check the Junk mailbox from time to time to make sure that Mail hasn't caught any *false positives*: legitimate messages marked as junk. If you do see a legit message, Ctrl+click or right-click the message, choose Mark ⇨ As Not Junk Mail, and then move the message back to the Inbox mailbox.

Genius

Checking the Junk mailbox is never fun because it means dealing directly with messages that are usually either offensive or annoying (or both). To make this distasteful chore less onerous, turn off the preview pane before displaying the Junk mailbox. To toggle the preview pane off and on, double-click the horizontal bar that separates the folder content from the preview pane.

If you don't want to bother with the often distasteful chore of deleting junk mail, you can get Mail to handle it for you automatically. Choose Mail ⇨ Preferences, click the Accounts icon, and then click the Mailbox Behaviors tab. In the Delete junk messages when list, select an interval after which spam gets canned: One day old, One week old, or One month old.

Leaving incoming messages on the server

In today's increasingly mobile world, it's not unusual to find you need to check the same e-mail account from multiple devices. For example, you might want to check your business account not only using your work computer, but also using your home computer or your notebook while traveling, or using a PDA or other portable device while commuting.

If you need to check e-mail on multiple devices, you can take advantage of how e-mail messages get delivered over the Internet. When someone sends you a message, it doesn't come directly to your Mac. Instead, it goes to the server that your ISP (or your company) has set up to handle incoming messages. This is often called a POP (Post Office Protocol) server. When you ask Apple Mail to check for new messages, it communicates with the POP server to see if any messages are waiting in your account. If so, Mail downloads those messages to your Mac, and then instructs the server to delete the copies of the messages that are stored on the server.

The trick, then, is to configure Mail so that it leaves a copy of the messages on the POP server after you download them. That way, the messages are still available when you check messages using another device. Fortunately, the intuitive folks who designed Mail must have understood this, because the program automatically sets up POP accounts to do just that. (A POP account is an account you have with an ISP; this doesn't apply to MobileMe accounts.) Specifically, after you download any messages from the POP server to your Mac, Apple Mail waits a week before deleting the messages.

However, if you have multiple Macs, this setting doesn't work well because you only want one of your Macs to control when messages get deleted from the server. Here's a good strategy that ensures you can download messages on all your devices, but prevents messages from piling up on the server:

- **Let your main Mac be the computer that controls deleting the messages from the server.** You can either leave the setting as the default (delete after one week), or you can adjust the timing, as described in the next set of steps.

- **Set up all your other devices to leave a copy of the messages on the server.**

If you want to adjust either how long your main Mac waits before deleting messages from the server, or if you want to configure a Mac (say, your Mac notebook) to leave messages on the server, follow these steps to configure this feature:

1. **Choose Mail ⇨ Preferences.**

2. **Click the Accounts icon.**

3. **In the Accounts list, click the icon for the POP account you want to work with.**

4. **Click the Advanced tab.**

5. **Perform one of the following actions, depending on how you want your Mac to treat messages on the server:**

    - **Delete server messages after a while.** Leave the Remove copy from server after retrieving a message check box selected, and then use the list below it to choose the interval you want to use: After one day, After one week, or After one month.

    - **Leave copies of messages on the server.** Deselect the Remove copy from server after retrieving a message check box, as shown in figure 7.6.

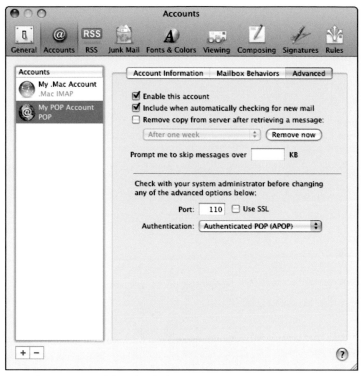

7.6 To leave a copy of downloaded messages on the server, deselect the Remove copy from server after retrieving a message check box.

Skipping really large incoming messages

Most POP mail hosts set a limit on the size of the e-mail messages they handle. It might be as small as 1MB or as large as 20MB, but whatever the number, any message larger than that won't go through. If your mail server has such a restriction, here's a problem you've probably encountered a time or two in your e-mail travels. Mail tries to download your messages, but it gets stuck because someone sent you a message that's too large for your mail server to handle. Mail can't get past the too-large message, so all your other messages get backed up behind it.

Solving this problem often requires a call to the mail host's tech support line (never a pleasant experience), but Mail offers a workaround: configure it to not download (or, more accurately, to ask you whether you want to download) messages that are larger than your POP mail server allows. Here's how it's done:

1. **Choose Mail ⇨ Preferences.**

2. **Click the Accounts icon.**

3. **In the Accounts list, click the icon for the POP account you want to work with.**

4. **Click the Advanced tab.**

5. **In the Prompt me to skip messages over text box, type the number of KB you want to use as a threshold.** For example, if your POP mail host restricts messages to 4MB, then you'd enter 4000 in the text box, as shown in figure 7.7.

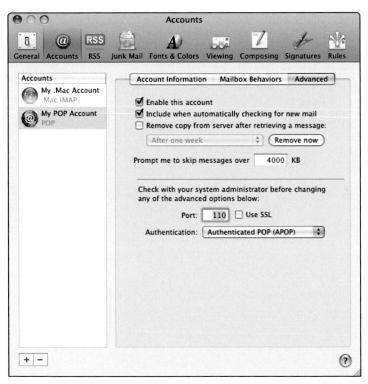

7.7 To avoid problems created by overly large messages, configure Mail so it prompts you before downloading messages larger than your POP mail server allows.

If there's a downside to setting this option, it's that Mail only gives you a few seconds to make your decision. When Mail checks for new messages (or when you click the Get Mail button in the toolbar) and it finds a too-large message waiting on the server, you see the dialog box shown in figure 7.8. You only have 15 seconds to click one of the following buttons:

7.8 Mail displays this dialog box when it detects an incoming message that's larger than the threshold you specified. Act fast!

- **Skip.** Leaves the message on the server. Note that Mail (sensibly) doesn't try to download the message again until your next Mail session.

- **Delete.** Permanently deletes the message.

- **Download.** Downloads the message to Mail. This is the default action that Mail takes after the 15 seconds are up.

Genius

Another good reason to skip large messages is when you're using a slow Internet connection. For example, if you're accessing the Internet over a dial-up connection, you might want to skip messages larger than, say, 100KB.

Sending e-mail with a different server port

For security reasons, some Internet Service Providers (ISPs) insist that all their customers' outgoing mail must be routed through the ISP's Simple Mail Transport Protocol (SMTP) server. This usually is not a big deal if you're using an e-mail account maintained by the ISP, but it can lead to the following problems if you are using an account provided by a third party (such as your Web site host):

- Your ISP might block messages sent using the third-party account because it thinks you're trying to relay the message through the ISP's server (a technique often used by spammers).

- You might incur extra charges if your ISP allows only a certain amount of SMTP bandwidth per month or a certain number of sent messages, whereas the third-party account offers higher limits or no restrictions at all.

- You might have performance problems, with the ISP's server taking much longer to route messages than the third-party host.

You might think that you can solve the problem by specifying the third-party host's SMTP server in the account settings. However, this doesn't usually work because outgoing e-mail is sent by default through port 25; when you use this port, you must also use the ISP's SMTP server.

To work around this problem, many third-party hosts offer access to their SMTP server via a port other than the standard port 25. For example, the MobileMe SMTP server (smtp.me.com) also accepts connects on port 587.

Here's how to use Mail to configure an e-mail account to use a nonstandard SMTP port:

1. **Choose Mail ⇨ Preferences.**

2. **Click the Accounts icon.**

3. **In the Accounts list, click the icon for the POP account you want to work with.**

4. **Click the Account Information tab.**

5. **In the Outgoing Mail Server (SMTP) list, choose Edit Server List.**

6. **In the list of SMTP servers, click the server you want to work with.**

7. **Click the Advanced tab.**

8. **Use the Server port text box to type the port number you want to use.** For example, figure 7.9 shows the MobileMe SMTP server configured to use port 587.

Sending all messages from the same account

If you have two or more e-mail accounts set up, then you may have noticed one of Mail's quirkier behaviors: When you compose a message, the account you see in the From list isn't always the same account. For example, if you

7.9 Use the Server port text box to specify the nonstandard port you want to use for the SMTP server.

have both a MobileMe account and a POP account set up, sometimes the From list shows the MobileMe account, and other times it shows the POP account. What's the story?

The background here is that Mail keeps track of the last mailbox you viewed, and it uses the account associated with that mailbox in the From list when you next go to compose a message. That actually makes a bit of sense when you think about it. For example, if you're currently working in a mailbox associated with your MobileMe account and you start a new message, there's at least a chance that you want to send that message using your MobileMe account.

However, it's much more likely that you want to use a single account to send most of your messages, so Mail's default behavior is inefficient. Here's how to fix it:

1. **Choose Mail ➪ Preferences.**

2. **Click the Composing icon.**

3. **Use the Send new mail from list to choose the account you want to set as the default sending account (see figure 7.10).**

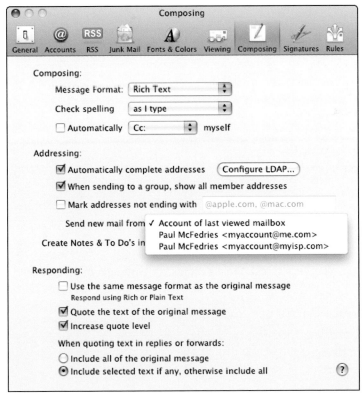

7.10 Use the Send new mail from list to choose the default account for sending messages.

Setting up rules to process incoming messages

With e-mail now fully entrenched on the business (and even home) landscape, e-mail chores probably take up more and more of your time. Besides composing, reading, and responding to e-mail,
basic e-mail maintenance — flagging, moving, deleting, and so on — also takes up large chunks of
otherwise-productive time.

To help ease the e-mail time crunch, Mail lets you set up rules that perform actions in response to
specific events. Here's just a few of the things you can do with them:

- Move an incoming message to a specific mailbox if the message contains a particular
  keyword in the subject or body, or if it's from a particular person.

- Automatically delete messages with a particular subject or from a particular person.

- Flag messages based on specific criteria (such as keywords in the subject line or body).

- Have Mail notify you when a high-priority message arrives either by playing a sound or
  by bouncing the Mail icon in the Dock.

For example, you may have noticed that any messages you get from Apple appear with a blue
background. That background gets applied because Mail comes with a predefined rule that looks
for messages from Apple and sets the background color of those messages to blue.

Genius

You can save yourself a bit of time by creating a rule based on an existing message.
For example, you could create a rule that uses the sender's address or the message's
Subject line. To do this, click the message you want to use before going through the
steps to set up your own rule.

Here's how you set up your own rule:

1. **If you want Mail to apply your new rule to the messages in a particular mailbox, select
   that mailbox.**

2. **Choose Mail ⇨ Preferences.** The Mail preferences appear.

3. **Click the Rules icon.**

4. **Click Add Rule.**

5. **Use the Description text box to type a name for the rule.**

6. **Specify a condition that an incoming message must satisfy to trigger the rule.** You use the leftmost list to select the message data that you want Mail to check, such as the message priority, the From address, the Subject line, or the message content. Whether you need to specify more information to complete the criterion depends on the data (see figure 7.11 for examples).

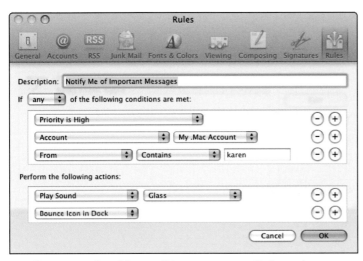

7.11 Some examples of the conditions you can specify for a rule.

- **Some data doesn't require more information.** For example, if you choose Priority is High, then the condition is met if an incoming message uses the High priority level.

- **Some data requires you to specify one other bit of information.** For example, if you choose Account, then you must also specify one of your mail accounts. The condition is met if an incoming message is sent to that account.

- **Some data requires both an operator and some specific information.** For example, if you choose From, then you must also specify an operator such as Contains or Is Equal To, and then some text. The condition is met if an incoming message has From text that matches what you specify.

7. **To add another condition, click the plus sign (+).**

8. **Repeat Steps 6 and 7 until you have specified all the conditions for your rule.**

9. **If you specified two or more conditions, use the If *X* of the following conditions are met list to decide how Mail applies the conditions:**

- **any.** Choose this item to have Mail trigger the rule only if an incoming message meets at least one of the conditions.

- **all.** Choose this item to have Mail trigger the rule only if an incoming message meets every one of the conditions.

10. **Use the controls in the Perform the following actions section to specify what you want Mail to do when an incoming message meets your conditions.** As with conditions, the action you choose may require you to specify more information (such as choosing a sound, as shown in figure 7.11).

11. **To add another action, click the plus sign (+).**

12. **Repeat Steps 10 and 11 until you have specified all the actions for your rule.**

13. **Click OK.** Mail asks if you want to apply the new rule to the messages in the current mailbox.

14. **Click Apply if you want to run the rule now; otherwise, click Don't Apply.**

Genius

If you want to create a new rule that's very similar to an existing rule, don't create the new rule from scratch. Instead, display the Rules preferences, click the existing rule, and then click Duplicate. Adjust the new rule as needed and then click OK.

Creating a smart mailbox

A *smart mailbox* is one that consolidates all of your messages that meet one or more conditions. It doesn't matter which mailbox the messages currently reside in: it could be any Inbox, the Sent mailbox, or even the Trash. After you set up a smart mailbox, Mail copies the applicable messages to the smart folder, and if any incoming messages meet the criteria they also get copied to the smart folder. (In both cases, the original messages remain in their current folders.) It's a great way to keep your messages organized without having to do any of the organizing yourself.

Follow these steps to set up your own smart mailbox:

1. **If you want to set up the smart mailbox based on the data in an existing message, click the message.**

2. **Choose Mailbox ⇨ New Smart Mailbox.**

3. **Use the Smart Mailbox Name text box to type a name for the smart mailbox.**

4. **Specify a condition that messages must satisfy to be put in the smart mailbox.** You use the leftmost list to select the message data that you want Mail to use, such as the message priority, the From address, the Subject line, or the message content. Whether you need to specify more information to complete the criterion depends on the data (see figure 7.12 for examples).

- **Some data doesn't require more information.** For example, if you choose Message is Flagged, then the condition is met if a message has a flag.

- **Some data requires you to specify one other bit of information.** For example, if you choose Sender is member of Group, then you must also specify one of your Address Book groups. The condition is met if a message was sent from someone in that group.

- **Some data requires both an operator and some specific information.** For example, if you choose Subject, then you must also specify an operator such as Contains or Begins With, and then some text. The condition is met if a message has Subject text that matches what you specify.

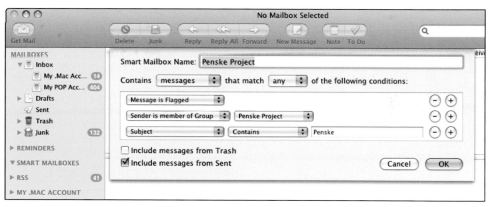

7.12 Some examples of the conditions you can specify for a smart mailbox.

5. **To add another condition, click the plus sign (+).**

6. **Repeat Steps 4 and 5 until you have specified all the conditions for your smart mailbox.**

7. **If you specified two or more conditions, use the Contains messages that match _X_ of the following conditions list to decide how Mail applies the conditions:**

- **any.** Choose this item to have Mail add a message to the smart mailbox if it meets at least one of the conditions.

- **all.** Choose this item to have Mail add a message to the smart mailbox if it meets all of the conditions.

8. **If you want to include any Trash mailbox messages that satisfy the conditions, select the Include messages from Trash check box.**

9. **If you want to include any Sent mailbox messages that satisfy the conditions, select the Include messages from Sent check box.**

10. **Click OK.** Mail creates the smart mailbox and populates with all the messages that meet your conditions.

Bouncing back an unwanted message

You've probably got your share of unwanted messages over the years. It could be marketing come-ons from a company you dealt with a while back, angry notes from an ex-friend or -lover, or menacing messages from your archenemy. Whatever the source, they aren't pleasant to deal with.

You could set up a rule to automatically delete messages from the sender, but sometimes a better approach is to make the company or person believe that your address is no longer legitimate. This should help stop the messages from coming your way, and it has just enough of a prankster whiff about it to make it fun.

Mail has a Bounce command that does this for you. In the e-mail world, a *bounce message* is one that a mail server automatically fires off to the sender of a message when a problem occurs with the delivery of the message. For example, if you send a message to a nonexistent address, you usually get a bounce message in return that includes a "User unknown" error message. This is what Mail's Bounce command does, only, of course, it does it because you said so, not because of an actual error.

Follow these steps to bounce a message back:

1. **Select the mailbox that contains the message you want to bounce back.**

2. **Choose Message ⇨ Bounce.** You can also press Shift+⌘+B. Mail asks if you're sure you want to return the message.

3. **Click Bounce.** Mail removes the message from the mailbox and then sends the bounce message.

Figure 7.13 shows an example of a bounce message returned by Mail.

7.13 An example of a bounce message that Mail sends back.

Note

The Bounce command will likely not work with junk mail because few spammers use legitimate return addresses.

Chatting and Videoconferencing

Whether the need is speed (wanting an instant connection) or sociability (wanting to hear a voice or see a face), when e-mail isn't quite right, many people turn to chat. With its immediate responses and actual conversations, chat is often the solution to e-mail's problems. However, chat has grown increasingly more sophisticated of late, and your Mac's iChat program is loaded with interesting features and options that can help you take chat beyond the basic exchange of simple text messages and to the next level.

Chatting over your network

For most chats, you need either a MobileMe account or an AOL Instant Messenger (AIM) account. However, if your Mac is connected to a local area network at home or at work, and if the person you want to chat with is on that network, your Mac may be able to locate that person using its Bonjour technology. (Bonjour, which used to be called Rendezvous, scours the local network looking for other computers and devices that provide services, and it then configures those services without requiring any input from you.)

Genius

You can get a free AOL screen name for chatting. Go to www.aimcreate.com, and click Sign up for a Free Account.

For this to work, your Mac must be configured to chat using Bonjour. Here's how you do that:

1. **Choose iChat ⇨ Preferences.**

2. **Click the Accounts icon.**

3. **In the Accounts list, click Bonjour.**

4. **Select the Use Bonjour Instant Messaging check box, as shown in figure 7.14.** iChat also displays the Bonjour List, which is the list of chat-enabled network users that Bonjour has detected.

7.14 To ensure that Bonjour discovers you, select the Use Bonjour Instant Messaging check box.

5. **If you see Offline under your name in the Bonjour List, click Offline and then click Available, as shown in figure 7.15.** You can also choose iChat ➪ Log in to Bonjour, or press ⌘+L.

The Bonjour List (which you can toggle on and off by choosing Windows ➪ Bonjour List or by pressing ⌘+2) now shows the other chat-enabled folks on your network, as shown in figure 7.16. Click the person you want to chat with and then click a button at the bottom of the window to choose the type of chat you want (text, audio, video, or screen sharing, although some of these may be disabled depending on the capabilities of the person's computer).

7.15 Make sure that you change your Bonjour status to Available.

7.16 The Bonjour List shows you the other chat-ready people on your network.

Genius

If you don't want the full MobileMe treatment (and the cost it involves), you can still get a free MobileMe chat account. Choose iChat ⇨ Preferences, and then click the Accounts icon. Click the plus sign (+) to start a new account and display the Account Setup dialog box. Click Get an iChat Account to launch Safari and navigate to the Apple iChat ID signup page. Sign up for MobileMe, and when the 60-day trial period ends, you get to keep your MobileMe member name for chatting.

Showing your iChat capabilities

What you can do with iChat depends on the equipment installed on your Mac. All Macs can exchange text messages, of course, but you need more stuff to handle more advanced chats:

- **Audio chat.** You need either a microphone — such as the microphones that are built into most Macs — or a headset (such as a Bluetooth headset, which I show you how to connect in Chapter 2).

- **Video chat.** You need a digital video camera, such as the iSight camera built into many Macs (such as the MacBook Pro and iMac), or an external video camera.

To find out what your Mac is capable of on the chat front, follow these steps:

1. **Pull down the Audio (or Video) menu and then chose Connection Doctor.**

2. **In the Show list, choose Capabilities.**

   Figure 7.17 shows the Capabilities list for a Mac with a microphone but no camera.

7.17 The Capabilities list for a Mac with a microphone but no camera.

Add a video camera to the mix, and there's no chat scenario that your Mac can't handle, as shown in figure 7.18.

How do you know what the other person can do? Your Bonjour List or AIM Buddy List tells you:

- **No icon.** This means the person doesn't have a microphone or video camera, so she can only exchange text messages, but she can hear or see your side of an audio or video chat.

- **Audio icon.** This icon (see figure 7.19) means that the person has a micro-phone, so you can initiate an audio chat. The person doesn't have a video cam-era, so he can only see your side of a video chat.

7.18 The Capabilities list for a Mac with a microphone and a camera.

- **Video icon.** This icon (also shown in figure 7.19) means that the person has a microphone and a video camera, so you can initiate any type of chat: text, audio, or video.

Setting up an audio chat

An audio chat is great because you get the immediate give-and-take of a phone conversation, but without tying up the phone. And if your buddy is somewhere in cyberspace, no long-distance charges apply: the audio is just another data stream being sent over the Internet. Best of all, it doesn't matter what type of Internet connection you or your buddy are using. Whether it's dial-up or broadband, you can still audio chat, although having broadband links at both ends gives you a higher quality conversation (at least as far as the audio goes).

7.19 David has a microphone but no video camera, while I have both, as indicated by the icons in the Bonjour List.

Note

If you have a fast network or Internet connection and you have a Mac that uses an Intel, G5, or 1GHz G4 processor, then you can set up an audio chat with up to ten peo-ple at once.

Note

To see the specific chat capabilities of a buddy, Ctrl+click or right-click the buddy and then choose Show Profile. The Info dialog box appears with the Profile tab displayed. This tab has a Capabilities section that tells you exactly what the person can do. For example, it will tell you whether you can share your screen with that person, whether that person can participate in multiperson conferencing, and more.

Connecting and configuring microphones

If your Mac doesn't have a built-in microphone (such as the one you get with an iMac or a MacBook Pro), then you need to connect one:

- **Microphone.** Connect the microphone to your Mac's Line In port.

- **Bluetooth headset.** Pair up your Mac and the headset, as I describe in Chapter 2. Note that you can initiate the pairing from iChat. Choose iChat ⇨ Preferences, click the Audio/Video icon, and then click Set Up Bluetooth Headset.

If your Mac happens to have either two microphones (for example, a built-in mic and a paired Bluetooth headset) or two sets of speakers (such as your Mac's internal speakers and a Bluetooth headset or headphones), then you need to configure which devices you want to use for audio chatting. Here's how:

1. **Choose iChat ⇨ Preferences.**

2. **Click the Audio/Video icon.** This tab's audio features are shown in figure 7.20.

3. **Use the Microphone list to select which microphone you want to speak into while audio chatting.**

4. **Use the Sound Output list to select which set of speakers you want to use to listen with while audio chatting.**

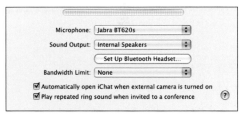

7.20 Use the Microphone and Sound Output lists to choose your audio chat devices.

Before you can chat, you must make sure your microphone is enabled: pull down the Audio (or Video) menu and if you don't see a check mark beside Microphone Enabled, choose that command.

Creating the chat session

Now that you have connected and enabled your microphone, you are ready to create an audio chat session. Follow these steps:

1. **Use either the AIM Buddy List (Window ⇨ AIM Buddy List, or press ⌘+1) or the Bonjour List (Window ⇨ Bonjour List, or press ⌘+2) to click the person you want to talk with.**

2. **Choose Buddies ⇨ Invite to Audio Chat.** You can also use any of these techniques:

   - Ctrl+click or right-click the person, and then click Invite to Audio Chat.

   - Click the Start an Audio Chat icon (the telephone icon) in the AIM Buddy List or Bonjour List.

   - If you see an audio icon (telephone) next to the buddy's picture, click that icon.

   - If you're currently in the middle of a text chat, choose Buddies ⇨ Invite to Audio Chat.

3. **To handle an audio chat invitation, click the invitation window that appears.** iChat displays the audio chat window shown in figure 7.21.

4. **Click Accept to initiate the audio chat.** If you can't chat right now, click Decline, instead.

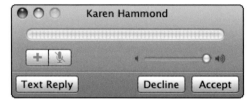

7.21 Click Accept to start the audio chat session.

5. **Use the audio chat window's volume slider to set the output volume as desired.** After you've set the volume to the correct level, you no longer need to see the audio chat window onscreen. Don't close the chat window, of course, or you'll cut off the session. Instead, click the minimize button to send the window to the Dock.

Genius

If you want to record the conversation, choose Audio ⇨ Record Chat. iChat asks your buddy for permission to record, and that person must click Allow to enable the recording. A red Recording icon appears in the chat window. When you're done, choose Audio ⇨ Stop Recording. When you complete the chat, iTunes opens and displays the recorded chat.

Setting up a video chat

Text chats require a lot of fast typing, and audio chats aren't all that much different from a good old-fashioned telephone conversation (although the free Internet-based "calling" is a major bonus). If you really want to crank up the chat wow factor, get a load of iChat's video chat feature. With a video chat, you not only get to talk to a buddy in real time, you also get to *see* your buddy, whether she's in another room, another city, or another country.

As you might imagine, you need a fast connection for this to happen with any smoothness. A local area network connection is plenty fast enough, but if you plan to video chat over the Internet, then you definitely need a fast broadband connection on both ends.

Note If you want to set up a video chat with two or more people, then you need a fast Mac to handle it. The Mac that invites folks to join the video chat must have an Intel or G5 processor, while any Mac that joins the video chat must have an Intel, G5, or 1GHz G4 processor.

If your Mac doesn't have a built-in video camera (such as the iSight camera that comes with an iMac or a MacBook Pro), then you need to connect one, which is described in Chapter 1.

It's not very likely, but if your Mac has two attached video cameras (for example, a built-in iSight camera and an external digital video camera), then you need to configure which camera you want to use for capturing the video. Follow these steps:

1. **Choose iChat ➪ Preferences.**

2. **Click the Audio/Video icon.**

3. **Use the Camera list to select which video camera you want to use for video audio chatting, as shown in figure 7.22.**

You should also make sure your camera is enabled: pull down the Video menu and if you don't see a check mark beside Camera Enabled, choose that command.

Follow these steps to get a video chat session up and running:

1. **Use either the AIM Buddy List (Window ➪ AIM Buddy List, or press ⌘+1) or the Bonjour List (Window ➪ Bonjour List, or press ⌘+2) to click the person you want to chat with.**

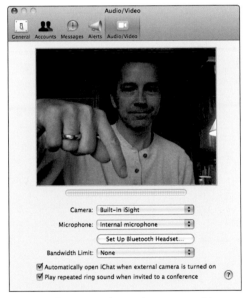

7.22 Use the Camera list to choose your video chat camera.

2. **Choose Buddies ⇨ Invite to Video Chat.** You can also use any of these techniques:

- Ctrl+click or right-click the person and then click Invite to Video Chat.

- Click the Start a Video Chat icon (the camera icon) in the AIM Buddy List or Bonjour List.

- If you see a video icon (camera) next to the buddy's picture, click that icon.

- If you're currently in the middle of a text chat, choose Buddies ⇨ Invite to Video Chat.

Genius

To take a snapshot of the current video chat, choose Video ⇨ Take Snapshot (or press Option+⌘+S). iChat creates a JPEG image of the current video chat and adds it to the desktop.

3. **To handle a video chat invitation, click the invitation window that appears.** iChat displays the video chat window shown in figure 7.23.

4. **Click Accept to initiate the video chat.** If you can't chat right now, click Decline, instead.

5. **Use the audio chat window's volume slider to set the output volume as desired.**

7.23 Click Accept to start the video chat session.

Note

If you want to record the video chat, choose Video ⇨ Record Chat. iChat asks your buddy for permission to record, and that person must click Allow to enable the recording. A red Recording icon appears in the upper-right corner of the chat window. When you're done, choose Video ⇨ Stop Recording. When you complete the chat, iTunes opens and displays the recorded chat.

Using iChat and a video camera to set up a security cam

When you want to monitor your home over the Internet, it usually requires expensive and complex packages that include a webcam, webcam software, a program to let you access the webcam, and so on. Fortunately, you're a Mac user, so you get all this as part of your Mac (except for the camera, if your Mac doesn't have one built in). Using iChat and your video camera, you can monitor a live video feed of some part of your house. This enables you to see what the dog is up to, check in on the nanny, or just keep an eye on things.

The basic idea is that you leave your Mac running at home with iChat open and have the Mac's video camera pointed at the spot you want to monitor. You then initiate a video chat session over the Internet. To make this work, you must do four things:

1. **On the Mac you plan to use as a monitor, select the MobileMe or AIM account you want to use.** Choose iChat ⇨ Preferences, click the Accounts tab, click the account you want to use, and then select the Use this account check box.

2. **Prevent your Mac from going into sleep mode.** Click Apple ⇨ System Preferences, click the Energy Saver icon, click Sleep, and then drag the sleep slider to Never.

Note You might also need to be concerned about your video camera going into sleep mode. This isn't a problem with an iSight camera or most webcams, but if you're using a camcorder, it might sleep after it has been idle for a while. See your manual, but in most cases you can prevent a camcorder from going to sleep by removing the tape.

3. **Configure iChat to automatically accept video chat invitations.** This is necessary because you won't be home to accept the invitation by hand. See the next section for the details on this step.

4. **Configure iChat security to only allow specific people to see you.** See the section on setting iChat security later in this chapter.

After you do all that, you're ready to start monitoring. On the remote Mac, find the iChat account used by your home Mac in your AIM Buddy List, and then initiate a video chat (as described earlier). Your home Mac accepts the invitation automatically and you get a live video feed of your home (in this case, a pet), as shown in figure 7.24.

7.24 With iChat and a video camera, you can monitor your home from a remote location.

Note

If your remote Mac has a video camera, you don't need to see its feed while you're monitoring your home. To turn it off, choose Video ➪ Hide Local Video.

Configuring iChat to automatically accept video chat invitations

Setting up your security cam requires that you initiate a video chat with your home computer. However, when you send a video chat invitation, the session doesn't start until the invitee clicks Accept. You won't be home to do that (and it's unlikely the dog will help), so how do you start the video chat?

The answer is that it's possible to configure iChat to accept incoming video chat invitations automatically. You can do this most easily in Leopard (OS X 10.5), as the following steps show:

1. **Choose iChat ➪ Preferences.**

2. **Click the Alerts tab.** The Alerts preferences appear.

3. **In the Event list, choose Video Invitation.**

4. **Select the Run AppleScript check box.**

5. **In the Run AppleScript list, choose Auto Accept.applescript, as shown in figure 7.25.**

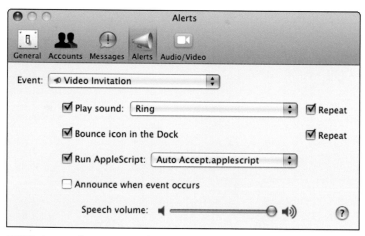

7.25 In Leopard, you can use the Auto Accept script to automatically accept incoming video invitations.

If you have an earlier version of OS X, then you need to use a different method:

1. **If iChat is open, choose iChat ➪ Quit iChat to close it.**

2. **In Finder, choose Applications ⇨ Utilities ⇨ Terminal.**

3. **At the Terminal prompt, type the following command: defaults write com.apple.ichat AutoAcceptVCInvitations 1.**

4. **Press Return to put the new setting into effect.**

To turn off the video chat automatic answer setting, run Terminal and enter the following command: defaults write com.apple.ichat AutoAcceptVCInvitations 0.

Setting iChat security

With your home Mac set up to automatically accept incoming video chat invitations, you probably don't want anyone just sending you an invitation. To prevent this, you need to configure your iChat account so only specific people on your Buddy List can see you. Here's how you do it:

1. **On your home Mac, choose iChat ⇨ Preferences.**

2. **Click the Accounts icon.**

3. **In the Accounts list, click the account you're using for the security cam.**

4. **Click the Security tab.**

5. **Select the Allow specific people option, as shown in figure 7.26.**

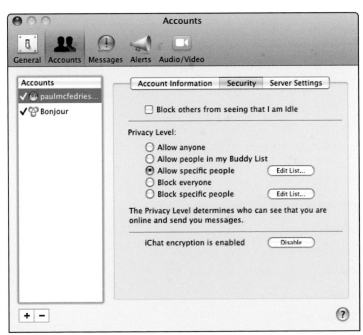

7.26 Configure your iChat account to only be seen by specific people.

Genius Be sure to include the address of whatever account you'll be using to send the video chat invitation. You can also add other addresses for people you trust.

6. **Click the Edit List button beside the Allow specific people option.** The Allow Specific People dialog box appears.

7. **Click the plus sign (+).**

8. **Type the MobileMe or AIM address of the person you want to allow, and then press Return.** iChat adds the address to the list, as shown in figure 7.27.

9. **Click Done.**

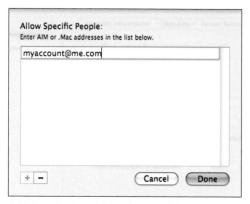

Allow Specific People:
Enter AIM or .Mac addresses in the list below.

myaccount@me.com

`+` `−` (Cancel) (Done)

7.27 Specify the address that you'll be using to issue the video chat invitation.

Sending camcorder video to a video chat

You'll almost always use a video chat for a conversation, but it doesn't have to be a communications tool. For example, you might have a camcorder video that demonstrates how to perform some task, shows a marketing message, or includes some other prerecorded scenes. If you want other people to see the video, you either need to send it via postal mail, or you need to convert it to digital video.

A much easier way to do this is to fire up a video chat session and then, instead of sending live video, send the output of the camcorder video. Here's how:

1. **Connect your camcorder to your Mac.**

2. **Use the camcorder controls to cue up the video.**

3. **Press Play on the camcorder.**

4. **In iChat, choose Video ⇨ Preview Video.** Make sure your running video appears in the preview window. If it doesn't, check your cable connections.

5. **Cue up the video once again.**

6. **Initiate your video chat session.**

7. **Press Play on the camcorder.** Your buddy sees the video playback.

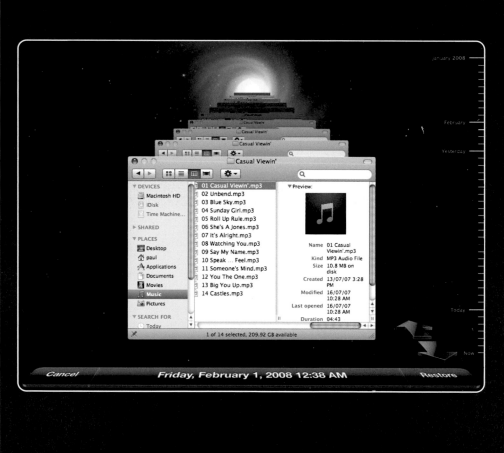

Unlike almost any other computer on the planet, your Mac just works; and it is far less likely to head south on you than most. However, all computers are complex beasts, and your Mac is as complex as they come. Its excellent design and engineering ensure a mostly trouble-free operation, but it doesn't hurt to do a little preventative maintenance. The techniques addressed in this chapter help ensure your Mac and the precious data it holds are far less likely to run into trouble.

Routine Mac Maintenance

Get your maintenance chores off to a solid start by examining a few tasks that I describe as *routine*, meaning you ought to perform them regularly to help keep your Mac running smoothly.

Emptying the Trash

You might not give a whole lot of thought to the Trash icon that's a permanent resident on the right edge of the Dock. You delete something, your Mac dutifully tosses it into the Trash, and you move on with your life.

However, while you're busy with other things, the Trash is slowly expanding with each new deleted file or folder. After a while, the Trash might contain several *gigabytes* worth of the data. What's the big deal, right? It's just the trash for goodness sake! Ah, but the Trash is actually a folder on your Mac hard disk. (It's a hidden folder located at /Users/*You*/.Trash, where *You* is your user folder name.) So the more space the Trash takes up, the less space you have to store episodes of your favorite shows.

To see just how much space the Trash is occupying, follow these steps:

1. **Ctrl+click (or right-click) the Trash icon in the Dock.**

2. **Click Open.**

3. **Choose File ➪ Get Info.** You can also click the Action icon and then click Get Info, or press ⌘+I. The Trash Info window appears.

4. **Read the Size value.**

In figure 8.1, you can see that the Trash contains a whopping 3.22GB of data.

So it makes sense to empty the Trash relatively often, perhaps once a month or once every two months, depending on how often you delete things. Here's the safe method of taking out the Trash:

1. **Ctrl+click (or right-click) the Trash icon in the Dock.**

2. **Click Open.**

8.1 The Trash Info window tells you how much hard disk space the Trash is currently using.

3. **Examine the Trash files to make sure there's nothing important that you deleted by accident.**

4. **If you see a file that you don't want deleted, click-and-drag the file and drop it on the Desktop for now.** After you're done emptying the Trash, you can figure out where the rescued file is supposed to go.

Caution Examining the contents of the Trash is crucial because after you empty the Trash, there's no turning back the clock — all those files will be permanently deleted and there will be nothing you can do to get any of them back.

5. **Choose Finder ⇨ Empty Trash.** You can also click the Empty button or press Shift+⌘+Delete. Your Mac asks you to confirm.

6. **Click OK.**

Genius When you delete a file from the Trash, your Mac actually leaves the file on the hard disk, but it tells the file system that the file's space is available for other files to use. If you don't like the idea of sensitive or private files lurking on your drive for who knows how long, choose Finder ⇨ Secure Empty Trash, instead. This tells your Mac to overwrite each file with gibberish data. However, see also the section on erasing your hard drive's free space later in this chapter.

Now I don't know about you, but after being so careful about making sure I'm not permanently deleting anything important, it bugs me that my Mac asks if I'm sure I want to go through with it. Of course, I'm sure! Fortunately, there are a couple of ways to work around this annoyance.

The easiest is to hold down the Option key while you choose Finder ⇨ Empty Trash or click the Empty button. If your fingers are limber enough, you can also press Option+Shift+⌘+Delete.

A more long-term solution is to tell your Mac not to bother with the confirmation message at all. Here are the steps to follow to turn off this message:

1. **In any Finder window, choose Finder ⇨ Preferences.** The Finder Preferences window appears.

2. **Click the Advanced icon.**

Genius Rather than try to remember to empty the Trash regularly, a program called Compost can do it for you. You can configure Compost to remove from the Trash any files that are older than a specified number of days or weeks. You can also set up Compost to impose a maximum size on the Trash, so you never have to worry about it taking over your hard disk. Download Compost from www.apple.com/downloads/macosx/system_disk_utilities/compost.html. Note that this is a free trial version that you can use for 30 days (after which you need to pay $19.95 to keep using the program).

3. **Deselect the Show warning before emptying the Trash check box, as shown in figure 8.2.** Note, too, that if you have Leopard (OS X 10.5) you can also select the Empty Trash securely check box to force your Mac to always overwrite files with gibberish data when you remove them from the Trash.

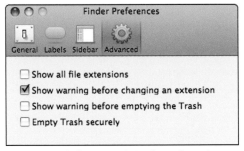

8.2 To get rid of your Mac's Trash confirmation prompts, deselect the Show warning before emptying the Trash check box.

Cleaning up your desktop

The Mac Desktop is a handy place to store things, and most Mac users aren't shy about doing just that, so they end up with dozens of icons scattered around the Desktop. This isn't a terrible thing, to be sure, but it's not very efficient. When you have more than, say, a dozen icons on your Desktop, finding the one you want becomes a real icon-needle-in-a-Desktop-haystack exercise.

So, periodically (say once every couple of weeks), you should tidy up your Desktop so that you can find things easily and keep the Desktop a useful tool. You can do a couple of things:

1. **Get rid of any icons you absolutely don't need on the Desktop.**
   - If you're still using the icon, move it to the appropriate folder in your user account.
   - If you don't need the icon anymore, off to the Trash it goes.

2. **Organize the remaining icons.**
   - If you don't care about the order of the icons, click the Desktop and then choose View ⇨ Clean Up. This lines up all the icons in neat columns and rows based on the Desktop's invisible grid.

- If you want to organize the icons by name, click the Desktop and then choose View ➪ Arrange By ➪ Name (or press Ctrl+⌘+1).

- If you want to apply a label to related icons, Ctrl+click (or right-click) the selection, and then click a label color. You can then sort the icon by label: click the Desktop and then choose View ➪ Arrange By ➪ Label (or press Ctrl+⌘+6).

Watching hard disk free space

Although it's true that hard disks are larger than ever these days, it's also true that files are getting larger, too. Music files are almost always multimegabyte affairs; a single half-hour TV show can usurp about 250MB, and movies can be three or four times as large. If you're not careful, it's easy to run out of hard disk space in a hurry.

To prevent that from happening, you should keep an eye on how much free space is left on your Mac's hard disk. One way to do this is to open any Finder window and click Macintosh HD. As you can see in figure 8.3, Finder displays the amount of space in the status bar at the bottom of the open window.

8.3 Click Macintosh HD in any Finder window to display the hard disk's free space in the status bar.

An even better way to keep your eyes peeled on the free hard disk space is to configure the Desktop to always show this information. Here's how:

1. **Click the Desktop.**

2. **Choose View ➪ Show View Options.** You can also press ⌘+J. The Desktop window appears.

Caution The Mac does most things right, but sometimes it's a bit brain-dead. For example, the Desktop icons only have so much room to display text, so the Macintosh HD icon might truncate the amount of free space. For example, if your Mac hard disk has a capacity of 232.57GB and you have 141.34GB free, the Macintosh HD icon displays this as follows: 232.57GB,...34GB free.

3. **Select the Show item info check box, as shown in figure 8.4.**

Finder now displays extra information under the name of each Desktop icon, such as the number of items in a folder and the dimensions of an image. In the case of the Macintosh HD icon, Finder shows the total size of the hard disk and the amount of free space, as shown in figure 8.5.

8.4 Select the Show item info check box.

8.5 The Macintosh HD icon now shows the total space and total free space.

Deleting unneeded files

I mentioned earlier that a neglected Trash folder can eat up lots of hard disk real estate. If you're minding your Mac's hard disk and you find that you're running low on hard disk free space, you should empty theTrash as a first step. You should also uninstall any programs you no longer use.

Other than that, I also suggest periodically rummaging through the folders in your user account to look for documents, downloads, and other files that you don't need. Send these items to the Trash and, when you're done, empty the Trash to recover the disk space. However, you should also consider backing up your system before you start trashing a lot of files.

Caution All the folders in your user account are fair game, except for the Library folder. Messing with the wrong files in this folder can cause your Mac or your programs to behave erratically or crash. Therefore, I highly recommend leaving the Library folder alone when purging old files.

Uninstalling unused applications

To free up some room on your Mac's hard disk, get rid of any installed applications that you no longer use. The great thing about uninstalling Mac software is that it's just so darn easy. If you've ever used Windows, you know that removing a program is a long, involved process that always requires a large number of mouse clicks. On your Mac, however, the uninstall process couldn't be simpler:

1. **In Finder, choose the Applications folder.** There's a chance the application you want to delete is in the Utilities folder, so you may need to choose that folder before continuing.

2. **Click and drag the folder of the application you want to get rid of, and then drop the folder on the Trash.**

Genius   Many applications also install files in your user account's Library/Application Support folder, or in the Macintosh HD/Library/Application Support folder. Check those locations and delete any folder that belongs to the application you removed.

Checking hard disk status

A hard disk can suddenly bite the dust thanks to a lightning strike, an accidental drop from a decent height, or an electronic component shorting out. However, most of the time hard disks die a slow death. Along the way, they almost always show some signs of decay, but a hard drive is hidden so how can you see these signs? Since about 1996, almost all hard-disk manufacturers have built into their drives a system called Self-Monitoring, Analysis, and Reporting Technology, or S.M.A.R.T. This system monitors a number of hard disk parameters, including the following:

- The spin-up time gradually slows
- The drive temperature increases
- The seek error rate increases
- The read error rate increases
- The write error rate increases
- The number of bad sectors increases
- An internal consistency check (called the cyclic redundancy check, or CRC) produces an increasing number of errors

Other factors that might indicate a potential failure are the number of times that the hard drive has been powered up, the number of hours in use, and the number of times the drive has started and stopped spinning. S.M.A.R.T. uses a sophisticated algorithm to combine these attributes into a value that represents the overall health of the disk. When that value goes beyond some predetermined threshold, S.M.A.R.T issues an alert that hard-disk failure might be imminent.

Although S.M.A.R.T has been around for a while and is now standard, taking advantage of S.M.A.R.T diagnostics originally meant using a third-party program. However, your Mac includes a component that can monitor S.M.A.R.T status and alert you if there's a problem. Here's how to use it:

1. **Click Finder in the Dock.**

2. **Choose Applications ⇨ Utilities ⇨ Disk Utility.** The Disk Utility window appears.

3. **Click your Mac's hard disk in the list of drives.**

4. **Read the S.M.A.R.T. Status value, as shown in figure 8.6.** This is located in the lower right of the window.

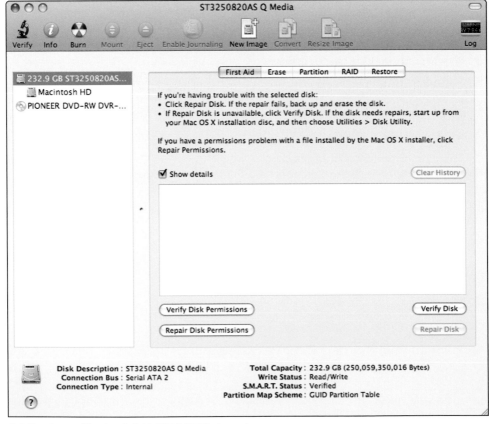

8.6 Check your Mac hard disk's S.M.A.R.T. Status value.

If all is well, the S.M.A.R.T. Status value says Verified. If, instead, you see either About to Fail or, worse, Failing, perform an immediate backup and then replace the hard disk, as described in Chapter 9.

Verifying the hard disk

The S.M.A.R.T. diagnostics (discussed in the previous section) look for catastrophic errors — those that might cause the entire hard disk to go belly up. However, hard disks can also fall prey to smaller maladies that, although they won't cause the hard disk to push up the daisies, could cause it to behave erratically or even damage files.

For example, your Mac maintains what it calls a Catalog file, which is a file that stores the overall structure of the hard disk, including all the folders and files. If that file gets corrupted, it might mean that you or an application can no longer access a folder or file.

You should check your Mac's hard disk for these types of errors every month or so. Here's how:

1. **Click Finder in the Dock.**

2. **Choose Applications ⇨ Utilities ⇨ Disk Utility.** The Disk Utility window appears.

3. **Click Macintosh HD in the list of drives.**

4. **Click Verify Disk.** The Disk Utility begins the verification check, which takes several minutes.

5. **When the check is complete, read the results, as shown in figure 8.7.**

6. **There are two possible results:**

   - **No problems.** Say "Whew!" and close the Disk Utility.

   - **Problems.** You need to repair the hard disk, as described in Chapter 9.

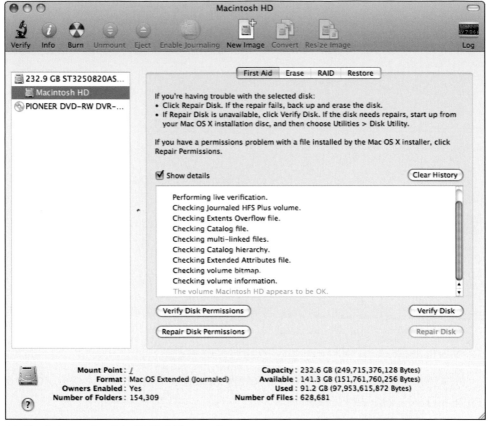

8.7 Check the results of the Verify Disk operation.

Setting the software update schedule

One of the most important things you can do to keep your Mac in the pink is to update its system software and applications. Apple is constantly improving its software by fixing bugs, adding features, closing security holes, and improving performance. So your Mac software is always in top shape if you install these updates regularly.

The good news is that your Mac checks for updates automatically. By default, your Mac does a weekly check, but you can change that if you'd prefer a shorter or longer schedule. Follow these steps:

1. **Click System Preferences in the Dock.** The System Preferences window appears.

2. **Click Software Update.** The Software Update window opens.

3. **Make sure the Check for updates check box is selected, as shown in figure 8.8.**

4. **Choose the frequency with which you want your Mac to check for new updates from the Check for updates list.** Your choices are Daily, Weekly, or Monthly.

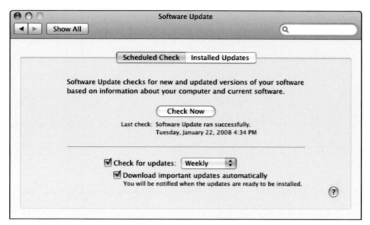

8.8 Select the Check for updates check box and then use the list to choose the update frequency.

Updating software by hand

If you configure Software Update to check for updates weekly or monthly, there may be times when this frequency isn't what you want.

- If your Mac is turned off when the time for the next scheduled update occurs, your Mac skips that check.
- If someone tells you that an important update is available, you might not want to wait until the next schedule check to get that update.

For these and similar scenarios, you can grab your Mac by the scruff of its electronic neck and force it to check for updates. There are two ways you can do this:

- Click System Preferences in the Dock, click Software Update, and then click Check Now.
- Click the Apple icon in the menu bar and then click Software Update.

Genius

Software Update applies only to Apple software. If you have other software installed on your Mac, see if the applications come with update features and, if so, make regular use of them. For Microsoft Office, for example, run the Microsoft AutoUpdate application (in Finder, choose Applications ⇨ Microsoft AutoUpdate).

Cycling your Mac notebook battery

If you have a MacBook Pro, MacBook Air, MacBook, or other Mac notebook, your computer comes with an internal battery that enables you to operate the computer without an electrical outlet. The battery also serves as a backup source of power should the electricity fail.

Older portable computers used rechargeable nickel metal hydride (NiMH) or nickel cadmium (NiCad) batteries. The NiMH and NiCad types are being phased out because they can suffer from a problem called the *memory effect*, where the battery loses capacity if you repeatedly recharge it without first fully discharging it.

All the latest Mac notebooks have rechargeable lithium-ion (Li-ion) batteries. Li-ion batteries are lighter and last longer than NiMH and NiCad batteries and, most importantly, Li-ion batteries don't suffer from the memory effect.

However, to get the most performance out of your Mac notebook's battery, you need to cycle it. *Cycling* a battery means letting it completely discharge and then fully recharging it again. To maintain optimal performance, you should cycle your Mac's battery once a month or so.

More Mac Maintenance

In addition to maintenance tasks that you should perform frequently to keep your Mac in fighting trim, there are other maintenance chores you can run. If you really want to get your Mac in tip-top shape, perform the tasks outlined in the following sections from time to time.

Removing login items

When you start your Mac, lots of behinds-the-scenes tasks get performed to set up the computer for your use. One of these tasks is that your Mac checks the list of items that are supposed to start automatically when you log in to your user account. These items are usually applications, but they can also be files, folders, and shared network locations. Appropriately, these are called *login items*.

Most login items are added by applications because they need some service running right from the get go. Typical examples include:

- **iTunesHelper.** This application is used by iTunes to detect when an iPod is connected to the Mac.
- **Transport Monitor.** This application is used by a Palm's HotSync Manager to detect when a Palm PDA is connected to the Mac.

- **Microsoft AU Daemon.** This application is used by Microsoft Office to check for available updates to the Office software.

As you can see, login items are usually quite important. However, not all login items are vital. For example, a login item might be associated with an application you no longer use, or it might open a file or folder that you no longer need at startup. Whatever the reason, these unneeded login items only serve to slow down your Mac's startup and to consume extra system memory. Therefore, you should from time to time check your user account's login items and remove those you no longer need.

Follow these steps to remove a login item:

1. **Click System Preferences in the Dock.** The System Preferences window opens.
2. **Click Accounts.** The Accounts preferences window opens.
3. **Click the lock icon, if the lock is closed.** If the lock icon is open, skip to Step 5.
4. **Type the name and password of an administrator account and then click OK.**
5. **Click the Login Items tab.** You see a list of login items, as shown in figure 8.9.
6. **Click the login item you want to remove.**
7. **Click the minus sign (-).** Your Mac removes the login item.
8. **Click the lock icon to prevent further changes in the Accounts preferences window.**

8.9 The Login Items tab shows a list of your user account's login items.

Erasing your hard disk's free space

If you regularly deal with files that contain private, sensitive, or secure data, I mentioned earlier that even if you delete those files and then empty the Trash, the files remain on the disk for an indeterminate amount of time. A person who steals or gains physical access to your computer and has the appropriate disk recovery software can easily recover those files.

You can use Leopard's Empty Trash Securely feature (choose Finder ➪ Preferences ➪ Advanced) to improve security by writing gibberish data over the files. You might think this would be pretty darn secure, but it turns out that professional disk recovery experts with high-end tools can *still* recover at least parts of the original files!

Genius

What about sensitive files that you haven't deleted? To protect those, you need to encrypt the contents of your hard disk using your Mac's FileVault encryption technology. Click System Preferences in the Dock, click the Security icon, and then click FileVault. Click Set Master Password to create a master password for your Mac. When that's done, click Turn On FileVault. However, note that if you forget your master password, you lose access to all your data! So, write down the master password and store it in a secure offsite location (such as a safety deposit box).

So is keeping deleted files secure an impossible goal? Fortunately, the answer is a resounding "No!" because your Mac comes with a great tool that can write over deleted files multiple times, thus ensuring that they can never be recovered. The tool is called Erase Free Space, and it's something you should run from time to time to ensure the security of any deleted files that contained important data. Here are the steps to follow:

1. **Click Finder in the Dock.**
2. **Choose Applications ➪ Utilities ➪ Disk Utility.**
3. **Click Macintosh HD in the list of drives.**
4. **Click the Erase tab.**
5. **Click Erase Free Space.** The Disk Utility displays the Erase Free Space Options dialog box, shown in figure 8.10.
6. **These options determine the number of times the hard disk free space gets overwritten.** Select the option you want to run.

- **Zero Out Deleted Files.** This option writes over the free space once. This is the quickest option, but it provides the least security and it will be possible for a sophisticated user to recover some of the data.

- **7-Pass Erase of Deleted Files.** This option writes over the free space seven times. This means the erasure takes seven times as long as the Zero Out option, but it gives you a highly secure (that is, government-grade) erasure. This is the option that's the best blend of convenience and security.

- **35-Pass Erase of Deleted Files.** This option writes over the free space 35 times. This means the erasure takes five times as long as the 7-Pass option and 35 times as long as the Zero Out option. It's likely that this will take a day or so to complete, but it gives you the highest possible security (military-grade).

7. **Click Erase Free Space.**

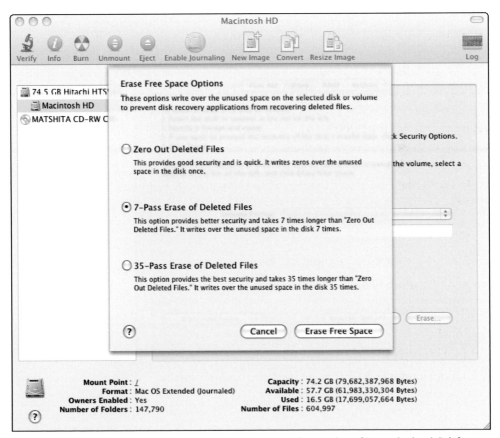

8.10 Use the Erase Free Space Options dialog box to choose the number of times the hard disk free space gets overwritten.

Note

The option is called "Zero Out" because your Mac overwrites the free space with a series of 0s.

Cleaning your Mac inside and out

Your Mac is a beautiful piece of technology, no doubt about it, but in the long run it's only as good looking as it is clean. Unfortunately, computers never stay clean for very long: screens get finger-prints on them; keyboards collect crumbs and other particles; mice get grimy; and, unless you've got some kind of heavy-duty air purifier on the job, all computer parts are world-class dust magnets.

To keep your Mac looking sharp, you should give it a thorough cleaning every so often (how often depends on your own cleanliness standards and outside factors such as how dusty your room is). The most frequent object of your cleaning duties will be the exterior, which you can do following these general steps:

1. **Turn off and unplug the Mac and the LCD monitor.**

2. **Use a soft, dry, clean cloth to wipe any excess dust from the screen, keyboard, and mouse.** If your Mac came with a cloth, use that cloth to do the wiping. If your components are still dirty (fingerprints, smudges, and so on), continue with the remaining steps.

3. **Take a soft, clean cloth and dampen it with water.** Be sure to merely dampen the cloth, because you don't want there to be any excess water that might drip off the cloth.

Caution

Never spray water or any other liquid onto an LCD screen. The liquid could seep into the monitor (or, in the case of the iMac and Mac notebooks, into the computer case) and damage the electronics.

4. **Use the damp cloth to wipe the screen and other components.**

5. **If you see any dust build-up around your Mac's ports, use a vacuum with a soft brush attachment to suck up the dust.** While you have the vacuum handy, use it on your key-board, as well, to suck up any dust or other particles that have settled in between (and even below) the keys.

The outside of your Mac may be nice and shiny now, but there's a good chance you can't say the same for the inside. The inside? You bet. Your Mac has interior fans that serve to flow air through the system and keep it cool. There's usually an intake fan that brings in cool air from the outside of the case, and an exhaust fan that blows out hot air from inside the case. Unfortunately, in most environments the intake fan brings in lots of junk along with the outside air: mostly dust, but also human hair, pet hair, carpet fibers, and whatever else might be hanging around at ground level. Most of this grime takes up residence inside the case, which can be very bad for your Mac's health:

- Dust collects on electrical connections, which can make those connections unreliable.

- A component that's covered in dust retains more heat, which could cause it to perform erratically or even to fail because of overheating.

- The excess heat that dusty components generate causes your overall system to run hotter. This can make your system louder (because the fans have to work harder to cool the system) and can shorten the lifespan of crucial components such as the processor.

Genius

If water seems too low-tech of a solution (pun intended), give Klear Screen a try. It comes in an Apple version (that's recommended by Apple itself), and the kit contains iKlear, an antistatic screen polish, and a soft chamois cloth. See www.klearscreen.com for more info.

Dust, clearly, is a bad thing. So once every six months or so, you should open up your Mac's case (as described in Chapter 9), and give the machine's innards a good cleaning. There are two ways to do this:

- **Canned air.** This is a can of air under pressure, and you use it to blow away dust and other debris. I'm not a huge fan of this method because all it tends to do is blow the dust back into the air where it will simply settle elsewhere. However, it's often useful for getting to dust in areas where a vacuum can't reach.

- **Vacuum.** Be sure to use an attachment that has soft bristles to avoid damaging any of the sensitive electronics inside your Mac. If you want to take things up a notch, get a computer vacuum, which has attachments specifically designed for cleaning computers. If you want to go the whole hog, get an electronics vacuum that has an antistatic feature (and a hefty price tag, too).

Backing Up Your Mac

The data you create on your Mac is as precious as gold not only because it's yours, but mostly because it's simply irreplaceable. Macs are reliable machines, but they do crash and all hard disks eventually die, so at some point your data will be at risk. To avoid losing that data forever, you need to back up your Mac, early and often.

Configuring Time Machine

If your Mac runs Leopard (OS X 10.5), then backing up your data has never been easier. That's because Leopard introduced Time Machine to the world. Time Machine is a backup application that's unlike anything you've seen before in the Mac world:

- The initial Time Machine backup includes your entire Mac.

- Time Machine runs another backup every hour, and this backup includes just those files and folders that you've changed or created since the most recent hourly backup.

- Time Machine runs a daily backup that includes only those files and folders that you've changed or created since the most recent daily backup.

- Time Machine runs a weekly backup that includes only those files and folders that you've changed or created since the most recent weekly backup.

All of this is completely automated, so Time Machine is a set-it-and-forget-it deal, which is exactly what you want in a backup application. However, Time Machine doesn't stop there: it also keeps old backups:

- It keeps the past 24 hourly backups.

- It keeps the last month's worth of daily backups.

- It keeps all the weekly backups until the backup location gets full, at which point it begins deleting the oldest backups to make room for more.

Keeping these old backups is what gives Time Machine its name. That is, it enables you to go back in time and restore not just a file, but also a *version* of a file. For example, let's say on Monday you created a document and added some text, and then spent Tuesday editing that text. If on Friday you realize that during Tuesday's edits you deleted some of the original text that you'd now give your eyeteeth to get back, there's no problem: simply restore the version from Monday.

Time Machine is so simple and so potentially useful, that you really ought to make it part of your backup toolkit. If there's a downside to Time Machine, it's that it only backs up to a second hard disk that is connected to your Mac. You can't, say, back up to a network folder. (If you want to back up to a network, then you need to get Apple's new Time Capsule device; see www.apple.com/timecapsule.)

When you first connect an external USB or FireWire hard disk, Time Machine sits up and takes notice, and it most likely displays the dialog box shown in figure 8.11. If you want to use the hard disk for your Time Machine backups, click Use as Backup Disk; otherwise, click Cancel to move on without configuring anything.

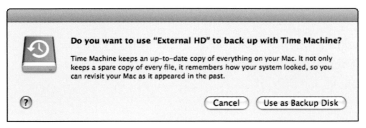

Do you want to use "External HD" to back up with Time Machine?

Time Machine keeps an up-to-date copy of everything on your Mac. It not only keeps a spare copy of every file, it remembers how your system looked, so you can revisit your Mac as it appeared in the past.

Cancel   Use as Backup Disk

8.11 Time Machine usually asks if you want to use a freshly connected hard disk as the backup disk.

If you didn't set up an external hard disk as the Time Machine backup disk, or if you want to use a different external disk as the backup disk, you can choose the disk by hand, as shown in the following steps:

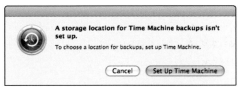

A storage location for Time Machine backups isn't set up.

To choose a location for backups, set up Time Machine.

Cancel   Set Up Time Machine

8.12 You see this dialog box if you've never configured Time Machine with a backup disk.

1. **Click the System Preferences in the Dock.**

2. **Click Time Machine.** If you've never set up a backup disk, the dialog box in figure 8.12 appears.

3. **Click Set Up Time Machine.** The Time Machine preferences window appears.

4. **Click Choose Backup Disk.** Time Machine displays a list of the hard disks on your system that you can use for backups, as shown in figure 8.13.

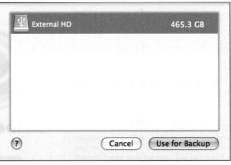

External HD   465.3 GB

Cancel   Use for Backup

8.13 Use this dialog box to choose which hard disk you want Time Machine to use for its backups.

5. **Click the hard disk you want to use.**

6. **Click Use for Backup.** If the hard disk has data on it, or if it has never been formatted, Time Machine warns you that it must erase (that is, format) the disk.

7. **Click Erase.** If you want to save the hard disk's data first, click Choose Another Disk, copy the drive data to another location, and then repeat this procedure.

When you get back to the Time Machine preferences window, you see that the Time Machine setting is set to ON, and the application immediately begins a 120-second countdown to the next backup. (If you don't want the backup to run right away, click the X icon beside the countdown.)

When you launch Time Machine preferences from now on, it shows you the current status (ON or OFF), how much space is left on the backup disk, and the dates and times of your oldest and most recent backups, as shown in figure 8.14.

8.14 The Time Machine window shows the backup device, its free space, and the dates of your oldest and newest backups.

The more data you have, the longer the initial backup takes. If you have data that you don't want included in your backups — for example, recorded TV shows that you'll delete after watching them — then it's a good idea to exclude the folders or files. Here's how it's done:

1. **In the Time Machine window, click Options.** Time Machine displays a list of items to exclude from the backups. (At first, this list includes the hard disk that Time Machine is using for the backups, which just makes sense.)

2. **Click the plus sign (+).**

Genius

If you exclude any items while a backup is running, Time Machine cancels the current backup and reschedules it. If you'd really prefer that the backup run right away, click Change Disk, choose None, and then click Stop Backing Up. Click Change Disk again, choose the hard disk you're using for backups, and then click Use for Backup. Time Machine then runs the backup after the 120-second countdown.

3. **Choose the folder or file that you want to exclude from the backups.**

4. **Click Exclude.** Time Machine adds the folder or file to the Do not back up list, as shown in figure 8.15.

5. **Follow Steps 2 through 4 to exclude any other folders and files that you don't want backed up.**

6. **Click Done.**

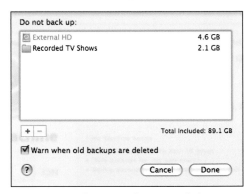

Backing up your hard disk to a disk image

8.15 You can tell Time Machine to exclude certain folders or files from the backups.

If you're using a version of Mac OS X earlier than Leopard, or if you'd rather back up your Mac to something other than another hard disk (such as a network folder), then you need a different backup strategy. One possibility is to create an *image* of your Mac's hard disk. A disk image is an exact copy of the disk. If your Mac hard disk gets corrupted, you can restore it from the disk image and you'll be back on your feet in no time.

Follow these steps to create a disk image for your Mac's hard disk:

1. **Click Finder in the Dock.**

2. **Choose Applications ⇨ Utilities ⇨ Disk Utility.**

3. **Click Macintosh HD, as shown in figure 8.16.**

4. **Click New Image.** The New Image from Folder dialog box appears.

5. **Use the Save As text box to type a name for the disk image.**

6. **Choose the location where you want the disk image saved.** For example, choose a shared folder on another computer on your network.

7. **In the Image Format list, choose read-only, as shown in figure 8.17.**

Caution The image file will be about the same size as the total used space on the hard disk. Therefore, be sure to choose a location that has enough free space to hold the image file.

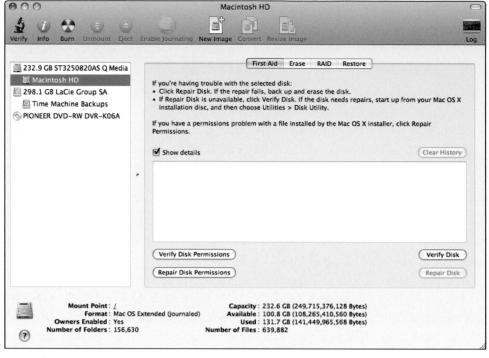

8.16 Choose Macintosh HD to make an image of your hard disk.

8.17 Use the New Image from Folder dialog box to name the disk image, set its location, and set its format.

8. **If you don't want other people to be able to read the contents of the image, choose 128-bit AES encryption in the Encryption list.**

9. **Click Save.** Disk Utility creates the disk image.

Note

Creating a disk image is a slow process that can take an hour or more depending on the size of your Mac's hard disk.

Backing up your files to a DVD

Another useful backup strategy is to back up your files to a DVD disc. The advantage here is that you can take the disc with you, so you have access to your file while you're away from your Mac. This also enables you to store the DVDs offsite for extra security.

You back up files to a DVD (or a CD) by first creating a *burn folder*, which is a special folder that contains aliases of whatever folders or files to add to it. You can then burn that folder to the disc to complete the backup. Follow these steps:

1. **Choose a location for the burn folder.**

   - If you want to place the burn folder on the Desktop, click any empty part of the Desktop. This is probably the best place for the burn folder because it's usually the easiest place to drag and drop files.

   - If you want to place the burn folder in some other folder, use Finder to open that folder.

2. **Choose File ⇨ New Burn Folder.** Your Mac creates a new burn folder.

3. **Type a name for the burn folder and then press Return.**

4. **Use Finder to locate a folder or file you want to burn.**

5. **Click and drag the folder or file and then drop it on the burn folder.** Your Mac creates an alias for the folder or file within the burn folder.

6. **Repeat Step 5 to add all the folders and files you want to burn.**

7. **Double-click the burn folder to open it.** Figure 8.18 shows an example of a burn folder.

Genius

You need to make sure that you don't add more files to the burn folder than can fit on the disc: 700MB for a CD, 4.7GB for a single layer DVD, and 8.5GB for a double layer DVD. To see the size of the items currently in the burn folder, double-click the burn folder to open it, and then examine the Minimum Disc Size value in the status bar (see figure 8.18).

8.18 A burn folder ready for burning to disc.

8. **Insert a writable DVD (or CD).**

9. **Click the Burn button.** The dialog box shown in figure 8.19 appears.

10. **Use the Disc Name text box to type a name for the disc.**

11. **Use the Burn Speed list to choose the burn rate.** If you have trouble burning, try again using a slower rate.

12. **Click Burn.** Your Mac burns the folders and files to the disc.

8.19 Specify a name and write speed for the burn.

Restoring files using Time Machine

If you delete a file by accident, you can always open the Trash to drag it back out. However, there are plenty of situations where recovering a file just isn't possible.

- You delete the file and then empty the trash.

- You overwrite the file with another file of the same name. If you notice the problem right away, you can choose Edit ⇨ Undo or press ⌘+Z to undo the file operation. But if you don't notice until later, you're stuck.

- Your hard disk develops a problem that corrupts the file.

- You make and save substantial edits to the file.

The good news is that if you've had Time Machine on the job for a while, you can probably go back in time, locate a version of the file, and then restore it to its original location. Time Machine even lets you keep the existing file if you still need the newer version. Note that I'm talking here about files, but you can also recover folders and even your entire hard disk.

Follow these steps to restore data from your Time Machine backups:

1. **Use Finder to choose the folder you want to restore, or the folder that contains the file you want to restore.** If you want to restore your entire hard disk, choose Macintosh HD in the Sidebar.

2. **Click the Time Machine icon in the Dock.** The Time Machine interface appears, as shown in figure 8.20.

Version windows

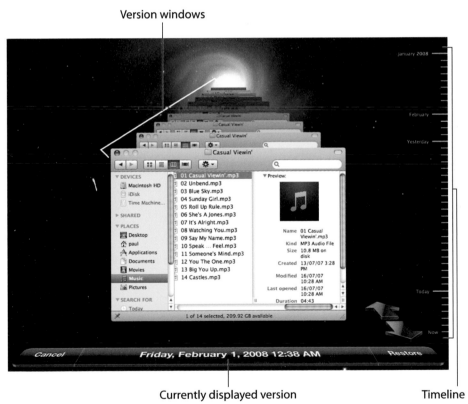

Currently displayed version   Timeline

8.20 Use the Time Machine interface to choose which version of the folder or file you want to restore.

3. **Navigate to the version you want by using any of the following techniques (the date and time of the backup appear at the bottom of the screen).**

   - Click the top arrow to jump to the earliest version; click the bottom arrow to return to the most recent version.

   - Hold down the ⌘ key and click the arrows to navigate through the backups one version at a time.

   - Use the timeline to click a specific version.

   - Click the version windows.

4. **Click the file and click Restore to restore a file.** Time Machine copies the version of the folder or file back to its original location. If the location already contains a folder or file with the same name, you see the dialog box shown in figure 8.21.

8.21 This dialog box appears if the restore location already has a folder or file with the same name.

5. **Click one of the following buttons.**

   - **Keep Original.** Cancels the restore and leaves the existing folder or file as is.

   - **Keep Both.** Restores the folder or file and keeps the existing folder or file as is. In this case, Time Machine restores the folder or file and adds the text (original) to the folder or file name.

   - **Replace.** Click this button to overwrite the existing folder or file with the restored folder or file.

Restoring your system

If disaster strikes and you can't start your Mac, then you need to restore your system to an earlier state when it was working properly. You can do this using either Time Machine or a disk image.

To recover your system, follow these steps:

1. **Insert your Mac OS X Install DVD.** The Mac OS X Install DVD window appears, as shown in figure 8.22.

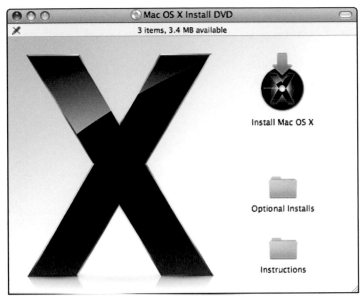

8.22 This window appears when you insert the Mac OS X installation DVD.

2. **Double-click Install Mac OS X.** The Install DVD tells you that your Mac needs to restart, as shown in figure 8.23.

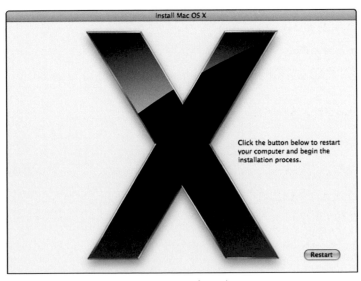

8.23 You need to restart your Mac to perform the system recovery.

3. **Click Restart.** Your Mac prompts you for an administrator username and password.

4. **Enter your administrator credentials and click OK.** Your Mac restarts and boots to the Mac OS X Install DVD.

5. **Select a language for the install.** The Install Mac OS X application appears.

6. **Chose Utilities ⇨ Restore System From Backup.** The Restore Your System window appears.

7. **Click Continue.** The Select a Backup Source window appears.

8. **Click the hard disk that contains your Time Machine backups.**

9. **Click Continue.** The Select a Backup window appears.

10. **Click the backup you want to use for the restore.**

11. **Click Continue.** The Select a Destination window appears.

12. **Click Macintosh HD.**

13. **Click Restore.** Install Mac OS X begins restoring your system.

To recover your system using a disk image, follow these steps:

1. **Follow Steps 1 through 5 in the previous set of steps.** You should be at the Install Mac OS X application window.

2. **Chose Utilities ⇨ Disk Utility.** The Disk Utility window appears.

3. **Click Restore.**

4. **Beside the Source box, click Image.**

5. **Choose your disk image and then click Open.**

6. **Click and drag Macintosh HD and drop it inside the Destination text box, as shown in figure 8.24.**

7. **Click Restore.** Disk Utility asks you to confirm.

8. **Click Restore.** Disk Utility begins restoring your system.

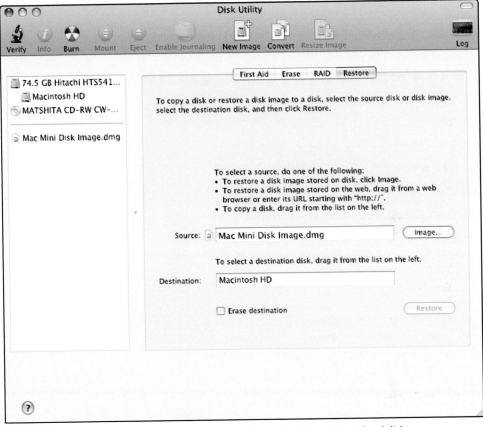

8.24 The restore source is your disk image, and the destination is your Mac's hard disk.

Macs look so stylish and work so well that it's easy to think of them as objects

of perfection. This is perhaps why most people never even think of upgrad-

ing their Mac's hardware, because who would want to mess with perfection?

Far be it from me to burst anyone's bubble, but most Macs, terrific machines

though they are, could stand a little upgrading. Whether it's a bit more mem-

ory, a larger (or second) hard drive, a more powerful graphics card, or a fresh

notebook battery, you *can* make your Mac better. In this chapter, I show you

how to get under your Mac's hood and what to do when you get there.

Using System Profiler to See Your Current Hardware

By definition, upgrading your Mac means replacing an existing component with another compo-nent that's faster, more powerful, or has a larger capacity. (In the case of the roomy Mac Pro, upgrading also means adding new devices, such as extra hard drives and new expansion cards.) So it makes sense that you can't really upgrade your Mac unless you know what existing components your Mac has.

If you're not sure what your Mac has going for it internally, that's not a problem because it has a handy program called System Profiler that gives you the full scoop. To launch System Profiler, fol-low these steps:

1. **Click Finder in the Dock.**

2. **Choose Applications ⇨ Utilities ⇨ System Profiler.** You see a System Profile window that's similar to the one shown in figure 9.1.

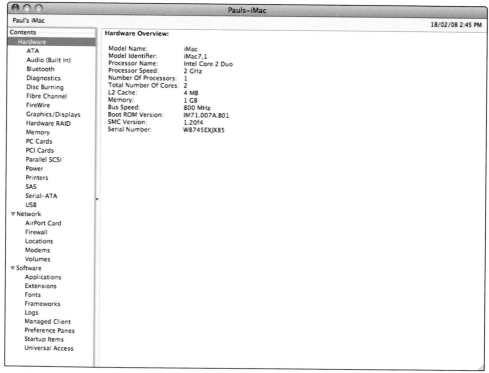

9.1 System Profiler lets you know what's inside your Mac.

By default, System Profiler starts off by displaying the contents of the main Hardware branch, which shows you, among other things, the type of Mac you have (the Model Name), the type of processor and the processor speed, and how much memory your Mac has. You can use the Hardware subbranches to get more detailed information about specific parts. For example, the Memory subbranch shows you the number of memory slots in your Mac, and how much memory is in each slot, as shown in figure 9.2.

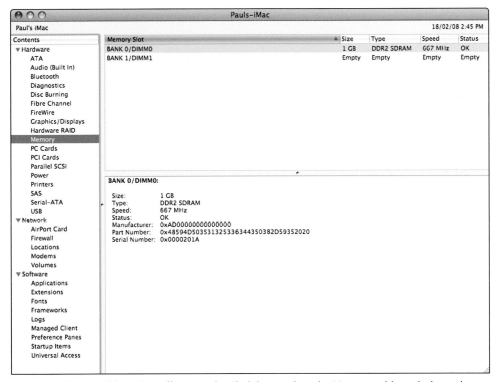

9.2 The Hardware subbranches offer more detailed data, such as the Memory subbranch shown here.

Upgrading Your iMac Memory

The iMac with its compact, curvaceous shape and integrated LCD display is one of the most beautiful computers ever built. However, that beauty comes at a price: the iMac has only limited upgrade potential for most people because Apple has made it extremely difficult to access the inside of the new iMacs. The one thing that you can easily do is upgrade the memory.

Getting Inside Your Intel-based iMac

The Intel-based iMacs are difficult to open, but not impossible. If you're technically savvy and you don't mind voiding your warranty, there are tutorials on the Web that tell you how to get inside an iMac. Here are two:

www.amfiteatar.org/content/view/155/57/lang,en

http://forums.macrumors.com/showthread.php?t=350120

Most Intel-based iMacs come with 1GB of memory installed, and that memory is usually in a single memory slot, with the other slot empty. This means you can drop in a second memory module to increase your system's memory and boost your Mac's performance. Note that the memory module you use must meet the following conditions:

- **Form factor.** 200-pin Small Outline Dual Inline Memory Module (SO-DIMM).
- **Memory type.** Double Data Rate 2 (DDR2) running at 667MHz (also known as PC2-5300).

Genius

Your iMac supports dual-channel memory, which essentially doubles the rate at which information is transferred to and from memory. To enable dual-channel memory, the two memory modules must be the same size, the same form factor, and the same type. For example, most iMacs come with a single 1GB DDR2 667MHz SO-DIMM memory module. To enable dual-channel mode, add a second memory module that's identical to the first.

Your iMac's memory is the easiest thing to upgrade because it doesn't require opening the case. Follow these steps:

1. **Choose Apple ⇨ Shut Down, and then click Shut Down to turn off your iMac.**
2. **Unplug the iMac's power cable and any other cables attached to the Mac, including USB, network, and FireWire cables.**
3. **Lay the iMac screen side down on a flat surface that's covered with a towel or other soft material.** Make sure the bottom edge of the iMac is facing you.
4. **Touch something metal to ground yourself.**

Caution It's vital to discharge your body's pent-up static electricity by touching a metal object. Otherwise, the static electricity discharges into your Mac and could damage one or more internal components.

5. **Use a Philips screwdriver to loosen the screw in the middle of the iMac's underside, as shown in figure 9.3.**

6. **Pull out the memory access door.**

7. **Unfurl the plastic tab from inside the memory area.**

8. **If you're replacing the existing memory module, pull the module's tab toward you to eject the module from its slot, and then pull out the module.**

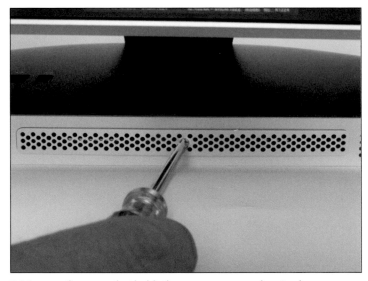

9.3 Loosen the screw that holds the memory access door in place.

Note If you find it difficult to remove the memory access door on your iMac, try using a pair of needle-nose pliers to grab the top and bottom edges of the door and yank it out.

233

9. **Take the new memory module and orient it in front of the memory compartment as follows (see figure 9.4).**

   - The gold contacts should be facing the memory slot.
   - The notch in the contacts should be toward the left.
   - The plastic tab should be under the module.

10. **Insert the memory module into the slot and use your thumbs to press gently but firmly on the back edge of the module until it snaps into place.**

Notch   Contacts

9.4 Orient the module as shown.

11. **Curl the plastic tab over the module and tuck it into the memory compartment.**

12. **Reattach the memory access door.**

13. **Return your iMac to the upright position, reattach all the cables, and then turn on the iMac.** If your iMac doesn't start but, instead, plays a series of three tones every few seconds, it means it doesn't like the memory you added. The most likely cause is that you didn't fully insert the memory module; however, you should also double-check that you used memory that's compatible with the iMac.

14. **Use System Profiler to confirm that your iMac recognizes the new memory.**

Upgrading Your MacBook Pro

The stylish and powerful Intel-based MacBook Pro is a great machine right out of the box, so you're no doubt happy with what you've got. However, even the MacBook Pro can be improved upon, although in only a limited way. That is, the most you can do is replace the battery and upgrade the memory. The next two sections take you through the steps required.

Replacing your MacBook Pro battery

If your MacBook Pro's battery won't charge or if it runs down very quickly when you're running the Mac without outlet power, then it's time to yank out the old battery and replace it with a new one. Follow these steps:

1. **Choose Apple ⇨ Shut Down and then click Shut Down to turn off your MacBook Pro.**

2. **Unplug the MacBook Pro's power cable and any other cables attached to the MacBook Pro, including USB, network, and FireWire cables.**

3. **Close the screen and lay the MacBook Pro upside down on a flat surface that's covered with a towel or other soft material.** For easiest access to the battery, turn the MacBook Pro so that the back of the computer is facing you.

4. **Touch something metal to ground yourself.**

5. **Slide the battery locking tabs toward you, as shown in figure 9.5.** The battery pops up slightly.

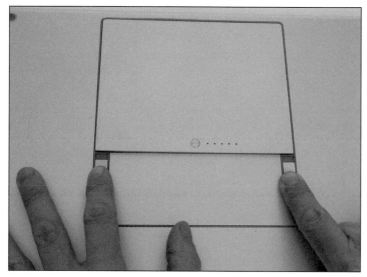

9.5 Release the battery by sliding the locking tabs toward you.

Caution It's vital to discharge your body's pent-up static electricity by touching a metal object. Otherwise, the static electricity discharges into your Mac and could damage one or more internal components.

6. **Remove the battery.** Figure 9.6 shows the MacBook Pro with the battery removed.

7. **Insert the new battery.**

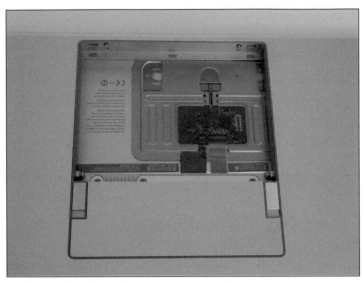

9.6 The MacBook Pro with the battery removed.

Upgrading your MacBook Pro memory

Most Intel-based MacBook Pros come with 1GB of memory installed. However, the MacBook Pro has two memory slots, so you can add a second memory module to increase your system's memory and boost your Mac's performance. Note that the memory module you use must meet the following conditions:

- **Form factor.** 200-pin Small Outline Dual Inline Memory Module (SO-DIMM).
- **Memory type.** Double Data Rate 2 (DDR2) running at 667MHz (also known as PC2-5300).
- **Memory size.** The memory module must be either 512MB or 1GB.

Follow these steps to add new memory or replace the existing memory in a MacBook Pro:

1. **Follow Steps 1 through 6 from the previous section to remove the battery.**
2. **Turn the MacBook Pro so that the front edge of the computer is facing you.**
3. **Use a precision Phillips screwdriver (that is, a Phillips #00) to remove the three screws that attach the RAM shield to the case, as shown in figure 9.7.**
4. **Lift off the RAM shield to expose the memory slots.**
5. **If you're replacing an existing memory module, push apart the metal clips that hold the sides of the memory module.** When you push the clips apart far enough, the memory

module pops up. Make sure the module pops up far enough that you can get a grip on it, as shown in figure 9.8.

6. **Remove the memory module by pulling it straight back from the slot, as shown in figure 9.8.**

Remove screws

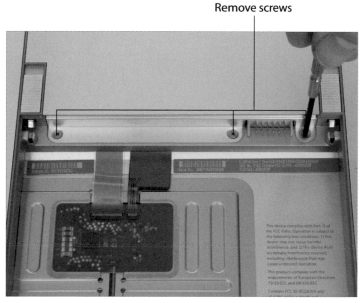

9.7 Remove the three screws that hold the RAM shield.

9.8 Pull the old memory module straight back to remove it from the slot.

237

7. **Take the new memory module and orient it to the lower memory slot as follows (see figure 9.9):**

   ● The gold contacts should be facing the memory slot.

   ● The notch in the contacts should be toward the left.

   ● The back of the module should be raised slightly.

8. **Insert the module into the slot as far as it will go.** The module is fully seated when it snaps into place.

9. **Press down on the module until the metal clips snap into place.**

10. **If you're installing a second memory module, repeat Steps 7 through 9 for the upper memory slot.**

11. **Reattach the RAM shield.**

12. **Reinsert the battery.**

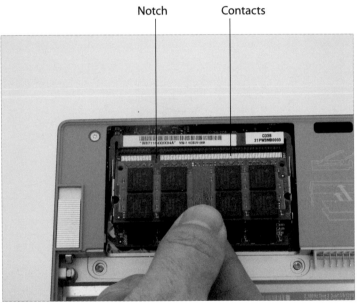

Notch   Contacts

9.9 Orient the module as shown here.

13. **Reattach all the cables and then turn on the MacBook Pro.** If your MacBook Pro doesn't start but, instead, the sleep light constantly blinks on and off, it means the MacBook Pro doesn't recognize the memory you added. The most likely cause is that you didn't fully insert the memory modules; however, you should also double-check that you used memory that's compatible with the MacBook Pro.

14. **Use System Profiler to confirm that your MacBook Pro recognizes the new memory.**

Upgrading Your MacBook

The Intel-based MacBook may not be as powerful as its older sibling the MacBook Pro, but it's still no slouch in the performance department and looks good in its own right. It even has one advantage over the MacBook Pro: it's more easily upgraded. That is, just like the MacBook Pro you can replace the battery and upgrade the RAM, but the MacBook also lets you replace the hard disk without working up a sweat.

Replacing your MacBook battery

If your MacBook's battery runs down quickly while not plugged into a power outlet, or if the battery won't take a charge, then it's definitely ready to be replaced. Follow these steps to replace the battery on most MacBook models:

1. **Choose Apple ⇨ Shut Down and then click Shut Down to turn off your MacBook.**

2. **Unplug the MacBook's power cable and any other cables attached to the MacBook, including USB, network, and FireWire cables.**

3. **Close the screen and lay the MacBook upside down on a flat surface that's covered with a towel or other soft material.**

4. **Touch something metal to ground yourself.**

5. **Use a coin or flat-head screwdriver to turn the battery's locking screw 90 degrees in the clockwise direction.** The battery pops up.

6. **Remove the battery.** Figure 9.10 shows the MacBook with the battery removed.

Locking screw

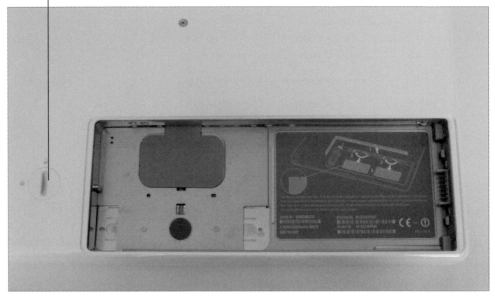

9.10 Release the locking screw and then lift out the old battery.

7. **Insert the new battery.**

8. **While holding the battery in place, use a coin or flat-head screwdriver to turn the battery's locking screw 90 degrees in the counter-clockwise direction.**

Caution It's vital to discharge your body's pent-up static electricity by touching a metal object. Otherwise, the static electricity can discharge into your Mac and could damage one or more internal components.

Upgrading your MacBook memory

Most MacBooks come with either 512MB or 1GB of memory installed. However, the MacBook has two memory slots, so you can add a second memory module to increase your system's memory and boost your Mac's performance. Note that the memory module you use must meet the following conditions:

- **Form factor.** 200-pin Small Outline Dual Inline Memory Module (SO-DIMM).

- **Memory type.** Double Data Rate 2 (DDR2) running at 667MHz (also known as PC2-5300).

- **Memory size.** The memory module must be either 512MB or 1GB.

Follow these steps to add new memory or replace the existing memory in a MacBook:

1. **Follow Steps 1 through 6 from the previous section to remove the battery.**

2. **Use a precision Phillips screwdriver (that is, a Phillips #00) to remove the three screws that attach the RAM shield to the case, as shown in figure 9.11.**

3. **Remove the RAM shield to expose the memory slots.**

4. **If you're removing an existing memory module, push the metal lever toward the middle of the slot.** The memory module pops out of the slot.

Remove these screws

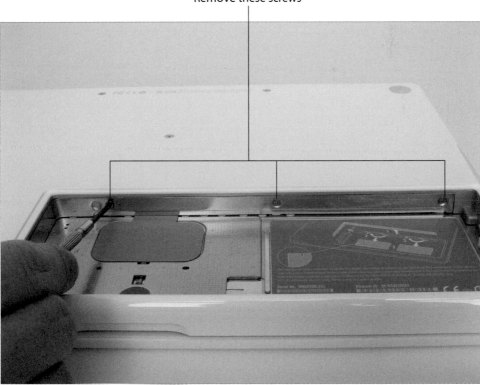

9.11 Remove the screws on the RAM shield.

5. **Remove the memory module from the slot.**

6. **Take the new memory module and orient it in front of the memory compartment as follows (see figure 9.12):**

   - The gold contacts should be facing the memory slot.

- The notch in the contacts should be toward the left.

- The plastic tab should be under the module.

7. **Insert the memory module into the slot and use your thumbs to press gently but firmly on the back edge of the module until it snaps into place.**

8. **Curl the plastic tab over the module and tuck it into the memory compartment.**

9. **Reattach the RAM shield.**

10. **Reinsert the battery.**

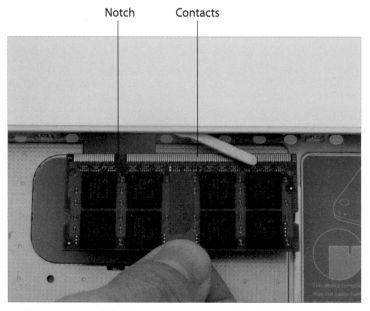

9.12 Orient the module as shown here.

11. **Reattach all the cables and then turn on the MacBook.** If your MacBook doesn't start but, instead, the sleep light constantly blinks on and off, it means the MacBook doesn't recognize the memory you added. The most likely cause is that you didn't fully insert the memory modules; however, you should also double-check that you used memory that's compatible with the MacBook.

12. **Use System Profiler to confirm that your MacBook recognizes the new memory.**

Upgrading your MacBook hard disk

One of the nice features you get with the MacBook is that the hard disk is easily accessible. So if your original hard disk goes belly up, or if you just want a larger hard disk, it doesn't take a ton of work to take out the old one and replace it with a new one.

Genius If you're replacing your MacBook's original hard disk and the hard disk still works, be sure to back up the hard disk using Time Machine or one of the other methods in Chapter 8. After you've installed the new hard disk, you can then restore your configuration from the backup.

Here's what you need:

- **Form factor.** 2.5-inches wide; this is called a *notebook hard disk* or a *laptop hard disk*.
- **Interface.** Serial Advanced Technology Attachment (SATA).
- **Bandwidth.** 1.5 gigabits per second (Gbps); this is also called SATA150.

 Note If you can only find a SATA300 hard disk (this is a SATA disk with a bandwidth of 3.0Gbps), that's okay because the hard disk will just operate at the slower rate of 1.5Gbps in your MacBook.

Follow these steps to upgrade your MacBook hard disk:

1. **Follow Steps 1 through 3 from the previous section to remove the RAM shield.**
2. **Use the plastic tab to pull out the hard disk assembly, as shown in figure 9.13.**

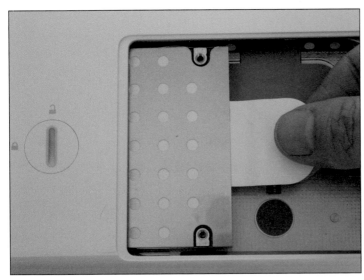

9.13 Pull the plastic tab to remove the hard disk assembly.

243

3. **Use a T8 Torx screwdriver to remove the four Torx screws that attach the bracket to the hard disk (two screws on each side), as shown in figure 9.14.**

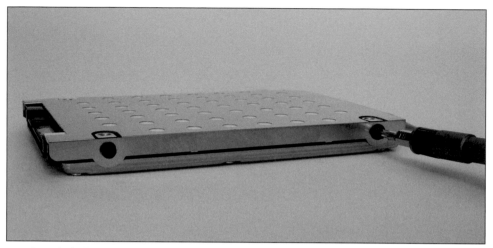

9.14 Detach the hard disk from the bracket by removing the four T8 Torx screws.

4. **Remove the old hard disk from the bracket.**

5. **Insert the new hard disk into the bracket as follows:**
   - The label on the hard disk should face up (away from the bottom of the bracket).
   - The hard disk's connectors should face the back of the bracket (the side away from the white plastic tab).
   - Align the holes on the sides of the hard disk with the holes on the sides of the bracket.

6. **Attach the hard disk to the bracket using the four T8 Torx screws.**

7. **Lay the hard disk/bracket assembly in the battery bay as follows:**
   - The label on the hard disk should face up.
   - The hard disk's connectors should face the hard drive bay.

8. **Slide the hard disk/bracket assembly into the hard disk bay, as shown in figure 9.15.** The hard disk snaps into place when it's fully seated.

9. **Tuck the plastic tab under the hard disk.**

10. **Reattach the RAM shield.**

11. **Reinsert the battery.**

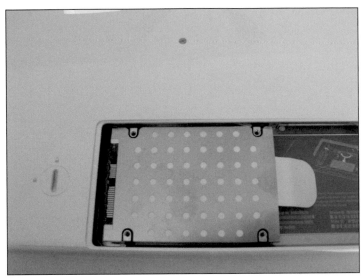

9.15 Lay the hard disk/bracket assembly into the battery bay as shown here, and then slide it into the hard disk bay.

Upgrading Your iBook

If you've got an old iBook G4 lying around, you can give it a new lease on life by upgrading it with a new battery, a new AirPort Extreme card, or more memory. The following sections give you the details.

Replacing your iBook battery

If your iBook's battery no longer holds a charge or gives you only a limited amount of power, then it's time to replace it. Follow these steps:

1. **Choose Apple ⇨ Shut Down and then click Shut Down to turn off your iBook.**

2. **Unplug the iBook's power cable and any other cables attached to the iBook, including USB, network, and FireWire cables.**

3. **Close the screen and lay the iBook upside down on a flat surface that's covered with a towel or other soft material.**

4. **Touch something metal to ground yourself.**

5. **Use a coin or flat-head screwdriver to turn the battery's locking screw 90 degrees in the clockwise direction.** The battery pops up.

Caution   It's vital to discharge your body's pent-up static electricity by touching a metal object. Otherwise, the static electricity can discharge into your Mac and could damage one or more internal components.

6. **Remove the battery.** Figure 9.16 shows the iBook with the battery removed.

Locking screw

9.16 Release the locking screw and then lift out the old battery.

7. **Insert the new battery.**

8. **While holding the battery in place, use a coin or flat-head screwdriver to turn the battery's locking screw 90 degrees in the counter-clockwise direction.**

Replacing your iBook AirPort Extreme card

If you're having trouble accessing wireless networks, a faulty AirPort Extreme card may be to blame. To replace the card, follow these steps:

1. **Follow Steps 1 through 6 from the previous section to remove the battery.**

2. **Turn the iBook over and open the cover so that you can see the keyboard.**

3. **Locate the keyboard release keys, as shown in figure 9.17.** One key is between Esc and F1. The other key is between F11 and F12.

Keyboard release keys

Keyboard locking screw

9.17 Use these keys to release the keyboard.

4. **Pull the release keys toward you and lift the keyboard away from the iBook.** Gently set the keyboard face down on the trackpad.

Note

If the keyboard won't budge, it's likely locked. Use a small flat-head screwdriver to rotate the keyboard locking screw (pointed out in figure 9.17) a half turn to unlock it.

5. **Release the metal clip that holds the AirPort Extreme Card in place, as shown in figure 9.18.**

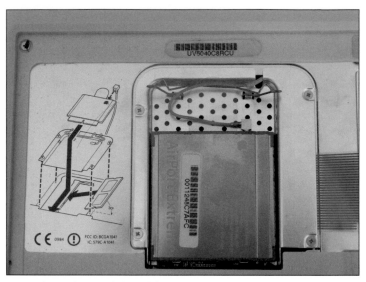

9.18 Release the metal clip holding the AirPort Extreme card.

6. **Grasp the plastic tab attached to the AirPort Extreme Card and pull it toward the screen to release the card.**

7. **Pull the antenna connector out of the AirPort Extreme card and attach it to the new AirPort Extreme card.**

8. **Insert the new AirPort Extreme card into the slot.**

9. **Reattach the metal clip.**

10. **Reattach the keyboard.**

11. **Reinsert the battery.**

12. **While holding the battery in place, use a coin or flat-head screwdriver to turn the battery's locking screw 90 degrees in the counter-clockwise direction.**

Upgrading your iBook memory

Most iBook G4s came with 512MB of internal RAM. However, they also have an extra memory module that can take up to 1GB of RAM, for a total of 1.5GB. Note that the memory module you use must meet the following conditions:

- **Form factor.** 200-pin Small Outline Dual Inline Memory Module (SO-DIMM).
- **Memory type.** Double Data Rate (DDR) running at 333MHz (also known as PC-2700).

Follow these steps:

1. **Follow Steps 1 through 6 from the previous section to remove the battery, keyboard, and AirPort Extreme card.**

2. **Use a precision Phillips screwdriver (that is, a Phillips #00) to remove the four screws that hold the RAM shield in place, as shown in figure 9.19.** Move the RAM shield and AirPort Extreme card off to the side.

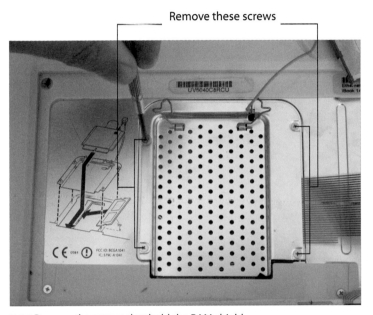

9.19 Remove the screws that hold the RAM shield.

3. **If you're replacing an existing memory module, push apart the metal clips that hold the sides of the module in place, and then lift out the module.**

4. **Align the new memory module as follows (see figure 9.20):**

   - The gold contacts should be facing the memory slot.
   - The notch in the contacts should be toward the left and aligned with the ridge in the memory slot.
   - The back of the module should be raised slightly.

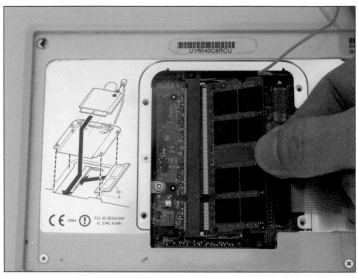

9.20 Align the memory module as shown.

5. **Insert the memory module into the slot as far as it will go, and then press down on the module until it snaps into place.**

6. **Reattach the RAM shield.** Make sure the AirPort Extreme card's antenna fits inside the notch in the RAM shield.

7. **Reinsert the AirPort Extreme card into the slot.**

8. **Reattach the metal clip.**

9. **Reattach the keyboard.**

10. **Reinsert the battery.**

11. **While holding the battery in place, use a coin or flat-head screwdriver to turn the battery's locking screw 90 degrees in the counter-clockwise direction.**

12. **Reattach all the cables and then turn on the iBook.** If your iBook doesn't start but, instead, the sleep light constantly blinks on and off, it means the iBook doesn't recognize the memory you added. The most likely cause is that you didn't fully insert the memory modules; however, you should also double-check that you used memory that's compatible with the iBook.

13. **Use System Profiler to confirm that your iBook recognizes the new memory.**

Upgrading Your Mac Pro

The Mac Pro is a behemoth of a machine, both in its heft (it weighs a ton) and in its power (this is one awesome computer). However, the Mac Pro also excels in another area: upgradeability. Unlike the cramped interiors of the iMac and the various Mac notebooks, the Mac Pro has tons of room inside, which enables you to easily add more memory, more hard disks, and extra expansion cards.

Opening the Mac Pro case

The Mac Pro is the only current Mac that uses a tower-style case. So, like all tower cases, you access the inside of the machine by removing the side panel. Here are the steps:

1. **Turn off and unplug the Mac Pro.**

2. **Put the Mac Pro upright on a solid surface, preferably one where the computer is within easy reach.**

3. **Pull up the lever on the back of the Mac Pro.** This unlocks the side panel, which is the panel on the left when you're looking at the back of the Mac Pro (see figure 9.21).

4. **Open the side panel from the top, and then pull the panel away from the case.**

9.21 Pull up the lever on the back of the Mac Pro to unlock the side panel.

Caution

It's important that you use memory modules designed for the Mac Pro, which come with a special heatsink to help the memory modules avoid overheating.

Upgrading your Mac Pro memory

The Mac Pro has eight memory module sockets, four each on two separate cards. You need to upgrade your memory two modules at a time, and use identical pairs of modules. The module sockets are numbered from DIMM1 to DIMM4, and you need to use up the module sockets in numeric order. For example, your Mac Pro probably already has two modules in the two DIMM1 sockets. In that case, if you're adding two more modules, you need to add them in the two DIMM2 sockets (see figure 9.22). 2007 Mac Pros use 667MHz modules (PC2-5300), while 2008 Mac Pros use 800MHz modules (PC2-6400). Check your System Profiler to learn what type of memory your Mac Pro uses.

Follow these steps to add two more memory modules to your Mac Pro:

1. **Turn off and unplug the Mac Pro, remove the side panel, as described earlier, and touch something metal to ground yourself.**

DIMM2 Sockets   Ejector tabs

9.22 The Mac Pro's memory module sockets are located on two separate riser cards.

Caution It's vital to discharge your body's pent-up static electricity by touching a metal object. Otherwise, the static electricity can discharge into your Mac and could damage one or more internal components.

2. **Place your index fingers in the two finger holes on one of the memory module cards (see figure 9.23) and then pull the card toward you to remove it from the motherboard.**

3. **Locate the memory socket you want to use.**

Fingerholes

9.23 Use the finger holes to pull out the memory riser card.

4. **If the memory socket's ejector tabs (shown in figure 9.22) are in the vertical position, open them by pivoting them away from the socket.**

5. **Orient the memory module over the memory socket so that the module's notch lines up with the socket's ridge.**

6. **Slide the memory module into the thin vertical channels on the ends of the socket.**

7. **Place your thumbs on the top edge of the module, one thumb on each side and press the module into the socket.** The ejector tabs automatically snap into the vertical position when the module is in completely.

8. **Slide the riser card back into the opening and gently press down until it snaps into place on the motherboard.**

9. **Repeat Steps 2 through 8 to install the second memory module in the same socket on the other riser card.**

Replacing a hard disk on the Mac Pro

If one of your Mac Pro hard disks dies, or if you want to upgrade to a larger hard disk, you can replace an existing hard disk by following these steps:

1. **Turn off and unplug the Mac Pro, remove the side panel, as described earlier, and touch something metal to ground yourself.**

2. **Locate the hard disk bay of the disk you want to replace.** Figure 9.24 shows the Mac Pro's four hard disk bays.

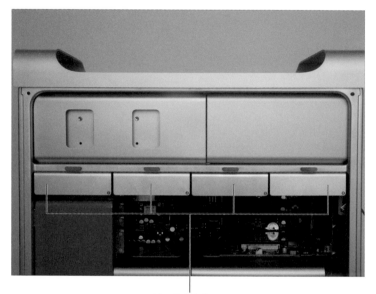

Hard disk bays

9.24 The Mac Pro's hard disk bays

3. **Pull out the hard disk bay bracket.** The hard disk is connected to the Mac Pro, so it takes a slight amount of force to unplug the hard disk.

4. **Remove the four screws from the bracket to release the hard disk.**

5. **Take your new hard disk and line up the four holes on the bottom of the disk with the four holes in the bracket.**

6. **Use the screws to attach the hard disk to the bracket.**

7. **Slide the bracket back into the bay (see figure 9.25) until the hard disk connectors snap into place.**

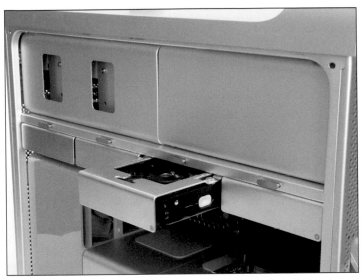

9.25 After you've attached the hard disk to the bracket, slide the bracket back into the bay.

Adding an extra hard disk to the Mac Pro

The Mac Pro can hold up to four SATA hard disks. If you need the extra storage, here's how to add another disk:

1. **Turn off and unplug the Mac Pro, remove the side panel, as described earlier, and touch something metal to ground yourself.**

2. **Pull out an empty hard disk bay bracket.**

3. **Remove the four screws from the bracket.**

4. **Line up the four holes on the bottom of the hard disk with the four holes in the bracket.**

5. **Use the screws to attach the hard disk to the bracket.**

6. **Slide the bracket back into the bay (see figure 9.25) until the hard disk connectors snap into place.**

Replacing your Mac Pro graphics card

If the Mac Pro has a weakness, it's the default video card, which is an ATI Radeon HD 2600 XT, with 256MB of graphics memory. This is a decent card, to be sure, but it's nowhere near the top-of-the-line. If you want the best possible graphics, then you need to get a first-rate video card, which means anything in the NVIDIA GeForce 8000 series, such as the GeForce 8800 GT or, if you don't want to spend a ton of money, the GeForce 8000 GTX. You should also get a minimum of 512MB of graphics memory.

After you have your new video card, follow these steps to replace the original card:

1. **Turn off and unplug the Mac Pro, remove the side panel, as described earlier, and touch something metal to ground yourself.**

2. **Remove the two screws that hold the slot bracket, as shown in figure 9.26, and then remove the bracket.**

Graphics card   Bracket screws

9.26 Remove the two screws that hold the slot bracket.

3. **Carefully remove the graphics card.** Here are some guidelines to follow:

   - Don't touch anything on the surface of the card; try to use the edges and empty spots on the card's surface.

   - To get the card started, it helps to push gently on the card's bracket, which is the part of the card that holds the video ports.

256

4. **Place the new graphics card so that its bracket is flush with the open slot cover, and slowly slide the card toward the slot.**

5. **When the card's connectors are touching the slot and are perfectly aligned with the slot opening, place your thumbs on the edge of the card and press the card gently but firmly into the slot.**

Genius

How do you know whether the card is completely inserted into the slot? The easiest way to tell is to look at the portion of the bracket that touches the case. If that portion isn't flush with the case, the card isn't fully inserted.

6. **Reattach the slot bracket.**

You can use these same steps to add a new expansion card to your Mac Pro. Locate an empty slot, remove its slot cover, and then insert the new card into the slot.

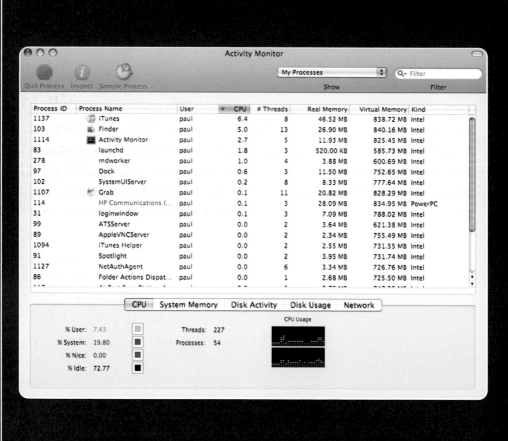

Somebody once proved mathematically that it was impossible to create a reasonably complex piece of software without introducing some bugs into the code. In other words, *all* software contains bugs, which means that all software at some time or another causes problems. Yes, even Mac software, which is by and large remarkably low on glitches, but is certainly not glitch-free. Fortunately, your Mac comes with all kinds of useful tools for investigating and resolving software problems. This chapter introduces you to some of those tools, and shows you how to solve a few specific software problems.

General Software Troubleshooting Techniques

One of the ongoing mysteries that all Mac users experience at one time or another is what might be called the "now-you-see-it-now-you-don't" problem. This gremlin plagues you for a while and then mysteriously vanishes without any intervention on your part. (It also tends not to occur when you ask a nearby user or someone from the IT department to look at it. Like the automotive problem that goes away when you take the car to a mechanic, computer problems often resolve themselves as soon as a knowledgeable user sits down at the keyboard.) When this happens, most people just shake their heads and resume working, grateful to no longer have to deal with the problem.

Tracking down the problem

Unfortunately, most computer ills don't just disappear. For more intractable problems, your first order of business is to track down the source of the glitch. There's no easy or set way to go about this, but it can be done if you take a systematic approach. Over the years, I've found that the best approach is to ask a series of questions designed to gather the required information and/or to narrow down what might be the culprit:

- **Did you get an error message?** Unfortunately, most computer error messages are obscure and do little to help you resolve a problem directly. However, error codes and error text can help you down the road, either by giving you something to search for in an online database or by providing information to a tech support person. Therefore, you should always write down the full text of any error message that appears.

Genius If the error message is lengthy and you can still use other programs on your Mac, don't bother writing down the full message. Instead, while the message is displayed, press Shift+⌘+3 to place an image of the current screen on the desktop.

- **Is there an error message in the Console?** If an error occurs behind the scenes, you don't see anything onscreen to tell you that something's amiss. However, there's a good chance that your Mac made a note of the error as a Console message. To check, open Finder and choose Applications ➪ Utilities ➪ Console. You should check both the Console log (choose File ➪ Open Console Log; see figure 10.1) and the system log (choose File ➪ Open ➪ System Log).

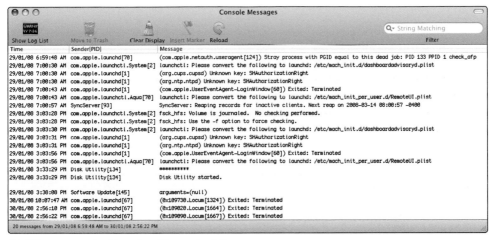

10.1 You can use the Console utility to check for error messages.

- **Did you recently change any application settings?** If so, try reversing the change to see whether doing so solves the problem. If that doesn't help, check the software developer's Web site to see whether an upgrade or patch is available. Otherwise, you could try uninstalling and then reinstalling the program.

- **Did you recently install a new program?** If you suspect a new program is causing system instability, restart your Mac and try operating the system for a while without using the new program. (If the program has any login items that load at startup, be sure to deactivate them, which you can learn about in Chapter 8.) If the problem doesn't reoccur, the new program is likely the culprit. Try using the program without any other programs running. You should also examine the program's readme file (if it has one) to look for known problems and possible workarounds. It's also a good idea to check for a version of the program that's compatible with your version of OS X. (For example, some new versions of Mac applications require Leopard — OS X 10.5 — or later.) Again, you can also try reinstalling the program. Similarly, if you recently upgraded an existing program, try uninstalling the upgrade.

Note

One common cause of program errors is having one or more program files corrupted because of hard disk errors. Before you reinstall a program, try repairing the Mac's hard disk, as described in Chapter 11.

- **Did you recently install a new device?** If you recently installed a new device or if you recently updated an existing device driver, the new device or driver might be causing the problem. Run through the general hardware troubleshooting techniques in Chapter 11.

⦿ **Did you recently install any updates?** It's an unfortunate fact of life that occasionally updates designed to fix one problem end up causing another problem. You can't uninstall a software update, so your only choice is to restore your Mac to a previous version, as described in Chapter 8.

⦿ **Did you recently change any System Preferences?** If the problem started after you changed your Mac's configuration, try reversing the change. Even something as seemingly innocent as activating a screensaver can cause problems, so don't rule anything out.

Performing basic troubleshooting steps

Figuring out the cause of a problem is often the hardest part of troubleshooting, but by itself it doesn't do you much good. When you know the source, you need to parlay that information into a fix for the problem. I discussed a few solutions in the previous section, but here are a few other general fixes you need to keep in mind:

⦿ **Close all programs.** You can often fix flaky behavior by shutting down all your open programs and starting again. This is a particularly useful fix for problems caused by low memory or low system resources.

⦿ **Log out.** Logging out clears the memory and so gives you a slightly cleaner slate than merely closing all your programs. Pull down the Apple menu and choose Log Out *User*, where *User* is your Mac username or press Shift+⌘+Q to logout quickly

⦿ **Restart your Mac.** If there are problems with some system files and devices, logging off won't help because these objects remain loaded. By restarting your Mac, you reload the entire system, which is often enough to solve many problems. I discuss various ways of restarting the Mac in Chapter 11.

Monitoring Your Mac to Look for Problems

If your Mac feels sluggish or an application is behaving erratically, what might the problem be? Perhaps the processor is busy with other tasks; perhaps your Mac is running low on memory; or perhaps there's a problem with the hard disk. It could be any of these things, but the only way to tell is to look under the hood, so to speak, and monitor these aspects of your Mac.

Your Mac's monitoring tools are useful troubleshooters, but they're also good for acquainting you with your Mac. Monitoring things such as the processor and memory usage regularly (not just when you have a problem) helps you get a feel for what's normal on your Mac, which then helps you better diagnose your Mac when you suspect a problem.

Monitoring CPU usage

The CPU (central processing unit or just processor) is the chip inside your Mac that acts as the computer's control and command center. Almost everything you do on your Mac and almost everything that happens within your Mac goes through the CPU. It is, in short, a pretty darned important component, and it pays to keep an eye on how much your Mac's CPU is being taxed by the system. If your Mac feels less responsive than usual, or if a program has become very slow, it could be because the CPU is running at or near full speed.

To see if that's the case, you can use Activity Monitor, which gives you a list of everything that's running on your Mac and tells you, among other things, what percentage of the CPU's resources are being used. Follow these steps to get started:

1. **Click Finder in the Dock.**

2. **Choose Applications ⇨ Utilities ⇨ Activity Monitor.**

3. **Click the CPU tab.**

Figure 10.2 shows the Activity Monitor window. The bulk of the window is taken up by a list of running programs, which Activity Monitor calls *processes*. A process is a running instance of an executable program. All the applications you have running are processes, of course, but so too are all the behind-the-scenes programs that your Mac and your applications require to function properly.

By default, Activity Monitor shows the processes that are associated with your user account: the applications you've launched, your user account's login items, and other programs that your Mac started when you logged in. However, this is by no means a complete list of the running processes. You can use the Show list to display a different set of processes. Here are the most important items in the Show list:

- **My Processes.** This displays the default list of processes, as shown in figure 10.2.

- **All Processes.** This displays a complete list of all the running processes.

- **Active Processes.** This displays just those processes that are currently or have recently used the CPU.

- **Inactive Processes.** This displays just those processes that are running but haven't used the CPU in a while.

- **Windowed Processes.** This displays just those processes associated with running programs that you can see in the Dock. (That is, the programs with open windows you can interact with.)

- **Selected Processes.** You can use this item to display specific processes. For example, if you want to watch certain processes, you'd choose them and then choose Selected Processes.

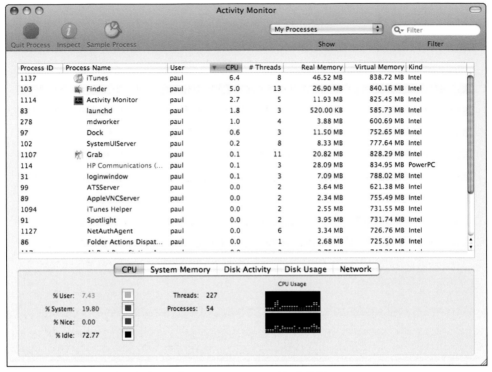

10.2 You can use Activity Monitor to keep an eye on your Mac's CPU usage.

Genius

The processes appear alphabetically by name, but you can change that order by clicking any column header. For example, to sort the processes by CPU usage, click the CPU column header. (This gives you an ascending sort; click the header again to get a descending sort.)

Whichever processes you display, the list itself is divided into a number of columns that give you information about the resources that each process is using. Here's a summary:

- **Process ID.** This column shows the process identifier, a unique numerical value that your Mac assigns to the process while it's running.

- **Process Name.** This is the name (usually the executable filename) of the process. You also see the icon for each windowed process.

- **User.** This value tells you the name of the user or service that launched the process.

- **CPU.** This is the key column for you in this section. The values here tell you the percentage of CPU resources that each process is using. If your system seems sluggish, look for a process that is consuming all or nearly all of the CPU's resources. Most programs will monopolize the CPU occasionally for short periods, but a program that is stuck at 100 (percent) for a long time most likely has some kind of problem. In that case, try shutting down the program or process, as described later in this chapter.

⦿ **Threads.** This value tells you the number of threads that each process is using. A *thread* is a program task that can run independently of and (usually) concurrently with other tasks in the same program (in which case the program is said to support *multithreading*). Multithreading improves program performance, but programs that have an unusually large number of threads can slow down the computer because it has to spend too much time switching from one thread of execution to another.

⦿ **Real Memory.** This value tells you approximately how much memory the process is using. This value is less useful because a process might genuinely require a lot of memory to operate. However, if this value is steadily increasing for a process that you're not using, it could indicate a problem, and you should shut down the process, as described later in this chapter.

Genius

You can control how often Activity Monitor refreshes its data. Choose View ⇨ Update Frequency, and then choose Very Often (Activity Monitor refreshes the data twice per second); Often (Activity Monitor refreshes the every second); Normally (Activity Monitor refreshes the data every two seconds; this is the default); or Less Often (Activity Monitor refreshes the data every five seconds).

⦿ **Virtual Memory.** This value shows the total amount of virtual memory that each process is using. Your computer can address memory beyond what is physically installed on the system. This nonphysical memory is called *virtual memory,* and it's implemented by using a piece of your hard disk that's set up to emulate physical memory. Again, seeing a steady increase in this value for a process that you're not using could be a sign of a problem, and you should shut down the process, as described later in this chapter.

⦿ **Kind.** This column shows you what type of CPU the process is programmed to run on: Intel or PowerPC.

⦿ **CPU Time.** Display this column by choosing View ⇨ Columns ⇨ CPU Time. It shows the total time, in days, hours, minutes, and seconds, that the process has used the CPU since the process was launched. If you see another process that seems to have used an inordinate amount of CPU time (for example, hours of CPU time when all other processes have used only minutes or seconds of CPU time), it could mean that the process is frozen or out of control and should be shut down, as described later in this chapter.

Changing Your Priorities

The priority of a process determines how much scheduling time the CPU gives to it: a higher priority process runs faster (because it gets more CPU time), and a lower priority process runs slower. By default, all processes are given the same priority. However, if you want to try changing a process priority (for example, to make the process run faster), choose Finder ⇨ Applications ⇨ Utilities ⇨ Terminal. In the Terminal window, type the following command: **sudo renice priority Process ID**.

Here, replace *priority* with a value between -20 (highest priority) and 20 (lowest priority); replace *Process ID* with the process identifier number of the process you want to work with. You need to enter an administrator's password for this to work.

The bottom part of the Activity Monitor window shows the CPU totals. For the percentage of CPU usage, you see separate percentages for User (processes running under your user account), System (processes that your Mac is using), Nice (processes that have had their priority changed), and Idle (the amount of resources available to the CPU, as a percentage of the total).

You want to monitor what percentage of the CPU is currently being used, but it's a hassle to always switch to Activity Monitor to check this. An easier way is to configure the Activity Monitor Dock icon as a graph that shows the current state of the CPU usage value. To do this, choose View ⇨ Dock Icon ⇨ Show CPU Usage. Figure 10.3 shows what it looks like.

Activity Monitor icon

10.3 You can configure the Activity Monitor Dock icon as a graph that shows the current CPU usage.

Monitoring memory usage

Memory is the lifeblood of any computer, and your Mac is no different. If your system runs low on memory, everything slows to a crawl, and programs may fail mysteriously. You can use Activity Monitor to examine how much real and virtual memory each running process is using. However, the total amount of memory being used is important, as well. To see that, you must click the System Memory tab in the Activity Monitor window, as shown in figure 10.4.

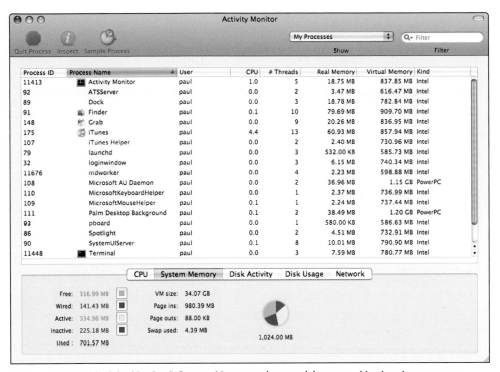

10.4 You can use Activity Monitor's System Memory tab to track how your Mac is using memory.

The pie chart shows how your Mac is currently allocating your computer's RAM, and the total amount of RAM available appears below the pie chart. These four types of RAM appear:

- **Free.** This is the number of megabytes that are currently available for processes. As this number gets lower, system performance slows because your Mac may reduce the memory used by each process. If this number (plus the Inactive number, described in this section) drops very low (a few megabytes), use the Activity Monitor to see if a process is using excessive amounts of memory. Otherwise, you may need to add RAM to your system, as described in Chapter 9.

- **Wired.** This is the number of megabytes that must stay in RAM and can't be stored on disk in virtual memory.

- **Active.** This is the number of megabytes that is currently being stored in RAM and is being used by processes.

- **Inactive.** This is the number of megabytes that is currently being stored in RAM and is no longer being used by processes. All of this data has also been paged out to virtual memory, so the RAM is available for another process to use.

267

Besides these four types of RAM, the System Memory tab also displays five other values:

- **Used.** This is the total number of megabytes of information currently being stored in RAM. It's the sum of the Wired, Active, and Inactive values.

- **VM size.** This is the size, in gigabytes, of the virtual memory cache on the hard disk.

- **Page ins.** This is the amount of data that the system has read in from virtual memory. If this number grows quite large, it means your Mac's performance is not what it could be because the system must retrieve data from the relatively slow hard disk. You need to either shut down some running programs or processes, or add RAM.

- **Page outs.** This is the amount of data that the system has had to write to the hard disk virtual memory to free up real memory. This value is likely 0 most of the time, but it's okay if it's not. However, if it starts to get large (hundreds of megabytes) in a short time, then it likely means that your system doesn't have enough real memory.

- **Swap used.** This is the size of the *swap file*, which is the area of virtual memory that your Mac is actually using. So even though the entire virtual memory cache may be 25 or 30GB, the swap file is (or should be) vastly smaller. It should actually be 0 most of the time, but it may grow to a few megabytes. If you see it grows to hundreds of megabytes over a short period, then your Mac likely doesn't have enough RAM.

Monitoring hard disk activity

Having enough RAM is crucial for system stability, but everything in RAM was originally stored on the hard disk. This means that it's nearly as important to monitor your hard disk activity. The crucial thing here is how often your system asks the hard disk to read data from the disk and write data to the disk:

- **Reading data from the hard disk.** Hard disks are extremely fast and they read data from the disk all the time. However, a hard disk is still relatively slow compared to RAM, so if the hard disk has to read data excessively, it slows down your system. Excessive disk reading is most often a sign that your hard disk is defragmented.

- **Writing data to the hard disk.** If your hard disk is writing data back to the disk excessively, it's usually a sign that your Mac doesn't have enough RAM.

Genius

Your Mac's files don't easily get defragmented (that is, broken into smaller chunks and spread around the hard disk). This is probably why your Mac doesn't come with a disk optimization utility to fix defragmentation. Defragmenting can happen, however, so to fix it you need a program such as iDefrag from Coriolis Systems (www.coriolis-systems.com), which costs $34.95, but there's a demo version that will defrag up to 100MB.

So if you quite often get the spinning wait cursor (the rainbow-colored spinning cursor that appears when the system is taking its sweet time to complete some task), excessive disk reads and writes could be the culprit. To check, run Activity Monitor (in Finder, choose Applications ⇨ Utilities ⇨ Activity Monitor) and then click the Disk Activity tab, shown in figure 10.5.

Note

Spinning wait cursor is Apple's yawn-inducing name for the dreaded "busy" icon. Much more fun names for it are *spinning pizza* and, my favorite, *spinning beach ball of death* (SBOD).

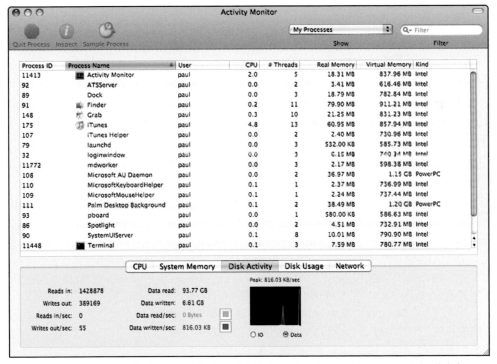

10.5 You can use Activity Monitor's Disk Activity tab to track how frequently your Mac's hard disk is reading and writing data.

There's lots of data here, but you only need to monitor two values:

- **Reads in.** This tells you the number of times per second the hard disk is reading data.
- **Writes out.** This tells you the number of times per second the hard disk is writing data.

These values should be 0 most of the time, but do jump up occasionally when you use your Mac. If you see these numbers jump up and stay up for an extended period, then you know you have a problem.

269

More Troubleshooting Techniques to Try

Computer troubleshooting is most often a question of trial and error: you try one thing to fix the problem, and if that doesn't work you try another. With that spirit in mind, the next few sections take you through a few more general troubleshooting techniques to add to your arsenal.

Checking for software updates

When Apple or a third-party software developer prepares an update to a program, they often include new features, support for new technologies, performance boosts, and security enhancements. However, the vast majority of items in a software update are fixes that squash bugs, provide more stability, and make the program more compatible with existing hardware.

In other words, if you're having consistent trouble with a program, chances are that other people have been having the same problem, the software developer knows about the problem, and they've taken steps to fix it. This means that installing the most recent update for the application can be the cure you've been seeking.

You have two ways to check for software updates:

- **For Apple software.** Pull down the Apple menu and choose Software Update.

- **For other software developers.** Go to the company's Web site. First find your program's product page and check out the latest version number. If it's later than the version you have, see if you're eligible for a free (or at least cheap) upgrade. Otherwise, go to the site's support pages and look around to see if a patch or other update is available for your application.

Genius

To find out what version of a program you have, start the program and then choose *Program* ➪ About *Program* (where *Program* is the name of the application). The dialog box that appears tells you the version number.

Bypassing your login items

It's always possible that flaky system behavior could be caused by one of your login items. To find out, it's possible to log in without loading any of your login items (this is called a *Safe Login*). If the problem goes away, then you're a step closer to locating the culprit.

First, follow these steps to log in without your login items:

1. **Pull down the Apple menu and choose Log Out *User*, where *User* is your username.** You can also press Shift+⌘+Q. Your Mac asks if you're sure.

2. **Click Log Out.** Your Mac logs you out and displays the login screen.

3. **Choose your user account (if necessary) and type your password.**

4. **Hold down the Shift key and then click Log In.** Your Mac logs you in without loading any of your login items.

5. **When you see the Desktop, release the Shift key.**

If the problem goes away, then you can be fairly certain that a login item is the cause. From here, disable the login items one at a time (as described in Chapter 8) until you find the one that's the source of your woes.

Deleting a program's preferences file

A *preferences file* is a document that stores options and other data that you've entered using the application's Preferences command. One of the most common causes of application flakiness is a preferences file that's somehow become damaged or corrupted (for example, its data is written with the wrong syntax). In that case, you can solve the problem by deleting (or moving) the preferences file so that the application has to rebuild it. On the downside, this may mean that you have to re-enter some preferences, but that's usually a fairly small price to pay for a stable application.

Preferences files use the .plist filename extension. In most cases, the filename uses the following general format: com.*company.application*.plist.

Here, *company* is the name of the software company that makes the application, and *application* is the name of the program. Here are some examples:

com.apple.iTunes.plist

com.microsoft.Word.plist

com.palm.HotSync.plist

Follow these steps to delete an application's preferences file.

1. **Quit the application if it's currently running.**

2. **In Finder, choose your username and then choose Library ⇨ Preferences.**

3. **Locate the application's preferences file.** If you can't find the preferences file, choose Macintosh HD ⇨ Library ⇨ Preferences and see if it appears in that folder.

Unfortunately, not every preferences file uses the com.*company.application*.plist format. If you can't find the preferences file you're looking for, type either the company name or the program name in the Search box.

4. **Click and drag the preferences file and drop it in another location.** The Desktop is probably the best spot for this. Note that if the application has multiple preferences files, you should move all of them to the new location.

5. **Run the application and see if the problem persists.**

   - **Problem resolved.** The preferences file was the source after all, so go ahead and move it to the Trash from the location you chose in Step 4. You need to re-enter your preferences.

   - **Problem remains.** The preferences file wasn't the culprit after all. Quit the application and move the preferences file back to the Preferences folder from the location you chose in Step 4.

Reinstalling Mac OS X

If worse comes to worst and your Mac won't start or if it's just completely unstable, then you need to bite the bullet and reinstall the operating system. As you see in the following steps, it's possible to have your data and settings transferred to the new installation using the Archive and Install option. However, if you still have access to the system, it's a good idea to make backups of your documents, just in case something goes wrong during the transfer. With that done, follow these steps to reinstall OS X:

1. **Insert your Mac OS X installation DVD.** The Mac OS X Install DVD window appears, as shown in figure 10.6.

2. **Double-click Install Mac OS X.** The Install DVD tells you that your Mac needs to restart, as shown in figure 10.7.

Genius If you have a small hard disk, then it may not have enough room for the reinstallation because the Archive and Install option moves all the old OS X System files to a separate folder called Previous System. In that case, the only way to reinstall OS X is to erase your hard disk and start from scratch (this is called the Erase and Install option). This means that if you don't back up your data, you lose it forever.

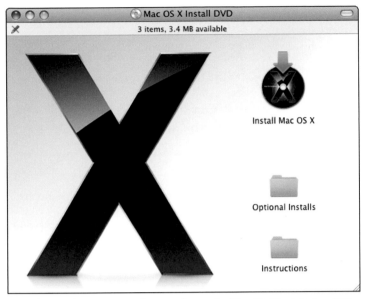

10.6 This window appears when you insert the Mac OS X installation DVD.

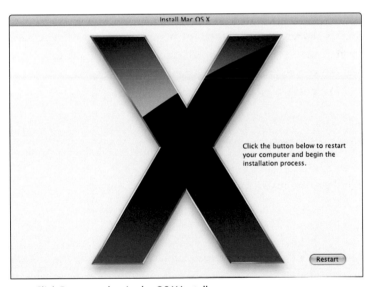

10.7 Click Restart to begin the OS X install.

273

3. **Click Restart.** Your Mac prompts you for an administrator username and password.

4. **Enter your administrator credentials and click OK.** Your Mac restarts and boots to the Mac OS X Install DVD.

5. **Select a language for the install.** The Install Mac OS X application appears.

6. **Click Continue.** The license agreement appears.

7. **Click Agree.** The Select a Destination window appears.

8. **Click Options.** This opens the dialog box that contains the installation options.

9. **Select the Archive and Install option and select the Preserve Users and Network Settings check box, the click OK.** Remember that if your hard disk doesn't have enough room for Archive and Install, you must select the Erase and Install option instead.

10. **Click the hard disk to which you want to install Mac OS X.**

11. **Click Continue.** The program begins installing Mac OS X.

Caution

The OS X installation program won't run unless your Mac has a mouse that's physically connected to the computer. The Apple Bluetooth mouse or some other wireless mouse won't work.

Mac Software Problems (and Their Solutions)

You've seen quite a few general solutions to software woes so far, but many problems require specific solutions. To that end, in the rest of this chapter, I take you through the solutions to some of the most common Mac software glitches.

You can't change some options in System Preferences

When you open System Preferences and click an icon, you may find that some or all of the controls in the resulting preferences window are disabled. This actually isn't a glitch or a bug at all. Instead, it's a security feature designed to prevent unauthorized users from making changes to sensitive system settings. (It's also designed to prevent you from making certain changes without at least having to think about them first.) For example, figure 10.8 shows what the Parental Controls preferences look like when a user without authorization displays the window.

To enable the controls, click the lock icon in the bottom-left corner of the window and then, if prompted, enter the username and password of an administrator account.

10.8 The Mac sometimes locks preferences to avoid unauthorized changes.

A program is stuck

When you're working away in a program, you may suddenly find that it's unresponsive and you're faced with the dreaded spinning wait cursor that just won't stop or go away. It's possible that your program is stuck, but that's not guaranteed.

- **The program could just be** *really* **busy.** Sometimes program operations take an inordinately long time. Recalculating a large spreadsheet, compiling a program, or rendering a 3-D object can takes minutes. Therefore, your first resort should be to wait for a while to see if the program works itself out of its trance.

- **Your Mac may be low on memory.** This can cause a program to seem stuck, when in fact it's really just trying to struggle through on limited resources. Try shutting down some of your other programs to free up some RAM.

If none of this works, then you have no choice but to force the program to quit. Here are the steps to follow:

1. **Pull down the Apple menu and choose Force Quit.** You can also press Option+⌘+Esc. You see the Force Quit Applications window shown in figure 10.9.

2. **Click the recalcitrant application.**

3. **Click Force Quit.** Your Mac asks if you're sure you want to do this.

4. **Click Force Quit.**

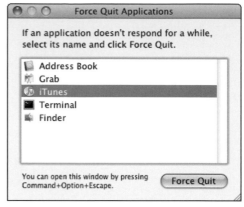

10.9 Use the Force Quit Applications window to shut down a misbehaving application.

Note

If the stubborn application *still* won't quit, try running the Force Quit command again. The second time is often the charm when forcing rogue applications to shut down. No go? Okay, now try quitting the application's process, as described in the next section. If the program remains running, shut down the rest of your applications and then restart your Mac.

A process is stuck

What happens if the Dock locks up or a Spotlight search hangs? In these cases, if you try the Force Quit command, you are out of luck because processes such as the Dock and Spotlight don't show up in the Force Quit Applications window.

However, they *do* show up in the Activity Monitor. You can use Activity Monitor to force these and any other stuck processes to quit. Here are the steps to follow:

1. **Click Finder in the Dock.**

2. **Choose Applications ⇨ Utilities ⇨ Activity Monitor.**

3. **Choose the process that you want to quit,** as shown in figure 10.10.

4. **Click Quit Process.** Activity Monitor asks you to confirm.

5. **Click Force Quit.**

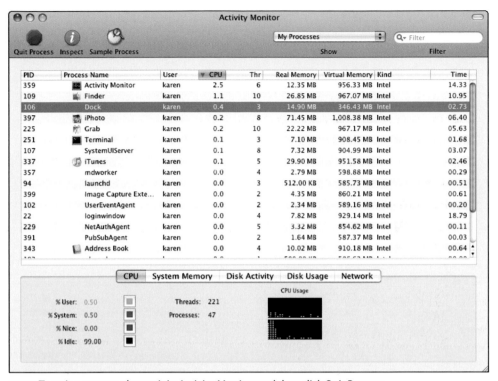

10.10 To quit a process, choose it in Activity Monitor and then click Quit Process.

Caution Processes used by the system itself usually appear as Root in the user column. These processes are critical to the functioning of your Mac, so don't quit any of them or you might lock up your machine.

A program crashes

One of the more frustrating Mac experiences is to be merrily working away in an application when, out of the blue, the program simply disappears from the screen. Apple says that the application "quit unexpectedly," but the rest of us call this a good old-fashioned program crash.

When an application crashes, you usually see a dialog box like the one shown in figure 10.11. Click Reopen to get your Mac to restart the application for you. In most cases, the program picks itself up, dusts itself off, and resumes working as though nothing bad had happened.

10.11 This dialog box appears when an application goes up in flames.

However, you may find that the program goes down for the count yet again. In this case, you see the dialog box shown in figure 10.12. Click Try Again.

At this point in the proceedings, your Mac is assuming that a corrupt preferences file is causing the problem. So when you click Try Again, your Mac does three things:

10.12 This dialog box appears when an application crashes a second time.

- **It creates a copy of the application's existing preferences file.** This copy has the same name as the original, with .saved tacked onto the end.

- **It deletes the application's existing preferences file.**

- **It restarts the application.** The application sees that new preferences file exists, so it creates a new, default preferences file.

This procedure is called *Safe Relaunch*. If your application runs without mishap now, then the preferences file was the troublemaker all along. Go ahead and enter your preferences again. When you exit the application, your Mac displays the dialog box shown in figure 10.13. Be sure to click Use new settings to save your new preferences file.

10.13 This dialog box appears when you shut down an application that started earlier with Safe Relaunch.

If the preferences file isn't the problem (that is, the application keeps crashing even after a Safe Relaunch), then use the following troubleshooting steps, in this order:

Genius

Before you get too involved in troubleshooting a program crash, consider a simpler explanation: Does the crash always occur when you're working with a particular file? If so, then there's an excellent chance that the problem lies not with the application itself, but with the file. If the file contains important data and you can work with the file for a time before the crash occurs, copy the data and paste it into a new file. Then trash the old file.

1. **Restart your Mac.**

2. **Install an update for the software, if one is available.**

3. **If it's a third-party application, reinstall the application.**

A program won't start

Occasionally you'll try to start a program and nothing happens. If you clicked a Dock icon to launch the application, all you see is the icon endlessly (and, eventually, maddeningly) bouncing up and down. This happened to me once when I tried to launch iWeb on a *brand new iMac*!

If this happens, try the following fixes, in this order:

1. **Restart your Mac.**

2. **Install an update for the software, if one is available.** (This solved my iWeb problem.)

3. **Delete the application's preferences file.** How to delete the preferences file is explained earlier in the chapter.

4. **If it's a third-party application, reinstall the application.**

You can't empty the Trash

When you attempt to empty the Trash, you may receive an error message such as the one shown in figure 10.14. To solve this problem, do what the dialog box says: Hold down the Option key while you choose the Empty Trash command.

10.14 You might see this dialog box when you try to empty the Trash.

Your Mac may also tell you that you don't have permission to delete a file. In this case, you need to follow these steps to solve the problem:

1. **In Finder, choose Applications ⇨ Utilities ⇨ Terminal.**

2. **Type** cd ~/.Trash **and press Return.**

3. **Type** sudo rm –rf **and then add a space at the end of the command, but** *don't* **press Return just yet.**

4. **Ctrl+click or right-click the Trash icon and then click Open.**

5. **Choose Edit ⇨ Select All.** You can also press ⌘+A.

6. **Click and drag the selected Trash files and drop them inside the Terminal window.**

7. **Return to the Terminal window and press Return.** Terminal prompts you for an administrator password.

8. **Type your password (it doesn't appear onscreen) and then press Return.** Terminal deletes all the files from the Trash.

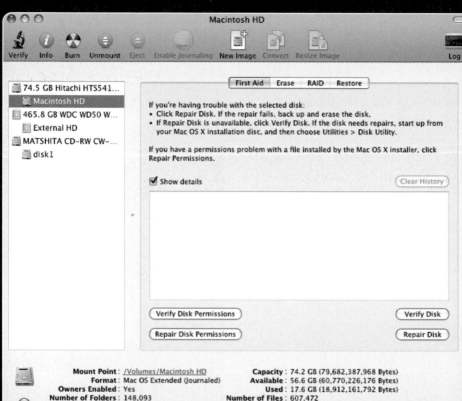

The good news about Mac problems — whether they're the software problems covered in Chapter 10 or the hardware problems covered in this chapter — is that they're relatively rare. The reason for such rarity is a simple one: application developers and device manufacturers only have to build their Mac products for machines made by a single company. This really simplifies things, and results in fewer problems. Not, however, *no* problems. As with programs, even in a Mac world, devices sometimes behave strangely or not at all. In this chapter, I give you some general troubleshooting techniques for hardware woes and also tackle a few specific problems.

Before the Fall: Preparing for Trouble

If, as the old saying has it, an ounce of prevention really is worth a pound of cure, then I suggest that your general state of mind when working with your Mac be what I call *ounce-of-prevention mode*. This means that you should assume that at some point your Mac will have a serious problem and so you should be prepared to handle it. Performing regular backups, as I discuss in Chapter 8, is a great start, but I also believe Mac users need to do two other things: create a user account with default settings and create a secondary boot device.

Creating a secondary user account

Your Mac lets you define multiple accounts, but if you're the sole user of the computer, then you don't need another account, right? True, but having a secondary account around is actually a useful troubleshooting device, as long as you don't customize, tweak, or in any way hack your Mac using that account. The idea is that you want the other user account to be pure in the sense that it uses only the default settings. That way, if your Mac starts acting up, you can log in to the secondary account and see if the problem persists. If it doesn't, then you know the problem is almost certainly related to any user-specific settings you applied in your main account.

Here are the steps to follow to set up a secondary user account on your Mac:

1. **Click System Preferences in the Dock.** The System Preferences window appears.
2. **Click the Accounts icon.**
3. **Click the lock icon, enter your Mac's administrator credentials, and then click OK.**
4. **In the New Account list, choose Administrator.**
5. **Use the Name text box to enter the account name.** For example, enter your full name.

Caution

Because you're creating an all-powerful administrator account, it's really important that you give this account a secure password. The password should be at least eight characters long with a mix of uppercase and lowercase letters, numbers, and symbols. Click the key icon beside the Password text box to check the strength of your password (a good password turns the Quality bar all green in the Quality bar).

6. **Use the Short Name text box to enter a short version of the account name.** For example, enter your first name (or some variation if you're already using your first name for your main account).

7. **Use the Password and Verify text boxes to type a secure password for the account.** Figure 11.1 shows the dialog box filled in so far.

8. **Use the password Hint text box to type a hint about your password, just in case you forget it.**

9. **Click Create Account.**

10. **Click the lock icon to prevent changes.**

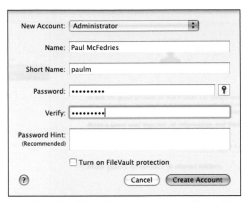

11.1 Use this dialog box to set up your Mac with a secondary administrator account for troubleshooting.

Creating a secondary boot device

If you want to paint the exterior of your house or wash the outside windows, you can't do either job from inside your house. This is analogous to performing certain troubleshooting tasks with your Mac, such a repairing the hard disk (described later in this chapter). You can't fix the disk while it's being used by the Mac operating system. Instead, you have to "step outside" of the Mac hard disk to repair it. How do you do that? By creating a secondary boot device that you can boot to instead of the internal Mac hard disk.

There are a number of ways to do this, but the following are the most common:

- **Your Mac OS X Install DVD.** This is the easiest option given you don't have to create anything, but it's also the slowest.

- **Another Mac connected by a FireWire cable.** You can start the other Mac in FireWire target disk mode, as described later in this chapter, and then boot to that Mac.

- **A second internal hard disk.** This is a suitable route if you have a Mac Pro, which can accommodate more than one hard disk.

- **An external FireWire or USB hard disk.** This is probably the best way to go if you have a Mac that can't take a second internal hard disk.

For the latter two options, you need to insert your Mac OS X Install DVD and install Mac OS X to the other drive. If you're going the external drive route, however, you need to set up the drive with a bootable partition. First, follow these steps to see if the drive is already bootable:

1. **Connect the external drive, if you haven't done so already.**

2. **In Finder, choose Applications ⇨ Utilities ⇨ Disk Utility.** The Disk Utility window opens.

3. **Click the external hard disk.**

4. **Click Partition.** You see a window similar to the one shown in figure 11.2.

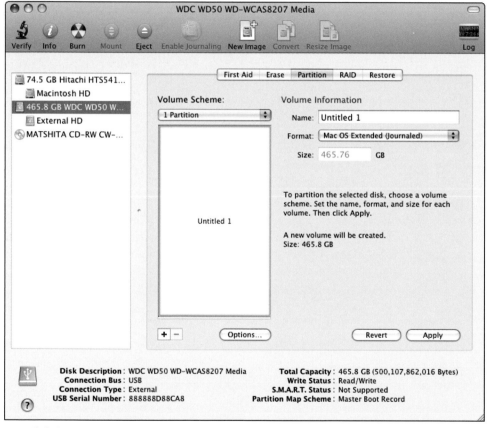

11.2 Click the external drive and then click Partition to check the drive's bootable status.

Examine the Partition Map Scheme value in the bottom-right corner of the window. There are three main possibilities:

● **GUID Partition Map.** This value tells you the drive is bootable only on an Intel-based Mac.

- **Apple Partition Map.** This value tells you the drive is bootable on a PowerPC-based Mac or as a non-boot drive on an Intel-based Mac.

- **Master Boot Record.** This value tells you the drive is bootable on a Windows-based PC.

If you see Master Boot Record or some other value not in the previous list, then you need to repartition the drive to make it bootable on your Mac. Here are the steps to follow:

Caution

Repartitioning erases all the data on the drive. So if you have any important stuff on the drive, copy it to a safe location before proceeding.

1. **In the Volume Scheme list, choose 1 Partition.**

2. **Use the Name text box to specify a name for the partition.**

3. **Click Options.** The dialog box shown in figure 11.3 appears.

4. **Select the partition scheme option you want to use.** For an Intel-based Mac, select GUID Partition Table; for a PowerPC-based Mac, select Apple Partition Map.

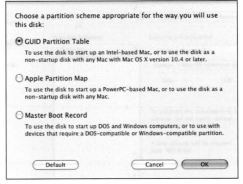

11.3 Select the partition scheme you want to use.

5. **Click OK.**

6. **Click Apply.** Disk Utility warns you that this will erase all the data on the disk.

7. **Click Partition.** Disk Utility partitions and then formats the drive. When Disk Utility is done, it remounts the drive, so you might see a prompt from Time Machine asking if you want to use the drive for backups.

8. **Click Cancel.**

If you're using either an external hard disk or a second internal hard disk as your secondary boot device, you now need to follow the steps in Chapter 10 for installing Mac OS X. In this case, however, instead of reinstalling Mac OS X on your main hard disk, you are installing a second copy on your secondary boot device. That is, when you get to the Select a Destination window, click the external or second internal hard disk and then continue the installation.

General Hardware Troubleshooting Techniques

If you're having trouble with a device attached to your Mac, the good news is that a fair chunk of hardware problems have a relatively limited set of causes, so you may be able to get the device back on its feet by attempting a few tried-and-true remedies that work quite often for many devices. The next few sections take you through these generic troubleshooting techniques.

Basic checklist

If it's not immediately obvious what the problem is, then your Mac hardware troubleshooting routine should always start with these very basic techniques:

- **Check connections, power switches, and so on.** Some of the most common (and some of the most embarrassing) causes of hardware problems are the simple physical things: making sure that a device is turned on; checking that cable connections are secure; and ensuring that insertable devices (such as a USB device) are properly inserted. For example, if you can't access the Internet or your network, make sure your network's router is turned on, and make sure that the network cable between your Mac and your router is properly connected.

- **Replace the batteries.** Wireless devices such as keyboards and mice really chew through batteries, so if either one is working intermittently or not at all, always try replacing the batteries to see if that solves the problem.

- **Turn the device off and then on again.** You *power cycle* a device by turning it off, waiting a few seconds for its innards to stop spinning, and then turning it back on again. You'd be amazed how often this simple procedure can get a device back up and running. Of course, not all devices have an on/off switch, but this technique works very well for devices such as external displays, printers, scanners, routers, switches, modems, external hard disks and optical drives, many USB and FireWire devices, and some wireless devices such as mice and keyboards. Many wireless mice have a reset button on the bottom, while some keyboards — notably the Apple Bluetooth keyboard — have an on/off switch. USB and FireWire devices often get their power directly from the USB or FireWire port. Power cycle these devices by unplugging them and then plugging them back in.

Genius

If you're getting a network error or you can't access the Internet, the router may be at fault. Power off the router and then power it on again. Wait until the status lights stabilize and then try accessing the network. If you still can't access the Internet, try the same thing with your modem.

- **Close all programs.** If you have lots of programs going, device drivers (the little programs that enable Mac OS X to communicate with devices, and vice versa) may get weird because there isn't enough memory or other resources. You can often fix flaky behavior by shutting down all your open programs and starting again.

- **Log out.** Logging off serves to clear the memory by shutting down your programs, but it also releases much of the stuff your Mac has loaded into memory, thus creating a slightly cleaner palette than just closing your programs. To log out, pull down the Apple menu and choose Log Out *User*, where *User* is your Mac username or just press Shift +⌘+Q.

- **Reset the device's default settings.** If you can configure a device, then perhaps some new setting is causing the problem. If you recently made a change, try returning the setting back to its original value. If that doesn't do the trick, most configurable devices have some kind of "Restore Default Settings" option that enables you to quickly return the device to its factory settings.

- **Upgrade the device's firmware.** Some devices come with *firmware*, a small program that runs inside the device and controls its internal functions. For example, all routers have firmware. Check with the manufacturer to see if a new version exists. If it does, download the new version and then see the device's manual to learn how to upgrade the firmware.

Restarting your Mac

If a hardware device is having a problem with some system files, logging off your Mac won't help because the system files remain loaded. By rebooting the system, you reload the entire system, which is often enough to solve many computer problems. You reboot your Mac by pulling down the Apple menu and choosing Restart.

Power cycling your Mac

For problem devices that don't have a power switch — basically, anything inside your Mac, including the display on your iMac or Mac notebook — restarting your Mac might not resolve the problem because the devices remain powered up the whole time. You can power cycle these devices as a group by power cycling the Mac:

1. **Close all running applications.**
2. **Pull down the Apple menu and choose Shut Down.** Your Mac asks you to confirm.
3. **Click Shut Down.**
4. **Wait for 30 seconds to give all devices time to spin down.**
5. **Turn the Mac back on.**

Forcing the issue: Making a stuck Mac restart or shut down

If things go seriously awry on your Mac, you may find that you can't do *anything*: your applications are frozen. You can bang away at the keyboard all you want but nothing happens; the mouse pointer doesn't even budge when you move the mouse. That's a major league lock-up you've got there, and your only recourse is to force you Mac to restart or shut down.

- **Forcing your Mac to restart.** Hold down the Ctrl and ⌘ keys and then press the power button.

- **Forcing your Mac to shut down.** Press and hold the power button until the Mac shuts off.

Every once in a great while, you can't even force your Mac to restart or shut down. Meaning you attempt the techniques in this section, your Mac's screen goes black, but it never really shuts down. When that happens, and you have an iMac, Mac mini, Mac Pro, or other desktop Mac that doesn't have an internal battery, your only option is to yank out the power cable.

Caution

As you might expect, forcing your Mac to restart or shut down doesn't give you any graceful way to close your running applications. This means that if you have unsaved changes in any open documents, you lose those changes. Therefore, it's a good idea to make sure your Mac is frozen and not just in a temporary state of suspended animation while it's waiting for some lengthy process to finish. If you're not sure, wait five minutes before forcing the restart or shutdown.

Restarting your Mac in Safe Mode

Login items — programs that run automatically when you log in to your Mac — can cause system problems by using up resources and creating memory conflicts. However, they're not the only behind-the-scenes components that can make your system wonky. Other processes used by your Mac and by your applications can run amok and cause trouble. To see whether such a process is at the root of your problem, you can perform a Safe Boot: starting your Mac in Safe Mode, which means that it doesn't load most of those behind-the-scenes components. If the problem still persists even in Safe Mode, then you know it's not caused by a hidden process. If the problem does go away, it's a bit harder to deal with because there's no way to disable individual components. So, you may need to reinstall Mac OS X.

Follow these steps to perform a Safe Boot:

1. **Pull down the Apple menu and choose Shut Down.** Your Mac asks if you're sure.

2. **Click Shut Down.** Your Mac logs you out and then shuts off.

3. **Press the power button to turn your Mac back on.**

4. **Hold down the Shift key until you see the Apple logo.** Your Mac loads with only a minimal set of components. When you get to the login screen, you see the words Safe Boot.

5. **Log in to your Mac.** Check to see if the problem is still present. If it is, then continue with the troubleshooting techniques in the following sections.

Note

Although you might think it would take your Mac less time to load without all those extra components, the opposite is actually the case: your Mac takes quite a bit longer to start up in Safe Mode. If you want to know why, see the following page: http://docs.info.apple.com/article.html?artnum=107392.

Starting your Mac using a secondary boot device

You can use a secondary boot device to boot your Mac when you need to troubleshoot or repair your main Mac hard disk. How you boot to this device depends on the device you're using:

- **Another Mac connected by a FireWire cable.** Connect the cable, restart the good Mac (that is, not the Mac that you want to troubleshoot or repair), and hold down T until you see the FireWire icon. That Mac is now in *FireWire target disk mode*. Restart the Mac that you want to troubleshoot and hold down Option until you see the Apple icon. This invokes the Startup Manager, which displays icons for the hard disks of both Macs. Double-click the icon for the other Mac (the icon has the FireWire logo on it) to boot to that Mac. When the other Mac's desktop appears, you see an icon for the hard disk of the Mac you want to troubleshoot.

Genius

Another way to restart the other Mac in target disk mode is to click System Preferences in the Dock, click the Startup Disk icon, and then click Target Disk Mode.

- **Your Mac OS X Install DVD.** Insert the DVD, restart your Mac, and hold down C until you see the Apple icon.

- **A second internal hard disk or an external FireWire or USB hard disk.** Connect the external drive (if necessary), restart your Mac, and hold down Option until you see the Apple icon. When the Startup Manager appears, double-click the icon for the secondary hard disk.

Note

To exit target disk mode, shut down the Mac you're troubleshooting, then turn off the Mac that's in target disk mode.

Running the Apple Hardware Test

If your Mac is running erratically, is locking up at random times, or is causing your applications to behave strangely, there are a number of things that could be wrong with the computer's memory, hard disk, processor, or some other internal component. To help you see whether faulty hardware is the source of these ills (and not wonky software), you can run the Apple Hardware Test. This program performs a thorough check of your system's innards to see if anything's amiss. If it finds a problem, it lets you know what component is acting up and it gives you an error code. However, Apple Hardware Test doesn't fix the problem. Instead, you're supposed to provide the error code to someone who knows what they're doing, and they ought to have enough information to fix the error.

On most Macs, the Apple Hardware Test isn't installed on the Mac. Instead, it's a separate program that resides on the Mac OS X Install Disc 1 that comes with each new Mac. (It's the gray disc.) You can't copy it to your Mac or run it directly from the disc. Instead, you need to reboot your Mac with the disc inserted. Follow these steps:

1. **Insert Mac OS X Install Disc 1 into your Mac.**
2. **Pull down the Apple menu and choose Restart.**
3. **When the Mac restarts, hold down D.** You see the Apple Hardware Test window.
4. **Click the language you prefer to use and then press Return.** The Apple Hardware Test opens.
5. **Select the Perform extended testing check box.**

Note

Performing the extended tests could take between one and two hours, so only run this test when you won't need your Mac for a while. You might be tempted to run just the regular tests, which take only a couple of minutes. However, if you're having problems, the extended test is better because it delves much more deeply into your hardware.

6. **Click Test or press T.** Apple Hardware Test begins testing your Mac. If Apple Hardware Test detects a problem, information about the problem appears in the Test Results area.

7. **Make a note of any problems found, particularly any error codes related to each issue.**

8. **Click Restart.**

Repairing the hard disk

If your Mac won't start, or if an application freezes, then it's possible that an error on the main hard disk is causing the problem. To see if this is the case, you need to repair the hard disk using your Mac's Disk Utility program. How are you supposed to do that if you can't even start your Mac? Good question! The answer is that you need to start your Mac using a secondary boot device (which is explained earlier in the chapter). You then run Disk Utility from that device, and that enables you to repair your main hard disk. Note, too, that even if you can start your Mac, you still need to boot to the secondary device because you can't repair the main hard disk while it's being used by your Mac.

Follow these steps to repair your hard disk:

1. **Restart your Mac using a secondary boot device.**

2. **Launch the Disk Utility.**

   - If you booted to an internal or external hard disk, or to a Mac in target disk mode, open Finder and choose Applications ➪ Utilities ➪ Disk Utility.

   - If you booted to your Mac OS X Install DVD, when you get to the Mac OS X Installer screen, choose Utilities ➪ Disk Utility.

3. **Choose the hard disk you want to repair.**

4. **Make sure the First Aid tab is selected, as shown in figure 11.4.**

5. **Click Repair Disk.** Disk Utility verifies that the disk is sound and fixes any problems that it finds.

Genius

Ideally, Disk Utility reports that "The volume Macintosh HD appears to be OK." In the worst-case scenario, Disk Utility reports that it found errors, but it can't fix them. In that case, you need to turn to a more heavy-duty solution: a third-party disk repair application. I recommend these two: DiskWarrior (www.alsoft.com) and TechTool Pro (www.micromat.com).

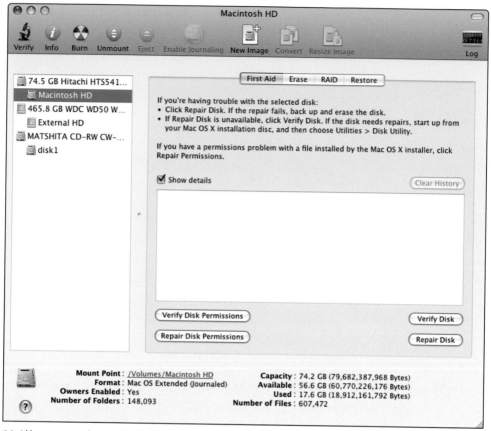

11.4 You can repair your Mac's hard disk by running Disk Utility from a secondary boot device.

Repairing disk permissions

All the files on your Mac have *permissions* applied to them. Permissions are a collection of settings that determine what users or groups of users can do with each file. For example, if a file implements read-only permissions, it means that all users can only read the contents of the file and can't make any changes to the file or delete it. For things like system files, particular permissions are set during installation and shouldn't ever be changed. If a system file's permissions *do* happen to change, it can cause all kinds of problems, including program lock-ups and flaky system behavior.

Fortunately, your Mac's Disk Utility has a feature that enables you to repair permissions for many of the files on your system. Here's how it works:

1. **If you can't start your Mac, boot using a secondary device.** Otherwise, boot your Mac normally.

2. **Launch the Disk Utility.**

- If you booted to an internal or external hard disk, or to a Mac in target disk mode, open Finder and choose Applications ⇨ Utilities ⇨ Disk Utility.

- If you booted to your Mac OS X Install DVD, when you get to the Mac OS X Installer screen, choose Utilities ⇨ Disk Utility.

3. **Choose the hard disk with the permissions you want to repair.**

4. **Make sure the First Aid tab is selected.**

5. **Click Repair Disk Permissions.** Disk Utility repairs the permissions.

Mac Hardware Problems (and Their Solutions)

The generic troubleshooting and repair techniques covered so far can solve all kinds of problems. However, there are always specific problems that require specific solutions. The rest of this chapter takes you through a few of the most common ones.

Your Mac won't start

Few problems are as frustrating as a Mac that can't get on its feet. Here are some ideas for troubleshooting this most vexing problem:

- **Check your connections.** If your Mac won't even turn on, make sure the power cord is properly connected at both ends. Also, if the power cord is plugged into a power bar or surge protector, make sure that device is turned on.

- **Unplug the Mac.** If the Mac freezes during startup, unplug the power cord, wait a few seconds, plug the cord back in, and then try starting the Mac.

- **Remove all non-essential devices.** Disconnect everything from your Mac except the keyboard and mouse. Ideally, replace a third-party mouse and keyboard with the original Apple devices. If your Mac starts successfully, one of the disconnected devices is likely the culprit. Reconnect the devices one at a time, restarting each time you connect another device. If after connecting one of the devices your Mac refuses to start, then that last device is the problem.

- **Run the Apple Hardware Test.** A non-starting Mac could be plagued by a memory problem or some other internal glitch, so running the Apple Hardware Test as described earlier in this chapter lets you know.

- **Try a Safe Mode boot and then restart.** One of the things a Safe Mode boot does is delete the cache that your Mac uses for storing fonts to improve performance. If that cache gets corrupted, it could cause startup headaches, so trashing the cache might do the trick.

- **Repair the hard disk.** A hard disk problem could be causing your startup woes, so boot to a secondary device and repair the hard disk.

- **Repair hard disk permissions.** Improper permissions aren't likely to cause a startup failure, but it's not out of the realm of possibility. Boot to a secondary device and repair the hard disk's permissions.

Your Mac tells you that you don't have enough memory

Macs don't run out of memory very often, but it can happen, particularly if you work with large files or many programs at once, and your Mac doesn't have tons of RAM (say, a gigabyte or less). Here are some things to try if your Mac is low on RAM:

- **Close large files.** If you have any extremely large files open, try closing them.

- **Close running applications.** Shut down any applications that you don't need.

Genius

One common cause for low RAM on a Mac is when you have a number of applications running that you don't know about. How can that happen? One way is to think you've shut down an application because you closed that application's window, but the application remains in memory. Check the Dock and look for icons of the applications that you thought you'd closed. If you see any, Ctrl+click or right-click the icon and then click Quit.

- **Log out.** This should help a lot because it shuts down all your open applications and documents.

- **Restart your Mac.** This is the ultimate way to clear out the RAM and get a fresh start.

If you continue to get low memory notices, then it's likely your Mac just doesn't have enough RAM installed. Chapter 9 explains how to upgrade your RAM.

Your Mac runs slowly

All Mac users want their Macs to be as speedy as the first day they got them, but sometimes that's not the case. If you find that your Mac has that molasses-in-January thing going, there are a few things you can try before you start pulling out your hair in clumps.

Sudden slowdown

If the slowdown is a recent and relatively sudden phenomenon, then it suggests one of the following remedies:

- **Shut down some running programs.** It's possible that you have too many programs running, which is causing your Mac to constantly swap data between RAM and the hard disk's virtual memory, which can really slow things down.

- **Look for a runaway application in Activity Monitor.** In Finder, choose Applications ⇨ Utilities ⇨ Activity Monitor and look for a process that's using up a large percentage of the CPU time. If you see one, shut it down (click the process and then click Quit Process).

Genius

While you're hanging around in Activity Monitor, take a look at the Kind column and see if there are any PowerPC processes listed. PowerPC-based programs often run very slowly on Intel-based Macs, and can even drag down the performance of other programs. Consider uninstalling the program or looking for an Intel-based upgrade for the program.

- **Uninstall a recently installed program.** If the slowdown coincided with a recent program installation, try uninstalling the program by dragging it to the Trash.

- **Repair the hard disk.** Some hard disk file system problems can cause system-wide slowdowns, so try a disk repair to see if that helps fix the problem.

Gradual slowdown

If your Mac has been getting slower gradually, then the usual cause is the accumulation over time of programs, widgets, add-ons, and other bric-a-brac that slowly take their toll on system performance. Here are some items to consider when trying to alleviate the slowdown:

- **Applications.** Installed applications often load files at startup, so they may take up precious resources even when you're not using them. Uninstall any application that you no longer use.

- **Login items.** Remove as many as you can, as described in Chapter 10.

- **Dashboard widgets.** Disable or remove any widgets that you don't use.

- **Browser add-ons.** These take up memory, so get rid of any you really don't need.

If your Mac is still sluggish after all this pruning, then it's likely that your system just doesn't have enough RAM. Consider upgrading your Mac to 2GB or more (which is described in Chapter 9).

Your mouse or keyboard doesn't work

Your mouse and keyboard are your sole connections with your Mac, so if they don't work, you're pretty much stuck. Even if just one of these devices goes on the fritz, using your Mac is next-to-impossible because few Mac operations can be performed using only one input device. Here are some suggested remedies to try in the face of recalcitrant input devices:

- **Wait for a bit.** Sometimes it only *seems* as though the mouse or keyboard is stuck when, in fact, it's actually waiting for some process to finish. Leave the devices be for a bit (particularly the keyboard; banging away on the keys won't solve anything) and then see if they respond.

- **Disconnect and reconnect.** If you're using a USB mouse or keyboard, disconnect the device, wait a short while (five or ten seconds is fine), and then reconnect the device.

- **Try a different port.** If you're using a USB mouse or keyboard, disconnect the device and then plug it into a different USB port. If the device works now, your USB port may be faulty.

- **Connect directly to the Mac.** If you're using a USB mouse or keyboard and the device is attached to a USB hub, disconnect the device from the hub and connect it to a USB port on your Mac. If the device works now, your USB hub might be wonky.

- **Try another device.** If you have a spare mouse or keyboard lying around, try connecting it to your Mac. If it works, then the original mouse or keyboard is broken.

- **Turn it on.** If you're using a Bluetooth mouse or keyboard, make sure the device is turned on.

- **Change the batteries.** If you're using a Bluetooth mouse or keyboard, try a fresh set of batteries.

- **Pair the device again.** If you're using a Bluetooth mouse or keyboard, try pairing the device and your Mac once again.

- **Restart.** Rebooting your Mac might just solve the problem.

Your display is garbled

If your display suddenly goes haywire, there are a number of things that could be the problem, but the following five are the most common:

- **It's a temporary glitch.** This is the usual cause of a wonky display, and you solve it by restarting your Mac. Because you can't see the Mac desktop, your mouse is no good to you, so you need to use the keyboard. First press Shift+⌘+Q to log out. If that doesn't work, hold down the Ctrl and ⌘ keys and then press the power button to force your Mac to restart.

- **For an external display, there's a loose connection.** If your Mac is connected to an external display, check the connection on the Mac side and on the monitor side. If the connector is loose, plugging it in properly should fix the problem right away. If not, turn the monitor off and then turn it back on again.

- **The display is using improper settings.** If your display somehow gets set to a resolution that it can't handle, you'll see a distorted screen image. To solve this problem, restart your Mac in Safe Mode, click System Preferences in the Dock, click the Displays icon, and then click an item in the Resolutions list.

- **The display shows white on black instead of the usual black on white.** This is actually a feature of the Mac's Universal Access preferences, and you (or another user) may have turned it on accidentally. Click System Preferences in the Dock, click the Universal Access icon, click Seeing, and then select the Black on White option. Note, too, that you can toggle between the settings by pressing Ctrl+Option+⌘+8.

- **The display's driver software is corrupted.** In this case, you either need to reinstall the driver software from the disc that came with the display, or you need to download the driver from the display manufacturer's Web site and then install it. In either case, you need to restart your Mac in Safe Mode.

How Do I Run Windows on My Mac?

Mac users are loath to admit it, but it's true: they live, for good or ill, in a Windows world. Most of the time that doesn't matter to dedicated Mac-heads because they have everything they need right in the comfy and stylish confines of their beloved Macs. Every now and then, however, this blissful state is intruded upon when they realize that — gasp! — they need Windows for something. It might be a program that doesn't have a Mac version, or it could be a file that won't open in any Mac application. Fortunately, if you don't have a Windows machine kicking around, you can do the next best thing and run Windows on your Mac. This chapter takes you through the two most popular methods for doing this — Boot Camp and Parallels Desktop.

Why Run Windows?

Unlike in those ubiquitous Apple commercials where a Mac and a PC are always together, these two worlds don't often collide in real life. The planet is divided (albeit rather unequally) into Mac and Windows camps, and it's a rare user who has a foot in both. Rare, yes, but nonexistent, no. The Mac and Windows worlds do intersect and here are just a few examples:

- **No Mac version of the software you need.** Thanks to the popularity of Windows, the vast majority of software developers create programs for Windows, so that operating system has by far the largest collection of available applications. Because many developers don't bother creating Mac versions of their programs, it's often the case that there's no Mac equivalent of a particular type of software. In that case, you need Windows to run one of those non-Mac programs.

- **The Mac equivalent just isn't the same for you.** If you use Windows at work, or if you used to run Windows at home, you might have a favorite Windows program that doesn't have a Mac version. Yes, there may be Mac applications that do something similar, but you really like the version you were using on Windows. In that case, you need Windows to install and run that program.

- **Better gaming opportunities.** If you like to play games, then you probably already know that the Mac isn't a great gaming platform. Windows is very game-friendly, however, and not only do most games run better under Windows than under Mac, but many (perhaps even most) of the best games don't have Mac versions. In that case, you need Windows for the optimum gaming experience.

- **Access to the full Office suite.** If you're an Office user, then you already know that the Mac version of Office doesn't come with Outlook (it has Entourage, instead) or the Access database program. If you really need to use either or both of these programs, then you need Windows to install Office 2007, Office 2003, or some other version of Office for Windows.

- **Viewing the Windows Internet platforms.** If you develop content for the Web, it's crucial to know what your content looks like on all the most popular platforms. And given Windows is the most popular operating system in the world, you'd be remiss in your duties of you didn't fire up your site (or whatever it is) using the Windows versions of Internet Explorer, Safari, and Firefox. In that case, you need Windows to view your content in these programs.

In all these examples, you probably only need to use Windows every now and then, or just for short periods each day. Buying a separate PC to run Windows will set you back hundreds of dollars (at least), which is more than likely wasteful for something that you won't be using all that often. On the other hand, of the two methods for running Windows on your Mac that I talk about in this chapter, one (Boot Camp) comes free with Mac OS X 10.5 (Leopard) and the other (Parallels Desktop) costs just $79.99 at the time of this writing. (In both cases, you also need a copy of either Windows XP Service Pack 2 or Windows Vista, so be sure to add that into your budget.) Either way, running Windows on your Mac is much more economical than using a separate PC, and you don't have to clutter your desk with multiple monitors, keyboards, and mice!

Dual-Boot or Virtualization (or Both!)?

When you run Windows on a Mac, Windows itself doesn't "know" that it's operating on Mac hardware. It "sees" an Intel processor, and all the other hardware components in your Mac — memory, hard drive, video card, DVD drive, and so on — aren't fundamentally different from the same components on a pure Windows PC. However, Windows (like any operating system) does insist that it have complete control over the computer. Before you decide how to go forward, you should know how the Mac's operating system (OS X) relinquishes control (or *appears* to relinquish control) because this defines how you use Windows and whether OS X and Windows can share data. You can dual-boot, go the visualization route, or even do both.

- **Dual-boot.** To *dual-boot* your Mac means to configure it with two different operating systems — Mac OS X and Windows — running on two separate sections (called *partitions*) on your Mac's hard drive. When you start your Mac, you have a choice to boot into either OS X or into Windows. If you choose to boot in OS X, then your Mac runs exactly as it does now. If you choose to boot into Windows, instead, then for all intents and purposes your Mac turns into a Windows PC. That is, you see the Windows desktop, Windows has control of the hardware, and your Mac OS is nowhere in sight. You use Apple's Boot Camp software (which comes with Mac OS 10.5 Leopard) to set up a dual-boot configuration with Windows.

- **Virtualization.** This method refers to running Windows on your Mac in a *virtual machine*: a software environment that simulates a physical computer. In this scenario, you boot into Mac OS X as usual, and then you run Windows essentially as an application in its own window. This virtual machine is configured in such a way that Windows is fooled into thinking that it's controlling an actual PC. There are several virtualization applications available, including the following:

- Parallels Desktop (www.parallels.com)

- Q (www.kju-app.org/kju/)

- VMWare Fusion (www.vmware.com/mac/)

So which method should you choose? That depends on a number of factors, including price, performance, compatibility, and data sharing.

You should dual-boot OS X and Windows if:

- **Your budget is tight.** Apple's Boot Camp dual-boot software comes free with Leopard, while most of the third-party virtualization programs are commercial products that you have to pay for (with the exception of Q, which is free).

Note   It's important to note that the performance hit when Windows is running in a virtual machine isn't onerous. That is, Windows runs at perhaps 80 to 90 percent of its top speed when it's running in a virtual machine.

- **You want maximum performance.** Dual-booting into Windows means that Windows gets to use all of the Mac's hardware resources, particularly the memory and processor. This means that Windows running on the Mac is just as fast as Windows running on a comparably equipped PC. Virtual machines share RAM and the processor with Mac OS X, so Windows performance suffers a bit as a result.

- **You want maximum compatibility.** Dual-booting into Windows means that Windows gets direct access to the Mac's hardware components, so Windows should recognize most if not all of those components and install the appropriate device drivers to work properly with them. When Windows is running in a virtual machine, however, it often installs only generic drivers for the virtual devices, and it may not recognize any other hardware on the system.

On the other hand, you should use virtualization to run Windows if:

- **You want easier access to Windows.** Having to reboot your Mac every time you need to use Windows is a major hassle. With virtualization, however, you can make Windows available all the time, and you can switch between OS X and Windows as easily as you can switch from one running application to another.

- **You want to run other versions of Windows.** Boot Camp only supports Windows XP Service Pack 2 (or later) and Windows Vista. Most virtualization applications support these Windows versions as well as older versions such as Windows 2000, Windows NT, and Windows 98.

- **You want to easily share data between OS X and Windows.** With Boot Camp, you can access files on your Windows partition when you're working in OS X, but you can't access OS X files while working with Windows. Also, you can't cut or copy data from an application running in one operating system and paste that data into an application running in the other operating system. Sharing data is usually much more straightforward under virtualization. To share files, you can either turn on Windows Sharing in OS X, or you can use the virtualization software's sharing feature (such as Parallel Desktop's Shared Folders command). Also you can cut or copy data in Windows and then paste that data into a Mac application (and vice versa).

Guarding Against Malware

Whichever method you choose to run Windows on your Mac, remember that where's there's Windows, there's malware, such as viruses and spyware. Therefore, your first chore after you get Windows running on your Mac is to install a top-of-the-line antivirus program. Here are some good ones to check into:

Norton Internet Security (www.symantec.com)

McAfee Internet Security Suite (www.mcafee.com)

AVG Internet Security (http://free.grisoft.com/)

avast! antivirus (www.avast.com)

Windows Vista comes with the antispyware program Windows Defender, but if you're running Windows XP then you need a third-party antispyware utility. The Norton, McAfee, and AVG suites that I mention here all come with antispyware components.

If you do happen to catch a virus or other form of malware on Windows, the good news is that the malware isn't contagious. That is, it's not possible for the virus (or whatever) to also infect your Mac.

Still not sure which method to use? That's not a problem because you can always use both! That is, you can set up a Boot Camp partition to dual-boot Windows and OS X, *and* you can install virtualization software, thus giving yourself the best of both worlds. The good news is that Parallels Desktop, which I discuss in this chapter, can use the same version of Windows that you've installed using Boot Camp, so you only have to configure and maintain one version of Windows.

Dual-Booting with Boot Camp

If you decide to go the dual-boot route, then it's just a matter of installing and configuring Boot Camp, and then installing Windows in the partition created by Boot Camp. For all this to work without a hitch, you need the following:

- **Mac OS X 10.5 or later.** Boot Camp is only available as a Leopard utility, and to install it you need either the Leopard installation disc or the Mac OS X Disc 1 that shipped with your OS 10.5-equipped Mac.

- **Windows XP or Windows Vista.** For XP, you need a 32-bit version of XP Home or XP Professional with Service Pack 2 or later; for Vista you need a 32-bit version of Home Basic, Home Premium, Business, or Ultimate. In all cases, you need the full installation disc for the full install, *not* an upgrade installation disc.

- **An Intel-based Mac.** Any Mac with an Intel processor will do.

- **Free hard disk space.** You should have at least 1.5GB free to install XP, and at least 15GB free to install Vista.

- **A wired mouse and keyboard.** The Windows install program won't recognize wireless input devices (particularly Bluetooth devices), so make sure you have a wired USB mouse and keyboard for the installation.

Creating a Windows partition

When you're ready to proceed, follow these steps to launch Boot Camp Assistant and create a new partition for Windows installation:

1. **If you're using a Mac notebook, connect the Mac to a power supply.**

2. **In Finder, choose Applications ⇨ Utilities ⇨ Boot Camp Assistant.** The Introduction window appears.

3. **Click Continue.** The Create a Partition for Windows screen appears, as shown in figure 12.1.

4. **Click and drag the dot separating the two partitions until the Windows partition is the size you want.**

Genius

Although 1.5GB and 15GB are the minimum partition sizes for XP and Vista, respectively, you need more space if you plan on installing programs in Vista, particularly large programs such as Microsoft Office.

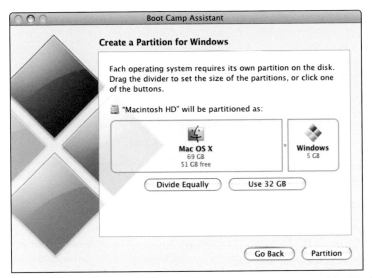

12.1 Use the Create a Partition for Windows screen to set the size of the Windows partition.

5. **Click Partition.** Mac OS X partitions the hard disk (this may take a while, depending on the size of the disk). When the partitioning is complete, you see a new desktop icon named BOOTCAMP, which represents the new partition.

Note

The partitioning process doesn't affect any of the data on your Mac. However, just to be safe, be sure your Mac is completely backed up before continuing.

Installing Windows

With the new partition ready to go, it's time to install Windows to that partition. The exact procedure varies according to which version of Windows you're using. The following are just the generic steps:

1. **Insert your Windows disc into your Mac's DVD drive.**

2. **In Boot Camp Assistant's Start Windows Installation screen, click Start Installation.** Your Mac reboots and the Windows installation program begins.

Genius

Boot Camp formats the BOOTCAMP partition using the FAT32 file system, which is fine for Windows XP partitions that are 32GB or less, but won't work for Windows Vista, which requires a different file system called NTFS. During the Vista install, when you get to the Where Do You Want to Install Windows? dialog box, click the BOOT-CAMP partition, click Drive Options, and then click Format.

3. **Follow the Windows installation screens as they appear.** Here are some things to bear in mind:

   - When the Windows setup program asks you where you want to install Windows, be sure to choose the BOOTCAMP partition.

     In Windows XP. Choose C: Partition 3 <BOOTCAMP>.

     In Windows Vista. Choose Disk 0 Partition 3 BOOTCAMP.

   - The Windows Setup program will automatically reboot your Mac a few times during the installation, and each time you'll see a screen that says the following:

     Press any key to boot from CD/DVD

     Do *not* press any key when you see this message, or you just start the installation process all over again.

   - Specify your username, password, time zone, and any other preferences that the setup program asks for.

4. **When the Windows installation is complete, insert your Leopard installation disc or Mac OS X Disc 1.** Windows prompts you to run setup.exe.

Note

In case you're wondering, a *file system* is a technology used by the operating system to keep track of the files stored on a disk, such as a hard disk. FAT32 (the FAT part is short for File Allocation Table) is a relatively simple file system used by some versions of Windows, while NTFS (New Technology File System) is a more sophisticated file system used by Windows Vista and other higher end versions of Windows (such as Windows Server). For the record, your Mac uses a file system called HFS+ (where HFS is short for Hierarchical File System).

5. **Run the setup.exe program.** If you're running Windows Vista, you need to provide User Account Control credentials to continue. The Boot Camp application appears, as shown in figure 12.2.

6. **Click Next.** The License Agreement dialog box appears.

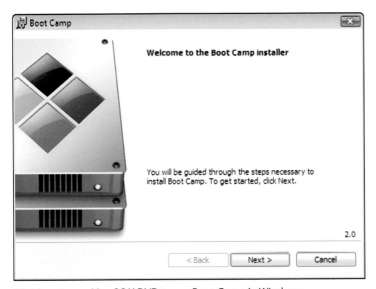

12.2 Insert your Mac OS X DVD to run Boot Camp in Windows.

7. **Select the I accept the terms in the license agreement option, and then click Next.**

8. **Make sure the Apple Software Update for Windows check box is selected, as shown in figure 12.3, and then click Install.** Boot Camp installs Apple Software Update for Windows.

9. **Click Finish.** Boot Camp lets you know that you need to restart the computer to put the changes into effect.

10. **Click Yes to restart your Mac.**

Genius

To use your Bluetooth mouse and keyboard with Windows, find the Bluetooth icon in the taskbar's notification area in the bottom-right corner of the Windows screen. Right-click the Bluetooth icon and then click Add a Bluetooth device. Select the My device is set up and ready to be found check box and click Next. If Windows doesn't find your devices, turn them off and then on again. Select a device and then click Next.

12.3 You need to install Apple Software Update for Windows to make sure your Mac hardware works properly with Windows.

Switching between Mac OS X and Windows

To switch between Mac OS X and Windows, you need to restart the Mac and then boot into whichever operating system you want to use. However, after you install Windows via Boot Camp, Windows sets itself up as the default startup volume, so just restarting your Mac only boots you into Windows. Here are the steps you need to follow to boot to Mac OS X:

1. **Start or restart your Mac. If you are currently in Windows, choose one of the following methods to restart:**

   - **In Windows Vista.** Click Start, click the Lock icon, and then click Restart.

   - **In Windows XP Home.** Click Start, click Turn Off Computer, and then click Restart.

   - **In Windows XP Professional.** Click Start, click Shut Down, choose Restart, and then click OK.

Genius

If you're in Windows, an easier way to boot into Mac OS X from Windows is to click the Boot Camp icon in the notification area and then click Restart in Mac OS X.

2. **Hold down the Option key until you see the Startup Manager.**

3. **Double-click the Macintosh HD icon.** Alternatively, if you want to boot into Windows, double-click the Windows icon.

Genius

If you usually boot to Mac OS X and only boot to Windows occasionally, it's a hassle to have to invoke Startup Manager every time you want to use Mac OS X. To fix this, boot to Mac OS X, click System Preferences in the Dock, click the Startup Disk icon, and then click Mac OS X *Ver* on Macintosh HD (where *Ver* is your OS X version number).

Renaming the Boot Camp partition

When you install Windows, it formats the Boot Camp partition, so you lose the original BOOTCAMP name. In its place, you end up with either UNTITLED (if the partition was formatted using NTFS) or NO NAME (if the partition was formatted using FAT or FAT32). Here's how to rename the partition:

- **In Windows.** Click Start ⇨ Computer (or My Computer in XP), right-click the hard drive, click Rename, type the new name, and then press Enter. In Vista, you need to enter your User Account Control credentials to make the change.

- **In Mac OS X.** If the partition is formatted as FAT or FAT32, Ctrl+click or right-click the partition's Desktop icon, click Get Info, and then edit the Name & Extension text.

Note

If you can't edit the partition name in Mac OS X, it means the partition is formatted using NTFS, which Mac OS X can't edit. In that case, you must use Windows to change the name.

Sharing files between Mac OS X and Windows

The major drawback with using Boot Camp is that you're limited in the amount of data you can share between Mac OS X and Windows, particularly if the Boot Camp partition is formatted using NTFS.

- **In Mac OS X.** You can see your Windows files by selecting the Boot Camp partition in Finder. For example, figure 12.4 shows Finder displaying the Windows Vista ⇨ Users ⇨ Paul folder (where Windows Vista is the name I'm using for my Boot Camp partition). If the partition is FAT or FAT32, you can work with the files just like they were local files: you can open files (assuming you have a compatible Mac application), edit files, add and delete files, and so on. If the partition is NTFS, you can only view the files; you can't make any changes to the existing files or add new files.

12.4 In Mac OS X, you can view the Windows files on the Boot Camp partition, and you can edit those files if the partition is FAT or FAT32.

- **In Windows.** Unfortunately, Windows can't work with the Macintosh HD format, so it's not possible to see the Mac hard drive in Windows. Here are a couple of alternatives for sharing files:

  - **Use an external hard drive.** Format the drive as FAT32 and you can see it in both Mac OS X and Windows.

  - **Use a common network share.** Store the files in a shared network folder that's accessible from both Mac OS X and Windows.

Running Windows with Parallels Desktop

If you'd rather have your Mac running all the time and just load Windows into a window whenever you need it, then virtualization software is the way to go. I mentioned earlier that there are several virtualization applications available, but the best of them (at least as I write this) is Parallels Desktop, so that's the one I talk about for the rest of this chapter.

Installing Parallels Desktop

Purchase the Parallels Desktop for Mac software from the Parallels site (www.parallels.com), or download the free trial if you just want to check it out. Don't bother with the Premium Edition, which is more expensive but doesn't offer anything you really need that the regular edition doesn't have.

When the download is complete, follow these steps to install Parallels Desktop for Mac:

1. **Open Safari's Downloads window, if it's not already onscreen, by choosing Window ⇨ Downloads.** You can also display the Downloads window by pressing Option+⌘+L.

2. **Double-click the Parallels Desktop icon.** Your Mac mounts the Parallels Desktop volume.

3. **Double-click the Install Parallels Desktop icon.** The Parallels Desktop Installer appears.

4. **Click Continue.** The Parallels Desktop Installer displays its release notes.

5. **Click Continue.** The Parallels Desktop Software License Agreement appears.

6. **Click Continue and then click Agree.**

7. **Click Install.** The Parallels Desktop Installer prompts you for your Mac administrative password.

8. **Type the password and then click OK.** Parallels Desktop Installer installs the program. If you see a dialog box telling you that New network interfaces have been detected, click Cancel.

9. **Click Close.**

Running Parallels Desktop

With Parallels Desktop installed, start the program by opening a Finder window and then choosing Applications ⇨ Parallels ⇨ Parallels Desktop. The first time you do this, you're prompted for your activation key, which you should have received via e-mail if you purchased the software. Click Enter Activation Key. (If you're using the trial version, click Later, instead.) Copy and paste the key in the Activation Key text box, click Activate, and then click OK.

Setting up Parallels Desktop with a Boot Camp virtual machine

If you previously installed Windows in a Boot Camp partition, the Parallels Desktop Installer recognizes that partition and sets it up as a virtual machine called My Boot Camp. Here are the steps to follow to set up Parallels Desktop to use that virtual machine:

1. **When you launch Parallels Desktop for the first time, the New Virtual Machine window appears and prompts you to select a virtual machine, as shown in figure 12.5.**

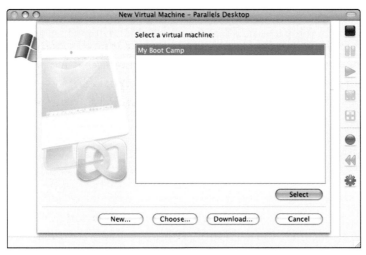

12.5 If you have Windows already installed in a Boot Camp partition, Parallels Desktop can use that partition as a virtual machine.

2. **Click the My Boot Camp virtual machine.**

3. **Click Select.** Parallels Desktop sets up the virtual machine, as shown in figure 12.6.

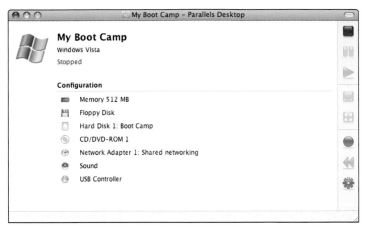

12.6 Parallels Desktop with Boot Camp's Windows partition set up as a virtual machine.

Installing Windows in a new virtual machine

If you don't already have a Boot Camp partition, then the first time you start Parallels Desktop you see the OS Installation Assistant, as shown in figure 12.7. You have three choices:

- **Windows Express.** This option installs Windows XP or Windows Vista in automatic mode, which means you're not prompted for any information during the installation. If you choose this option, you need to enter your Windows product key before starting the install. This is a good option to choose if you want to run the installation unattended, or if you want to create a new Windows installation.

- **Typical.** This option installs Windows XP or Windows Vista using a default virtual machine. I don't recommend this route because you don't get to customize the virtual machine.

- **Custom.** This option installs Windows XP or Windows Vista in a virtual machine that you can customize. No Windows information is specified in advance, so you must enter your Windows preferences during the installation. This is a good option to choose if you already have a Windows installation on your Mac (such as a Boot Camp Windows installation).

Note

If you see the New Virtual Machine window at startup, you can launch the OS Installation Assistant by clicking New. If Parallels Desktop displays an existing virtual machine at startup, launch the OS Installation Assistant by choosing File ⇨ New.

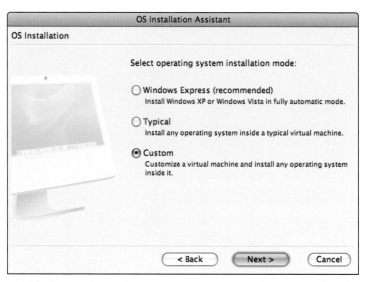

12.7 The OS Installation Assistant appears automatically when you first start Parallels Desktop.

The following steps take you through the Custom option:

1. **In the initial OS Installation Assistant dialog box, select the Custom option and click Next.** The OS Installation Assistant asks you for the OS Type and OS Version, as shown in figure 12.8.

2. **Choose Windows in the OS Type list, choose the version of Windows you want to install in the OS Version list, and then click Next.** The OS Installation Assistant asks you to specify how much RAM you want to give to the virtual machine, as shown in figure 12.9.

3. **Type the number of MB you want Windows to use, or click and drag the slider, and then click Next.** The OS Installation Assistant asks you to choose a virtual hard disk option.

Genius

The amount of RAM you specify depends on the version of Windows you're using and how much total RAM your Mac has to offer. If you only have 1GB total, then give Windows XP and earlier 256MB and Windows Vista 512MB (which is the Vista minimum). If you have 2GB, then give Windows XP and earlier 512MB and Windows Vista 1GB.

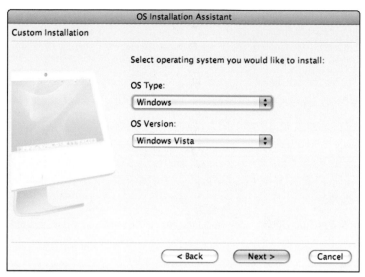

12.8 The OS Installation Assistant appears automatically when you first start Parallels Desktop.

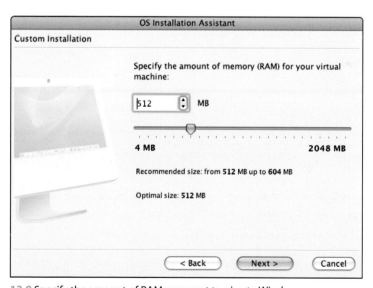

12.9 Specify the amount of RAM you want to give to Windows.

Caution

Don't specify a RAM amount that's larger than the highest recommended amount or the virtual machine won't be able to start.

4. **Select one of the following options and then click Next:**

- **Create a new hard disk image.** Select this option to set up a new virtual hard disk on which to install Windows. This is usually the preferred option for an initial install of Windows, unless you want to use an existing Boot Camp partition.

- **Use an existing hard disk image.** Select this option if you previously created a hard disk image and want to reuse it to save space on your Mac's hard drive.

- **Use Boot Camp.** Select this option if you want Parallels Desktop to use an existing Boot Camp partition as a virtual hard disk. This is the best option if you've already installed and configured Windows using Boot Camp because it allows Parallels Desktop to use the same Windows installation.

- **Do not add any hard disk.** This option is for an operating system (such as some versions of Linux) that can run off a CD instead of a hard drive. This doesn't apply to Windows, so you can ignore this option.

5. **If you opted to create a new hard disk in Step 4, the OS Installation Assistant asks you to specify the size and format of the hard disk, as shown in figure 12.10.**

- **Size.** Type the size in MB of the hard disk.

- **Format.** I recommend selecting the Expanding option, which gives the hard disk only as much room as it needs.

Click Next when you've made your choices.

6. **In the networking options, select Shared Networking and click Next.**

7. **Type a name for the virtual machine and select the sharing options you want to use.**

- **Enable file sharing.** Select this check box to enable Windows to see your Mac home folder.

- **Enable user profile sharing.** Select this check box to use your Mac user profile folders (including the Desktop) in Windows. Note that this option is disabled if you're using a Boot Camp partition as your Parallels Desktop virtual machine.

Click Next when you're done.

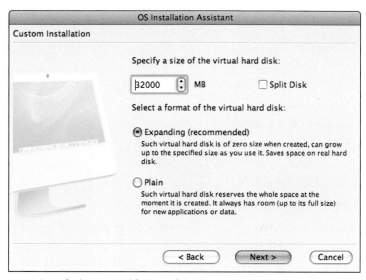

OS Installation Assistant

Custom Installation

Specify a size of the virtual hard disk:

[32000 ▼] MB   ☐ Split Disk

Select a format of the virtual hard disk:

⦿ Expanding (recommended)

Such virtual hard disk is of zero size when created, can grow up to the specified size as you use it. Saves space on real hard disk.

◯ Plain

Such virtual hard disk reserves the whole space at the moment it is created. It always has room (up to its full size) for new applications or data.

(< Back)   (Next >)   (Cancel)

12.10 Specify the size and format of the new virtual hard disk.

8. **In the optimize options, select Virtual machine and click Next.**

9. **Insert your Windows installation disc.**

10. **Click Finish.** Parallels Desktop installs Windows.

11. **Follow the Windows installation screens as they appear.** Here are some things to keep in mind:

- To use your mouse inside the virtual machine, click inside the Parallels Desktop window to activate the mouse.

- To use your mouse outside of the virtual machine, press Ctrl+Alt.

- Specify your username, password, time zone, and any other preferences that the setup program asks for.

12. **Install Parallel Tools by choosing Actions ⇨ Install Parallel Tools.** These tools ensure that all device drivers are installed correctly and they make it easier to share data between Mac OS X and Windows.

Figure 12.11 shows Windows Vista running in a virtual machine window on the Mac OS X Desktop.

12.11 Windows Vista running in a virtual machine in Mac OS X.

Configuring the virtual machine

If you need to make changes to the Windows virtual machine, first shut down the virtual machine by choosing Actions ⇨ Stop, and then click Yes when Parallels Desktop asks you to confirm.

When the virtual machine is stopped, choose Edit ⇨ Virtual Machine to open the Configuration Editor, shown in figure 12.12. Use the Resource list on the left to choose the item you want to configure, and then use the options on the right to make your changes. Click OK when you're done.

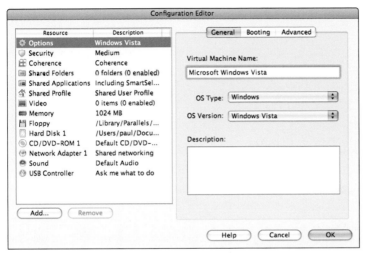

12.12 Use the Configuration Editor to make changes to the Windows virtual machine.

Sharing files between Mac OS X and Windows

Sharing files and data between Mac OS X and Windows is much easier and more versatile when Windows is running in a virtual machine. Here's a summary of the main ways that you can share files and data:

- **Clipboard.** Parallels Tools has a feature called Clipboard Synchronization. When you cut or copy a file, folder, or other data in either Windows or Mac OS X, you can switch to the other operating system and then paste the data.

- **In Windows.** If you selected the Enable user profile sharing check box, choose Start, Computer and you see an icon called .Home. Double-click this icon to see your Mac user profile folders and work with the files.

● **In Mac OS X.** Parallels Tools creates a device for the Windows hard drive named [C]
   Virtual Machine, where *Virtual Machine* is the name you supplied for the virtual machine.
   Click this device in Finder to access the Windows files, as shown in figure 12.13.

● **Drag and drop.** Select the object you want to share in either Windows or Mac OS X, click
   and drag the object from the source location and then drop it inside a window in the
   other operating system (or on the desktop).

12.13 You can access the Windows virtual machine via Finder.

Appendix A

Mac Online Resources

The Internet is chock full of Mac-related sites, many of which are exceptionally good and reflect the passion that most Mac users feel toward their beloved machines. This appendix lists a few of the best sites for great information on all things Mac, from tips to troubleshooting and more. Most of these sites have been online for a while, so they should still be up and running when you read this. That said, things do change constantly on the Web, so don't be too surprised if one or two have gone sneaker's up.

Official Apple Sites

If you like your information straight from the horse's mouth, here are a few useful Mac sites maintained by the good geeks at Apple.

www.apple.com/mac

This is your starting point for Mac-related stuff on the Apple site. You'll find the latest Mac news, the top downloads, and the latest Mac ads (always a great time-waster).

www.apple.com/imac

This is the official Apple site for the stylish iMac.

www.apple.com/macmini

This is Apple's official page for the almost-too-cute Mac mini.

www.apple.com/macbook

Head to this page to learn more about the MacBook.

www.apple.com/macbookair

This is the home page of the MacBook Air, "the world's thinnest notebook."

www.apple.com/macbookpro

This is the official page of the technolust-inducing MacBook Pro.

www.apple.com/macpro

This is the home page for the mighty Mac Pro.

www.apple.com/support/hardware

Head here for user guides, software updates, how-to articles, and troubleshooting tips for each different type of Mac.

http://discussions.apple.com

This site contains Apple's discussion forums, where you can talk to other Mac fans and ask questions.

More Mac Sites

If you feel like surfing off the beaten track, there are plenty of third-party Mac sites maintained by Mac enthusiasts.

http://db.tidbits.com

This it the best place to find news and commentary related to what's going on in the Mac universe.

www.download.com

This site has a huge selection of Mac software downloads.

www.macfixit.com

This site offers troubleshooting solutions for your Mac.

www.macintouch.com

You can find the latest news from the world of Mac here.

www.macosxhints.com

This site provides a massive database of user-generated tips for the Mac.

www.macrumors.com

You can find more news, and more than a few rumors, about the Mac on this site.

www.macworld.com

Go to this site to find articles, tips, and discussions from the publisher of *Macworld* magazine.

www.tucows.com/Macintosh

Thousands of Mac-related software downloads.

www.ultimatemac.com

Go to this site for Mac news, tips, troubleshooting, software reviews, and much more.

www.xlr8yourmac.com

You can find hundreds of great tips and how-to articles for getting more out of your Mac here.

Appendix B

Mac Shortcut Keys

Although your Mac was built with the mouse in mind, it comes with lots of keyboard shortcuts that can save you time and make many operations easier and faster. The tables in this appendix summarize the most useful Mac keyboard shortcuts.

Table B.1 Startup Shortcuts

Shortcut	Description
C	Press and hold to boot from the inserted CD or DVD
T	Press and hold to invoke FireWire Target Disk mode
Option	Press and hold to display the Startup Manager
Shift	Press and hold before the Apple screen comes up to boot into Safe Mode
Shift	Press and hold after the Apple screen comes up but before login to bypass login items
Shift	Press and hold after login to boot into Safe Login mode

Table B.2 Restart and Shutdown Shortcuts

Shortcut	Description
Shift+⌘+Q	Log out (with confirmation dialog box)
Option+Shift+⌘+Q	Log out (without confirmation dialog box)
Ctrl+Eject	Display the Restart/Sleep/Shut Down confirmation dialog box
Power	Notebooks only; Display the Restart/Sleep/Shut Down confirmation dialog box
Option+⌘+Eject	Put the Mac into Sleep mode (without confirmation dialog box)
Ctrl+⌘+Eject	Restart the Mac (without confirmation dialog box, but you can save changes in open documents)

Shortcut	Description
Ctrl+Option+⌘+Eject	Shut down the Mac (without confirmation dialog box, but you can save changes in open documents)
Ctrl+⌘+Power	Force the Mac to restart (without confirmation dialog box, and you can't save changes in open documents)
Power	Press and hold to force the Mac to shut down (without confirmation dialog box, and you can't save changes in open documents)

Table B.3 Application Shortcuts

Shortcut	Description
⌘+Tab	Cycle forward through active application icons with each press of the Tab key; release ⌘ to switch to the selected application
Shift+⌘+Tab	Cycle backward through active application icons with each press of the Tab key; release ⌘ to switch to the selected application
⌘+`	Cycle forward through the current application's open windows
Shift+⌘+`	Cycle backward through the current application's open windows
⌘+,	Open the current application's preferences
⌘ ı H	Hide the current application
Option+⌘+H	Hide all applications except the current one
⌘+M	Minimize the current window to the Dock
Option+⌘+M	Minimize all windows in active application to the Dock
⌘+Q	Quit the current application
Option+⌘+Esc	Display the Force Quit Applications window

Table B.4 Finder Shortcuts

Shortcut	Description
⌘+1	Switch the active window to Icons view
⌘+2	Switch the active window to List Flow view
⌘+3	Switch the active window to Columns view
⌘+4	Switch the active window to Cover Flow view
⌘+A	Select all items in the current window
⌘+D	Duplicate the selected item
⌘+E	Eject the current disc
⌘+F	Display the Find dialog box
⌘+I	Display the Get Info window for the selected item

continued

325

Table B.4 continued

Shortcut	Description
⌘+J	Display the View options
⌘+L	Create an alias for the selected item
⌘+N	Open a new Finder window
⌘+O	Open the selected item
⌘+R	Show the original item for the current alias
⌘+T	Add the current item to the Sidebar
⌘+W	Close the current Finder window
Shift+⌘+A	Go to the Applications folder
Shift+⌘+C	Go to the Computer folder
Shift+⌘+D	Go to the Desktop folder
Shift+⌘+G	Display the Go to Folder dialog box
Shift+⌘+H	Go to the Home folder
Shift+⌘+I	Go to the iDisk folder
Shift+⌘+K	Go to the Network folder
Shift+⌘+N	Create a new folder in the current Finder window
Option+⌘+N	Create a new Smart Folder in the current Finder window
Shift+⌘+U	Go to the Utilities folder
Option+⌘+W	Close all open Finder windows
⌘+Delete	Move the selected item to the Trash
Shift+⌘+Delete	Empty the Trash (with the confirmation dialog box)
Option+Shift+⌘+Delete	Empty the Trash (without the confirmation dialog box)

Table B.5 Safari Shortcuts

Shortcut	Description
⌘+I	E-mail the contents of the current page
⌘+L	Select the Address bar text
⌘+N	Open a new window
⌘+O	Open a file
⌘+R	Reload the current page

Shortcut	Description
⌘+T	Open a new tab
⌘+W	Close the current tab
⌘+n	Open the nth item on the Bookmarks bar, where n is a number between 1 and 9
⌘+}	Select the next tab
⌘+{	Select the previous tab
⌘+.	Stop loading the current page
⌘++	Make the text bigger on the current page
⌘+0	Make the text normal size on the current page
⌘+-	Make the text smaller on the current page
⌘+D	Add the current page to the Bookmarks
Option+⌘+D	Add the current page to the Bookmarks (without the Bookmark dialog box)
Option+⌘+B	Display the Bookmarks window
Option+⌘+L	Display the Downloads window
⌘+[	Navigate back
⌘+]	Navigate forward
Shift+⌘+H	Navigate to the Home page
Shift+⌘+T	Toggle the Tab bar on and off (only works if you have one tab open)
Shift+⌘+W	Close the current window
Shift+⌘+I	E-mail a link to the current page
Shift+⌘+K	Toggle pop-up blocking on and off
Shift+⌘+L	Run a Google search on the selected text
⌘+Return	Open the Address bar URL in a background tab
Shift+⌘+Return	Open the Address bar URL in a foreground tab
⌘	Click a link to open it in a background tab
Shift+⌘	Click a link to open it in a foreground tab
Option+⌘	Click a link to open it in a background window
Shift+Option+⌘	Click a link to open it in a foreground window
Option+⌘+Return	Open the Address bar URL in a background window
Shift+Option+⌘+Return	Open the Address bar URL in a foreground window

Table B.6 Miscellaneous Shortcuts

Shortcut	Description
⌘+X	Cut the selected objects or data
⌘+C	Copy the selected objects or data
⌘+V	Paste the most recently cut or copied objects or data
⌘+Z	Undo the most recent action
Option+Volume up/down/mute	Display the Sound preferences
Option+Brightness up/down	Display the Display preferences
F12	Press and hold to eject an inserted disc
Ctrl+F2	(Desktops only) Give keyboard control to the menu bar
Fn+Ctrl+F2	(Notebooks only) Give keyboard control to the menu bar
Ctrl+F3	(Desktops only) Give keyboard control to the Dock
Fn+Ctrl+F3	(Notebooks only) Give keyboard control to the Dock
Option+⌘+D	Toggle Dock hiding on and off
Shift+⌘+3	Capture an image of the screen
Shift+⌘+4	Drag the mouse to capture an image of the selected area of the screen
Shift+⌘+4	Press Spacebar and then click an object to capture an image of that object

Glossary

access point A networking device that enables two or more Macs to connect over a wireless network.

ad hoc wireless network See *computer-to-computer wireless network*.

AdSense An ad network run by Google where the ad server automatically examines the content of your page and generates one or more ads that are related in some way to that content.

archive See *Web archive*.

Bluetooth A wireless networking technology that enables you to exchange data between two devices using radio frequencies when the devices are within range of each other (usually within about 10 meters).

Bonjour A technology that scours the local network looking for other computers and devices that provide services, and then configures those services without requiring any input from you.

bookmark An Internet site saved in Safari so that you can access the site quickly in future browsing sessions.

bounce message An e-mail message that a mail server automatically fires off to the sender of a message when a problem occurs with the delivery of the message.

computer-to-computer wireless network A wireless network that doesn't use an access point. See also *infrastructure wireless network*.

crossover cable A cable used to connect two Macs directly using their network ports. See also *straight-through cable*.

deep link To navigate to a Web page that's buried several layers down in the site's folder hierarchy, rather than to the site's home page.

discoverable Describes a device that has its Bluetooth feature turned on so that other Bluetooth devices can connect to it.

dual-channel memory A memory technology that essentially doubles the rate at which information is transferred to and from memory, as long as the system has pairs of memory modules that are the same size, the same form factor, and the same type.

dual-link A Digital Video Interface (DVI) cable that uses two transmitters. See also *single-link*.

emulator A software application that simulates a hardware device or system.

event An appointment or meeting that you've scheduled in iCal.

extended desktop mode An external display mode where your Mac's desktop is extended onto the external display. See also *video mirroring*.

false positives A legitimate e-mail message that has been marked as spam.

female connector A cable connector with holes. See also *male connector*.

FireWire target disk mode A startup mode that enables you to use a Mac to view the hard disk of another Mac via a FireWire connection.

firmware A small program that runs inside the device and controls its internal functions.

Gbps Gigabits per second (billions of bits per second).

group A collection of Address Book contacts. See also *smart group*.

guest operating system An operating system that runs inside a virtual machine using virtualization software.

HTML See *Hypertext Markup Language*.

Hypertext Markup Language A collection of codes — called tags — that define the underlying structure of, and to some extent the formatting on, a Web page.

infrastructure wireless network A standard wireless network that uses an access point. See also *computer-to-computer wireless network*.

keychain A list of saved passwords.

login items The applications, files, folders, network shares, and other items that start automatically when you log in to your user account.

male connector A cable connector with pins. See also *female connector*.

memory effect The process where a battery loses capacity over time if you repeatedly recharge it without first fully discharging it.

multithreading Running two or more threads in a single program at the same time.

notebook hard disk A 2.5-inch-wide hard disk often used in notebooks such as the MacBook.

pair To connect one Bluetooth device with another by entering a passkey.

partition A subset of a hard disk onto which you install an operating system (such as Mac OS X in one partition and Windows in another).

permissions A collection of settings that determine what users or groups of users can do with a file.

piconet An ad hoc wireless network created by two Bluetooth devices.

port forwarding Taking data that comes in to the router on a specific port and sending it to a specified computer on the network.

power cycle To turn a device off, wait a few seconds for its inner components to stop spinning, and then turn it back on again.

preferences The options and settings, and other data that you've configured for your Mac via System Preferences.

preferences file A document that stores options and other data that you've entered using an application's Preferences command.

private browsing Surfing the Web with Safari configured not to store sites on the history list, not to save search box text or AutoFill text, and where no files are added to the Downloads window.

private IP address The IP address of the router's network connection. See also *public IP address*.

process A running instance of an executable program.

public IP address The IP address of the router's Internet connection as assigned by your Internet service provider. See also *private IP address*.

rich text Text that includes formatting features such as fonts, colors, and styles.

Safe Boot To start your Mac in Safe Mode.

Safe Login A login that doesn't load any of your login items.

Safe Mode A startup mode where your Mac doesn't load most of its behind-the-scenes components.

SATA See *Serial Advanced Technology Attachment*.

SATA/150 A SATA interface standard that transfers data at 1.5Gbps.

SATA/300 A SATA interface standard that transfers data at 3.0Gbps.

Serial Advanced Technology Attachment The current standard for transferring data between a hard disk and the rest of your Mac.

single-link A DVI cable that uses one transmitter. See also *dual-link*.

smart group A collection of Address Book contacts where each member has one or more things in common, and where Address Book adds or deletes members automatically as you add, edit, and delete contacts.

smart mailbox A mail folder that consolidates all of your messages that meet one or more conditions, and where Mail Book adds or deletes messages automatically as you receive and delete messages.

SMTP server The Simple Mail Transport Protocol server that an Internet service provider uses to process outgoing e-mail messages.

straight-through cable A cable used for regular network connections. See also *crossover cable*.

synchronization A process that ensures that data such as contacts, e-mail accounts, and events on your Mac is the same as the data on other devices such as cell phones and PDAs.

thread A program task that can run independently of and (usually) concurrently with other tasks in the same program. See also *multithreading*.

twisted-pair cable Network cable, so-called because it consists of four pairs of twisted copper wires that together form a circuit that can transmit data.

Universal Plug and Play A technology standard that enables a system such as your Mac to recognize, interrogate, and configure a hardware device.

UPnP See *Universal Plug and Play*.

user agent A string that a Web browser uses to identify itself to a Web server.

vCard A file that contains a person's contact information.

video mirroring An external display mode where the same image that appears on the Mac's main or built-in display also appears on the external display. See also *extended desktop mode*.

virtual machine A software environment that simulates a physical computer.

virtual memory Memory that your Mac can address beyond what is physically installed on the system by using a piece of your hard disk that's set up to emulate physical memory.

virtualization Running a guest operating system (such as Windows on a Mac) in a virtual machine.

Web archive A copy of the current content of a Web page.

Web bug An image that resides on a remote server and is added to an HTML-formatted e-mail message by referencing a remote server address that includes a code that identifies your e-mail address and so proves that your e-mail address is legitimate.

widget A small program that runs in your Mac's Dashboard application.

workflow A script created with Automator that implements a series of actions where the data returned by one action is passed along to the next.

Index

The Genius is in.

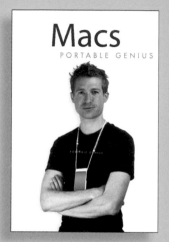

978-0-470-29052-1

978-0-470-29050-7

978-0-470-38108-3

978-0-470-29169-6

978-0-470-29170-2

The essentials for every forward-thinking Apple user are now available on the go. Designed for easy access to tools and shortcuts, the *Portable Genius* series has all the information you need to maximize your digital lifestyle. With a full-color interior and easy-to-navigate content, the *Portable Genius* series offers innovative tips and tricks as well as savvy advice that will save you time and increase your productivity.

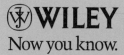

Available wherever books are sold.